Losing Our Heads

Losing Our Heads

Beheadings in Literature and Culture

Regina Janes

NEW YORK UNIVERSITY PRESS

New York and London

NEW YORK UNIVERSITY PRESS
New York and London
www.nyupress.org

Library of Congress Cataloging-in-Publication Data
Janes, Regina, 1946–
Losing our heads : beheadings in literature and culture /
Regina Janes.
p. cm.
Includes bibliographical references and index.
ISBN-13: 978–0–8147–4269–3 (cloth : alk. paper)
ISBN-10: 0–8147–4269–6 (cloth : alk. paper)
ISBN-13: 978–0–8147–4270–9 (pbk. : alk. paper)
ISBN-10: 0–8147–4270–X (pbk. : alk. paper)
1. Beheading—History.   2. Beheading in literature.
3. Executions and executioners in art.   I. Title.
HV8552.J34   2005
306.9—dc22   2005006791

*For Dale, who prefers that people keep their heads,
and Charles, who can spot a Salome dancing
in the remotest cathedral window.*

Contents

Preface

Why should anyone, especially nice people like you and me, be interested in a topic so repellent as beheadings?

Why should anyone, especially sophisticated people like you and me, regard so widespread a cultural practice as beheadings as repellent?

About 160,000 years ago, *homo sapiens idaltu* separated heads from bodies.[1] *Homo sapiens sapiens* still does. Disagreeable, fascinating, horrific, laughable, headless bodies and bodiless heads are all around us. Tim Burton, whose *Sleepy Hollow* (1999) sent heads flying, claims severed heads create unease that one cannot put one's finger on.[2] Garrison Keillor begins the millennium with a snowboarding beheading in Lake Wobegon where "we don't have many beheadings."[3] Snoopy horrifies himself by accidentally beheading a snowman. Decapitating murderers horrify the rest of us, populating our prisons, our films, and our fictions. Horror or comedy: decapitation owes its current characteristic shudder to the placement of violence within the modern ideology of the body. Decapitation, like other mutilations, makes visible a violence that the west has been campaigning to make invisible since the seventeenth century, when our body-based ideology begins to emerge.

We have faith in the materiality of the body and believe in its rights. We suspect that body is more important than soul, and we know "that bodily being [is] most real, most pressing, most undeniable."[4] Our selves are bodied, and among the body's rights is protection from violence. Central to heroic, aristocratic, or military society, violence, circumscribed, shifts to the margins of commercial, democratic, domesticated society, where the borders are to be defended. It does not stay there, however, but leaks back in, dominates popular media, decimates neighborhoods, destroys nations, and serves up the week's headless corpse in the news. A practice to be repressed, controlled, "disciplined," rather than fostered, encouraged, and enjoyed, violence is what sex used to be—a dirty secret that entices and sells, a horrid necessity that nice people do without and avoid regarding, a torrid fantasy that frees and individuates. Like sexuality, violence connects us to an ineluctable "nature" that we are unlikely ever to be able to do without, but about which we must always make culturally defined choices. A dominant modern trope for loss of a bodily-embodied self, decapitation strikes at our identification with our bodies. But that is not what decapitation has always meant or always means. Decapitation demonstrates the dangerous primacy of symbolism: people will do anything so long as it can be made to mean.

A severed head is the first sign that hominids are thinking in symbols. Never a solitary act (until modern times), removing a head as a communal act defines body and head as separable, affirms a preference for the head over other body parts, and asserts a desire to possess the good represented by the head. The head, seat of breath, and (later) soul, remains a site of power and a locus of desire. Reuniting the living and the dead over the gap created by death, pre-human decapitations make visible the rift that constitutes symbolization, the gap between value and object, word and thing, signifier and signified-referent, that makes imagination so hungry and so insatiable. Symbolization creates the crack in reality that it is always trying to heal.

Yet from our perspective such exegesis produces the antithesis of what severed heads must really mean. Life? Surely a severed head is nothing if not dead.

Such conflicts between life and death over heads concern us here: the deeply held, viscerally felt conviction that severed heads mean some particular thing, and the odd fact that heads are always turning over into meaning something else. Their meaning will be found at some crux near the ideological core of the culture, for where the head is, other values are as well. Theoretically, the head's mobility illustrates "nature" cannibalized by "culture," the innate by the constructed. That the head means is a constant; what it means and how it is used are contingent, temporal, historical, cultural, and contradictory. Paradoxically, the constancy of the head undercuts our view of the body as fundamental. The body always coexists with symbolization that always ultimately overrides the claims of the body in itself. Simply put, the body makes no claims for itself; the symbolizing head makes claims on its behalf, and that symbolizing head often prefers something else to the body, even its own body. "I'll stake my head" on it.

Part of the burgeoning literature on violence and the body, this study is indebted in its origins to works that made it possible to consider decapitation as more than castration, from outside Freudian bounds: Norbert Elias's *The Civilizing Process,* Michel Foucault's *Discipline and Punish,* and Pieter Spierenberg's *The Spectacle of Suffering.* There exists a vast literature on specialized aspects of decapitation—the guillotine, Roman headhunting, the conjunction of Beowulf and Judith in a single Old English manuscript, ethnographic studies of headhunting in the Americas, Africa, and Pacific, histories of decapitation in recent times in the near Orient, histories of executioners, and individual studies of famous decapitations or decapitators, from Medusa, Anne Boleyn and Charles I to Salome and Judith.[5] Such studies recognize how enormously rewarding it is to heave and handle a favorite, puzzling, irreducible head. Yet their example is rarely followed in general critical analysis. When a severed head drops into a work, most literary criticism falls into the imitative fallacy: the critic blinks, registers the blow, reuses the head for dramatic effect, and moves on.[6] The head becomes a stunning piece of punctuation, and critic and reader alike go blind at the shock—they do not look at the head. Heads deserve better.

The Prologue considers, briefly, why heads? Beheadings bother us because heads interest us, so what is it about heads that makes them matter? Freudian theory, even the Lacanian variety with its mirror stage (where facial recognition might seem primary), deals in phalluses and bodies, not heads, so it is necessary to look elsewhere for current answers to this ancient question, to evolutionary and developmental psychology, to the head's role in self-formation and social identity. Psychoanalysis fielded a unified theory of sexuality, identity, and aggression, but Sigmund Freud's seductive fin-de-siècle "death drive" has been displaced in the natural and social sciences and popular discourse by genetic codes and Darwinian evolutionary psychology, adumbrated in *Totem and Taboo.* When Freud's drives are replaced by Watson, Crick, and Franklin's DNA, as in Steven Pinker's stimulating synthesis of current scientific and social scientific findings *The Blank Slate: The Modern Denial of Human Nature* (2002), the questions research asks change, but the cultural placement of violence remains still to be explicated. If violence is "in" us genetically, why does it take so many different forms?

Like language, violence is biologically based, structured, differential, capable of infinite variation, from the simplest practical uses to the most elaborate symbolic ones. Some forms of human violence obviously re-produce animal predation and territoriality. Wolf packs occasionally kill their alpha male or alpha female.[7] Other forms only pacifists or vegetarians recognize as violence—just wars or cracking and beating innocent eggs to make a mayonnaise for tortured, salted cod. Beheadings everyone recognizes as violent, but they repel with greater force because they are symbolic, a work of human culture, not animal nature. Heads would remain securely on human shoulders were we not "the symbolic species."[8]

Chapter 1 proposes respect, though not imitation, for beheading as an ancient human cultural practice. Distinguishing the types of traditionally severed heads: venerated, trophy, sacrificial, presentation, and judicial, the chapter brings headhunting home to Europe and the west's ancestral headhunters, Greek, Celtic, and Roman. Pre-modern cultures kept heads as trophies—or threw them away; they presented severed heads to their enemies—or to their friends; they used them to make new friends and conciliate enemies—or to signify the rupture of an alliance and the opening of hostilities; they revered them as sacred or abhorred them as sacred; they preserved the heads of their enemies, or of their fathers. In sum, they used heads as powerful signs whose terror, to the taker, the taken, and the spectator, constituted part of their value. The symbolic systems that supported those activities having been displaced by another (modernity's foundational body), they no longer form part of an authorized repertoire of behaviors, but have moved to fascinating transgression in fantasy, crime in practice.

Chapters 2 and 3 take up decapitation's curious disappearance and phoenix-like revival in enlightened England and France. The enlightenment anticipated a pressing twentieth-century question: Why, now that we are so humane that we no longer put heads on bridges, do we kill each other in greater numbers with more efficiency? Why does mutilation perturb us more than death? These modern conundrums had become reality by the end of the eighteenth century when the guillotine in France improved the delivery of death, and the English, with great reluctance, gave up their axe.

Chapter 2 takes the bouncing head, rolling on the scaffold, as an impudent marker of the emergence of the new ideology of the body. In a process traditionally called the advance of humanitarianism, the body shifts from part of a larger symbolic order to the foundation of self, society, and politics. Developing in the period from 1650 to 1680 and fully visible after 1750,[9] the new attitudes are epitomized by John Locke, psychologist, for whom the body is protected by contract theory from violence, circumscribed by rights, defended by law, engaged in commerce, defined as property, and theorized as sympathetic. The conscious struggle between the old symbolic order and the new private body lasted well into the nineteenth century, much longer than is commonly remembered. In chapter 3 the severed head reasserts its symbolic, now political, power, and it does not bounce. In France, when revolution toppled absolutism, the people appropriated decollation, taking over as their own that sign of absolute power. The transfer of the sign secured its survival until the late 1970s.

Chapters 4, 5, and the Epilogue turn from real beheadings to tropes: Salome and the head of John the Baptist, the headless native of imperial fictions, and the peculiar headlessness of the present. Like a regime, when a discourse is in crisis, a severed head is likely to turn up. Severing heads, the nineteenth century worked through its major crises: gender, faith, race and empire, the advent of feminism, the death of God, the elaboration of scientific racism, the triumph of imperialism. Our own era plays with the crisis of its self.

Chapter 4 takes up the Salome topos from the perspective of the unmarked object that defines it: the Baptist's head. No head has had so many meanings as the Baptist's, twisting from an object of divine meditation in the Renaissance, through a sacrifice to the rights of man in the French Revolution, to a new apotheosis in the late nineteenth century as re-divinized, but marginalized masculinity. That last cultural reconfiguration produces the Freudian formula "decapitation = castration," dominating interpretation for a century. When Freud reduces the head to the penis, he elevates the sign of manhood once again, apotheosizing the male sexual part, identifying it as self, and depreciating female parts. Once Freud takes the cover off the fascinating manly part undone by Salome, self and sexuality depart for other venues, leaving St. John's head behind. In this magician's trick, once the interpretation is easy, it is no longer interesting. Worship has fled to the body, abandoning the head on its platter.

Chapter 5 considers severed heads as a cultural marker separating the civilized from the barbarians. Although common sense tells us this opposition is eternal and universal, it is neither. For Homer's Greeks and for European explorers through the sixteenth century, the primordial marker of terrifying otherness was the cannibal. Replacing cannibalism among Roman and eighteenth-century European imperialists, decapitation focalizes hierarchy, justifying an imperial authority that displaces native authority, but leaves the body intact. In its nineteenth-century variant, imperial authority projects decapitation's violence onto native peoples as both victims and perpetrators, producing the popular European topos of savage natives severing native heads. Once the natives take up writing, they take on the topos. Joseph Conrad's *Heart of Darkness* severs African heads both subtly and normatively, while two generations of Nigerian writers, Chinua Achebe, Amos Tutuola, and Ben Okri, write heads otherwise.

The Epilogue sets the reader down amidst defiant modern asseverations of headlessness. Denying primacy to any particular head, modernity's egalitarian ideologies simultaneously affirm and deny the value of all other individual heads. The result is an explosion of metaphoric discomfort, articulated through images of beheadings, severed heads or headless bodies, turning up everywhere as writers and artists probe limits and find, to everyone's dismay, that nothing is forbidden. From a world with one head to a world without any, we move from hierarchy to the market, the Web, and the gene pool. When the world had one head, it was horrified by the hydra, that many-headed monster. Now it embraces acephalic man.

I would like to thank Richard Wendorf and R. H. Peterson for their early enthusiasm for this project, my colleagues Sheldon Solomon and Joan Douglas for guidance on developmental psychology, Penny Jolly on art history, Michael Ennis-McMillan on modern headhunting, Undine Giguere for help with German, Marilyn Sheffer and Amy Syrell for their indefatigability on interlibrary loans, and Steve Otrembiak, Steve Dinyer, and Skidmore Media Services for assistance with illustrations. At the Metropolitan Museum, Eileen Sullivan and Perrin Stein helped with Denon, and Eliza Callard made Salome her own. For the misuse of their assistance, I alone am responsible.

Finally, I should like to wash my hands of some heads and return theirs to friends and colleagues. Some found a place in the text, others it would be a pity to leave unmentioned. So, returning heads to senders, a head-spinning miscellany: to Carolyn Anderson, Ionesco's *Leader*; Liz Bohls, Lady Margaret Pennyman's St. Dennis; Phil Boshoff, a prisoner with a dotted line tattooed around his neck with the inscription "Please cut here" beneath it; Ralph Ciancio, Nabokov's *Invitation to a Beheading*; Lee Coleman, Jayne Mansfield, headless in her convertible; Mary Correa, headhunters in business suits; Mark Slouka for his decapitated snapping turtles in "Feather and Bone"; Kathryn Davis, Turgenev's blink; Anne Diggory, querying the habits of cats and *Wonderland Revisited,* a headless rabbit beside the croquet set; Terence Diggory, Donatello's David; James Dixon, Kurosawa's *Ran,* Arnold Schwarzenegger's *Conan* movies, and John Carpenter's *The Thing*; Giuseppe Faustini, Bertran de Born in Dante's *Inferno*; Robert Ferguson, Melville's "Benito Cereno"; Kate Greenspan, a flurry of medieval martyrs and *Beowulf*; Harry Gaugh, Emily Dickinson's "If I feel physically as if the top of my head were taken off, I know that is poetry"; Catherine Golden, the Red Queen in *Alice in Wonderland*; Barry Goldensohn, Titian's *David and Goliath,* Cindy Sherman's *Judith*; Charlotte Goodman, Jean Stafford's maiden guillotine; Ann Hurley, *Sir Gawain and the Green Knight*; Robert Koeth, III, St. Paul; Susan Kress, Lovat's axe, Delaroche's Lady Jane Grey, and a guillotine-making kit; Patrick Kurp, speeding motorcyclists and barbed-wire fences; Patricia Ann Lee, "proper Heads and subHeads"; Tom Lewis, Rabelais's Epistemon; Robert Mahony, Lafcadio Hearn's "Diplomacy"; Michael Marx, "Human Head Kept Alive for 20 Days! Decapitated wreck victim blinks to communicate with doctors!" *Weekly World News,* and *Excalibur*; Barbara Melville, "'le dernier cri' in techno-political decapitation," exploding videocassette recorders: "After five minutes . . . boom, you saw a man carrying a video without a head," in *Newsweek*; Steven Millhauser, photographs of magicians' floating heads; Parthasarathy, Thomas Mann's *Transposed Heads: A Legend of India* and Girish Karnad's *Hayavadana*; David Porter, English folksongs and Cocteau's *Orphée*; Richard Rainey, *Phantom Forces,* especially Maxentius displayed by Constantine, Romans by Venedoti, Cromwell, Charles I, and Pancho Villa; Jon Ramsey, Melville's "Benito Cereno"; Phyllis Roth, the huge head of Marx on his tomb at Highgate; Joel Smith, *On Having No Head*; Richard Wendorf, Margaret Wharton's *Execution,* a "book transformation" that turns a book entitled *Creative Aggression* into a guillotine; Alan Wheelock, the Nazis of the White Rose, the American air-crew captured in the Doolittle raid over Tokyo, 1942, and General Charles "Chinese" Gordon in Khartoum.

Prologue
Head Matters

Head of the page, head of state.
> —"Go to the Head of the Class," a board game

You will be the head, and they will be the tail.
> —Deuteronomy 28:13

The head of every man is Christ, and the head of the woman is
the man.   —I Corinthians 11:3

Human beings have often cut off one another's heads. They do not always
cut off another's head. They often strenuously disapprove cutting off
heads, yet someone somewhere is always cutting off someone else's head
for some reason. Why?

Evolutionary and sociobiologists say it is "nature," articulated in the
genetic code, expressed in brain function as a response to experience. Edward O. Wilson argues that headhunting confers evolutionary advantages on skilled practitioners and tribes. Robin Fox proposes man as a
hunting primate whose innate violence and aggression are only loosely
controlled by culture. Steven Pinker includes "a drive for dominance and
a willingness to use violence to attain goals" among innate, genetically
coded social behaviors and individual abilities.[1] Given the frequency, distribution, and persistence of decapitation, there seems to be something to
the "nature" argument. Taking off someone's head suggests a successfully
concluded "drive for dominance" and requires "willingness to use violence" to accomplish it. Since the action takes place both with and with-

1

out social approval, some irrepressible, irreducible "nature" must be asserting itself, regardless of cultural support or rejection.

Such a position seems commonsensical enough. Heads get cut off, really and virtually, in fact and in representation, because violence, like sex,
is part of our being that we need to control and cannot do without. Although we know as yet very little about genes and violence, we do know
that one genetic variation correlates with violent behavior, if experience
triggers it.[2] If people differ in their aptitudes for art, music, mathematics,
and wine tasting, they are likely to differ in their aptitude for violence (or
sex). We do not question genetic variety when its effects are benign,
though we find it troubling when behavior advantageous or pleasurable
to one is destructive of others. Whether or not a gene exists that, in on or
off position, leads some people to sever heads and others not to, cutting
off heads doubtless confers an evolutionary advantage on those who cut
off heads over those whose heads are cut off. Yet decapitation turns on its
head any attempt to attribute decapitation to a resurgent "nature" our
"culture" has not yet mastered.

There is nothing natural about decapitation. The deliberate separation
of a head from its body is exclusively cultural. Not only is decapitation
exclusively cultural, but it is also the first sign of the symbolic processes
that mark our species as distinctively human or at least hominid. Decapitation as we now know it resembles other forms of violence—sometimes
promoted, sometimes disallowed, always subject to social control, yet
also always eluding it, and then designated crime. Unlike other forms of
violence, however, decapitation, defined as the deliberate separation of a
head from its body, does not occur outside human culture. Natural decapitations are by-products or accidents.

As by-products, drowned heads float free from the body when decom-
position separates the vertebrae.[3] Carcasses picked clean by buzzards
come apart at the neck. Domestic cats present headless bodies to mark a
relationship, but they have not deliberately severed the head for presentation. There is no longer any head. Domestic cats, specialists in decapitation who always attack at the neck, have curved canines that leverage
apart the vertebrae of the prey's spinal column, killing with a single bite
through the spinal chord. They then eat their prey starting at the head, so
the hair lies flat, avoiding toothfuls of fur or feathers.[4] The whole spar-
row or mouse may be presented with no difference in intention, only in
appetite. Preying mantises also have special mandibles for their special
mating practices. For primates, it is not easy to sever a head. Chim-

panzees eating the brains of baboon babies do not even try. Instead of attempting to break apart the head and body, they enlarge the opening between vertebral column and skull, and scoop out the brains with an index finger.[5] Separating a head from a body requires some skill, more strength, and a tool.

Icy rivers allegedly performed accidental decapitations until the modern era, when high speed and metal joined to make such accidents more frequent. In the *Anthologia Latina,* a Thracian boy falls through a frozen river; the river carries away his body and leaves his head on the ice. Finding it, his mother burns the head, saying, "This I bore for the flames, the rest for the water. Woe is me! The river has the greater part, leaving me enough to tell me that my son has perished!" Salome, who asked for John the Baptist's head, lost hers to ice. The tale from the ecclesiastical history of Nicephorus Callistus Xanthopoulos (ca. 1256–1335) was printed in France in 1586, retold in a footnote by Henry Vaughan in the seventeenth century, by Thomas Newton as "by Whitby from Nicephorus" in the eighteenth, and at length in a poem by "Michael Field" in the nineteenth.[6] A matronly apple seller loses her head to the frozen Thames in John Gay's *Trivia* (1716). Modern accidental decapitations feature high speed and metal, the most famous case being the death of Jayne Mansfield. Technologically facilitated, culturally specific accidental decapitations occur far more frequently than nature's.

Humans create severed heads only with difficulty, but with a will.[7] Severing a head requires that the head possess an already developed and elaborated system of meanings that can be appropriated with the head when the head is appropriated. Otherwise, why bother?

Decapitation as symbolic practice precedes decapitation as violence, and decapitation as violence (like decapitation by accident) flourishes with culture, dependent on technological advances. *Homo sapiens idaltu* carefully cut the heads from corpses: the skulls show the marks of his efforts. In those marks, the first symbol manifests itself. A symbol, whether an object, mark, or action, stands for or represents something beyond itself. The head of a dead animal sports a few chewy outside tidbits and encloses juicy brains. Like a bigger and better nut, the skull houses a delectable piece of meat. Smashed open for eating, a head is not symbolic. It represents nothing, and violence against it signifies only desire for its contents. Separating a head from a dead body or setting it in a ring of skulls serves no culinary, reproductive, or defensive purpose. Yet the head's separation demands effort, and the effort the action requires shows conscious purpose. Some motive beyond reproduction or survival is at work. Symbolization begins or, more precisely, *appears* in that gap between use and action, when we propose a difference between utility and activity.

What did the head symbolize? *What* the head meant is perhaps less important than *that* it meant. As Dan Sperber suggests, symbols are not explicable. They simply accrue exegesis.[8] Yet "life," replying to the puzzles that death poses, seems probable. Where did the light and movement of the eyes go? What has become of the breath of the nostrils? If "the symbol is the murder of the thing," as Jacques Lacan has it, then the "thing" murdered by this first, pre-human symbol is death.[9] Absence produces the attribution of presence; the fact of death produces the concept of life.

With *homo sapiens idaltu* and the Neanderthals, we can safely characterize head-severing as "inhuman"—they are another species. Initially a non-violent act, performed on the already dead, decapitation becomes increasingly violent as human technology and culture develop, until it finally becomes the capital symbolic act of violence, equally invigorating and horrifying. By the time evidence appears for humans' decapitations, any intrinsic uselessness of a severed head has been entirely overlaid by symbolic processes.

Apart from a skull's ability to hold drink, severed heads serve no practical function in any hominid activity: eating, hunting, gathering (agriculture), strife, sex, and burial. To eat the good bits in a head, one need not sever it; one need only slice, tear, pop, bash, or jimmy. Heads do not make useful weapons or tools for digging; they facilitate neither reproduction nor corpse disposal. Yet humans, unlike less symbol-ridden creatures, have used severed heads for cups, for hunting, for fertility (human, animal, and plant), for dowries, for building, for worship, for healing, for panicking enemies, and for law enforcement.

Still, why heads? As Mary Douglas observes, "Most symbolic behaviour must work through the human body . . . common to us all."[10] As the locus of four senses (sight, hearing, taste, smell), the brain, and the mouth, faced by the face, the head carries many species' social identity. Wasps recognize one another by facial markings and attack nest mates with painted-over markings until their rank is settled. Then they adjust to the new faces.[11] By human faces, seagulls identify intruding human predators who band their young. When motivated to do so, seagulls read faces across species-boundary lines. So do goats. Choosing his love object from the face of his mother, a male goat with a sheep foster-mother always prefers a sheep to a goat face when he seeks a mate.[12] Humans and other primates possess nerve cells specific for faces, first discovered in 1972 in macaques, located in the fusiform gyrus area in the cerebral cortex.[13] Facial recognition is part of our basic wiring, our standard equipment, and much depends upon it—for us as well as for wasps, seagulls, goats, and macaques.

Human infants focus on faces from their first hours of life, and the first abstraction they recognize is a human face: a hair line, a chin line, two eyes, and a mouth. Those phallic substitutes, noses and ears (vid. Sterne and Swift), are otiose. Within a few hours of birth, infants prefer schematic drawings of human faces to other patterns.[14] Focus and recognition have vital social and biological functions, for the infant's attention to the mother's face keeps her there, tending and attending to the infant.[15] The infant's smile, beginning at two to four months, elicits more intense attention and affection from adults.[16] Difficulty recognizing faces and lack of interest in faces characterize autism and its stunted affect.[17] Faces establish bonds that comprehend reciprocal dependence, desire, and control from the very beginning.

Human interest in faces is not confined to infancy. Aristotle asserted that the simplest chalk portrait is more compelling than the brightest colors at random. Confirming ancient intuitions, abstract expressionism has not crossed over into advertising. Darwin recognized the priority of faces when, of sixteen queries for investigating human expression, only three concerned the body. The remaining thirteen addressed expressions written only in the face, where "the different races of man express their emotions and sensations with remarkable uniformity throughout the world."[18] The races of men also reinforce their facial expressions of emotion less with their bodies' physical posture than do other primates.[19]

Studies of human eye movements show that the eye looking at an image, moves first to the head, makes brief excursions to other parts of the image, and keeps returning to the head. At the head, the eye watches the eye and mouth, glances at ears, hair, chin, and recurs to eye and mouth.[20] Not only does the eye watch the eye, but it learns to watch what the eye watches and to insert itself within another's eye. The existence of social, culture-transmitting groups depends upon this network of gazes, regulating intra-group behavior, establishing sympathetic bonds, enabling murderous cooperation against outsiders and prey, and making the head valuable.

Such attentiveness has social uses. As social primates, human beings are inevitably, though flexibly, hierarchical. Even the most hopefully egalitarian accounts of our primate cousins recognize a difference between "charismatic chimpanzees of both sexes and other more dependent members."[21] Recognition of place in the hierarchy depends on recognizing individuals, as in the folkloric motif of the disguised prince. Recognition of individuals depends in turn on the head, since the head's identity shows where the body belongs in the hierarchy. Affirming the primacy of the head as sign, high-ranking or valued heads appear on coins, stamps, magazine covers, in photographs, paintings, and sculptures. The more highly valued the head, the higher its facial prominence: so men and whites have more "face" in media photographs than do women and blacks.[22]

If the lineaments of the face enable us to recognize members of our species as members of our species and to tell one of us from the next, to differentiate members of the species, head size and shape enable anthropologists to tell one species of us from the next: *Australopithecus* from *homo habilis, homo habilis* from *homo erectus*. Three to four million years ago, preceding the enlargement of human cranial capacity by several million years,[23] bipedalism put the rounded head on top, rather than merely at the other, almost equally interesting,[24] end of the body. About two million years ago, the face of *homo erectus* retreated under the braincase, moving toward the globular head Edward O. Wilson claims "a perceptive Martian zoologist would regard . . . as a most significant clue to human biology."[25] The uniquely rounded head occupies a unique position relative to the genitalia, vertical and frontal, simultaneously visible. Covering the genitalia—the first self-conscious cultural act according to Genesis—enhances the head's prominence, interest, and vulnerability. Uncovered, the male genitalia protrude from the body at the legs, like the head at the shoulders. The Greek herm reduces the male body to stone head and genitals. Female genitalia are homologous with the whole torso, the "body" proper: breasts/eyes, vagina/mouth. Visiting a Turkish bath in 1717, Lady Mary Wortley Montagu observed that "if 'twas the fashion to go naked, the face would be hardly observed."[26] So archeologists identify as "fertility figures" conspicuously female bodies whose faces are hardly sculpted.

Gawking discreetly, Lady Mary inadvertently reveals that the head never sees itself. For moderns, the head's chief accomplishment is its role in self-formation. From infancy the self is formed by the responsive heads of others. Reversing Freud's hypothesis that the child experiences oceanic one-ness and lack of differentiation from his mother, many developmental psychologists now maintain with Colwyn Trevarthen that infants are born with an innate sense of "the virtual other." Daniel Stern, having rejected that view in favor of the fuller cognitive emergence at nine months, has come around to the strong view that self/other distinctions are present from birth and perhaps before. For Michael Tomasello, the infant already aware of self-other distinctions becomes capable at nine months of conceptualizing the other-as-self, a change visible in a move from dyadic behavior to triadic interactions.[27] Between nine and twelve months, the child looks to the adult's face to check that the other is attending to the same object as the self; between eleven and fourteen months the child follows the adult's gaze, putting herself in the other's situation to see what the other sees.[28] As Tomasello puts it, "Human cognition, including cognition of the self, is in large measure a social enterprise."[29]

Because the enterprise is social, it is also self-alienated. At about six months, infants reach "the mirror stage" and recognize themselves in mirrors. As Jacques Lacan insists, the self that recognizes itself sees itself in something other than itself—the mirror image.[30] Self-recognition is simultaneously self-alienation. The child discovers that she is *one*, a self, only by identifying herself with what is *other* than she, the speculary, spectral image in the mirror: *I am that; that is I*. The self is precisely the subject never at one with its own reality. The self defines itself by what it is not, a negation, in order to affirm a sense of its own identity that is always a lie: *I am that; that is I*.[31]

Common discourse understands the self as defined through the other in the expression "that boy just needs to find himself." The expression supposes that self awaits the boy in something outside himself, other than himself, that he can latch onto and disappear inside. The happiness of finding oneself is that one loses the self and has no sense of anything lost at all.

After the mirror stage, children learn to see through the eyes of the other, to follow the trajectory of the other's gaze in order to identify her intentions and object of attention. Studying the infant, the researcher follows the infant's face and the infant's gaze with her own. That power of self-alienated looking underlies both the ability to deceive and the empathy to which Jean Piaget ascribes moral reasoning.[32] To see as the other sees is to see as not-me and as me, simultaneously. The gaze founds a distinctively human sociality, proceeding beyond the cementing of social relationships, shared with other primates, and linking intentions via gazes, enabling, as Tomasello argues, the deliberate transmission of culture. Only humans hold up objects and point to them or bring them to others to show them.[33]

So goes the contemporary version of an ancient pastime: explaining the primacy of the head. Earlier accounts proceeded by analogy between the body and the cosmos or the social structure. In Indo-European mythologies, from head and skull issued the heavens, the vault of the sky, or, in Aryan mythology, the ruling castes.[34] In *Timaeus*, reversing Indo-European dismemberment and privileging geometry, Plato proposes that the perfect round head was created first, and the body followed, to serve the head. Plato's demiurge creates the universe as a perfect sphere, implicitly modeled on the head that, in turn, reproduces the round universe.[35] Isidore of Seville (ca. 560–636), proceeding more biologically, has a Christian's respect for the body to be resurrected: "The first part of the body is the head, and it received this name, *caput*, because all the feelings and nerves [*sensus omnes et nervi*] have their origin there [*initium capiunt*] and because all the well-springs of strength emanate from it."[36] Empirically, both Plato and Isidore had it right: heads indeed precede bodies in vertebrates (see the Epilogue), but that is not what they had in mind.

Head as hierarchy traditionally abuts head as person, life, the whole. For Plato, "the most sovereign" of man's three souls in head, chest, and liver dwells "in the summit of our body and lifts us from earth towards our celestial affinity." The neck separates that soul from the body so as not "to pollute the divine part."[37] So intent is Plato on unity and divinity that his text adds the differentiating genitalia to the body only at the last possible moment. For Plato the face figures hierarchy. "On the globe of the head" where are fixed "organs for all the forethought of the soul," the face is "the part having leadership."[38] The head as hierarchy survives in common use and in its Roman affiliates from *caput*: chief, chef, capital, capitol, capitalize, capitalism.

For Homer and the Romans, the head was the person, in life or in death. Carrying Hector's corpse, Priam redeems Hector's "head," while "the passionless heads of the dead," fleeting *psyche*, breath-souls, flit faceless through Hades.[39] The head as life persists in "capital punishment." The head as the whole person persists in common usage through the eighteenth century and survives in modern African English, but is largely ossified in current Anglo-American English, as in pricing "per head" or a "head count." Somewhat egalitarian (Roman slaves did not have "heads"; only citizens did), the head as whole person has been largely displaced by body, as in "body count," and its role assumed by "face."

When faces are understood to found sociality through sympathy, their politics become less hierarchical. The head abandoned for its connotations of domination shifts to the more egalitarian, affective, dyadic "face." Unlike heads, faces engage in interactive situations. The face enters conflicts that privilege the underdog: "He faced them down." The face acknowledges responsibilities to others: "She faced up to what she had done." The face transforms conflict into harmony: "Let's face the music and dance." Plato's "leadership" with its implicitly hierarchical and individualist politics becomes only one part of what faces do. The head is for itself and over others; the face is for others and to them.

Although decapitation, like death, seems simple, single, natural, and primitive, separating heads from bodies marks the consciousness of death that enables us to identify human consciousness or consciousness' becoming human. Lacan observes that "the first symbol in which we recognize humanity in its vestigial traces is the sepulture," and among the earliest signs of sepulture are skull rings.[40] If the separated head is the first sign that hominids are thinking in symbols, it is equally true that severed heads do not appear until hominids have begun to symbolize. In their absence of violence, the first separated heads contradict Freud's fable of the primal murder or René Girard's of the initial sacrifice.[41] Having acquired meaning, however, heads acquired value, and the development of better technologies for severing heads stimulated acquisitiveness. From our metaphors to Plato's cosmos, the greatest compliment paid to the head has been the frequency with which it is cut off. Privilege has its price. Decapitation bobs up as the decorative flourish to acts of violence, the finial on the spire, motivated not by bestiality since beasts do not decapitate, but by the irresistibility of symbolism, grounded in the body and coded by culture. Without symbolism, human heads would be safe from human hands.

1

Introduction to a Beheading

A Head Is Always a Sign of Something

Beheading is among the most ancient, widespread, and enduring of human cultural practices. Examples occur in every place, time, and level of culture. In Ashurbanipal's Nineveh, seventh-century B.C.E. Assyrians heaped heads beneath palm trees, the harvested fruits of victory, tallied by meticulous scribes (fig. 1.1). In his fourteenth-century progresses, Tamerlane piled heads into monitory mountains. Heads were carried aloft by Japanese warriors of the twelfth century, shrunk by Jivaro in the twentieth, tossed by Aztecs in their ball games, collected in baskets by Jehu and the Nazis, preserved in niches by pre-Roman Celts. Headsmen took them off throughout Europe until the end of the eighteenth century, when the guillotine modernized the practice until the end of the twentieth. The Third Reich decapitated the traitors of the White Rose during World War II; the French last used their guillotine to execute a capital sentence in 1977. Saudi executioners still decapitate with a sword, and western newspapers and Internet sites eagerly report it.

In spontaneous political actions, medieval peasants, Burmese rebels, Latin American death squads, enlightened British officers, and genial U.S. soldiers have severed heads for display. In September 1988, popular risings in Burma produced the people's decapitations of numerous public officials, their heads hung from tree limbs. In 1990, in South Africa, the leader of a criminal gang in the townships was seized, killed, and decapitated. His head was circulated through the schools in the township as a warning. In 1998 Indonesians hunted and decapitated ninjas to halt their sorcery. In 1945 American troops decollated a Japanese and propped his head on their tank as a trophy; *Life* magazine chose not to print the photograph. In 1991, American troops decollated an Iraqi and propped his head on their tank as a trophy; *Life* chose to print the photograph.[1]

Fig. 1.1. King Ashurbanipal triumphs over the allies of Shamash-Shum-Ukin. From the North Palace of Ashurbanipal at Nineveh. (© Copyright The British Museum)

Historically, decapitation is a public and social act, with public uses, functions, and audience. Beheading occurs in authorized forms as a tactic in warfare, an aspect of a legal system, or an access to mystical empowerment. Its unauthorized forms seek to redeploy, for public or for private uses, the magical, symbolic, and real power monopolized by authority.

Representations of decapitation are still more pervasive than the practice. They appear in every possible medium: stone walls, photographs, epics, paintings, histories, films, comic strips, mustard pots, coffee cups, and newspapers. From nursery rhymes to Nabokov, Botticelli to Louise Bourgeois, the Celtic beheading game to Mortal Kombat, unattached heads are all about us—in fish tanks in horror movies, on Saturday morning cartoons (Beetlejuice does a lot with his head), in French-language video learning programs such as "La Guillotine" (if you miss the vocabulary word, the guillotine cuts off the aristocrat's head), in scandalous video arcade games (Mortal Kombat's once notorious, now banal "final move"), in popular movies from the first full-length *Ben Hur* to *Braveheart, Mononoke Hime,* and *Kill Bill Vol. I.*

In medieval literature, the challenger in the Beheading Game of Irish folktales acts a superhuman fantasy of power. He can put his head back on when someone else cuts it off. In Peggy Glanville Hicks's opera *The Exchanged Heads,* a bereaved wife makes the ultimate Freudian slip. Restoring her husband and his best friend to life, she puts the heads on the wrong bodies. Judith displays Holofernes's head; her ephebic cousin David carries Goliath's; Perseus makes off with Medusa's, and Salome attends St. John's. The severed head in contemporary western culture is a grisly and uncanny object. In other cultures, as once in our own, it is an object of mystical veneration.

Beheading always signifies, but always signifies differently within specific codes supplied by culture. In many cultures, the head is the life.[2] In ours, for a century, the head has been the penis. In all, the head is a sign. Neither essential flesh nor irreducible bone, heads are plastic. Taking meaning from the discourse in which they are inserted, heads make meanings within that discourse. In terms of Saussure's distinction in the sign between the signified and the signifier, a head is a signifier, and its signified depends on the discursive system into which it is inserted.[3] Setting no limit on the utterances, the body provides a universal grammar, with morphology (forms) and syntax (arrangement of parts).

Beheading is the body's catachresis: a violation of the rules of the body's grammar that generates a sensation of dismay, horror, delight, or absurdity. "Catachresis" names the shocking literary figure that goes "against use": *kata chresthai.* Abusing the order of meaning, catachresis wrenches words from their proper contexts and puts them where they do not belong. Wrenched from its body, a head no longer performs its usual acts and is no longer available for self-confirming, assertive, or responsive uses. Its open eyes no longer move. Selves know themselves only through the body of the other ("Head Matters"), and such catachreses undo the claims of community, founded on sympathetic identification with others who define us.

With a severed head, the self, defined and confirmed from infancy by the responses of others, encounters an other that fails to give the accustomed, mutually defining responses. As a sign, the severed head communicates aborted communication. Others' heads, smiling, speaking, listening, responding, establish our reality. From them, we learn that we are, and how we are doing. A head that does not respond is a mirror that gives back no reflection although we stand before it, searching for ourselves in the other. When something is wrong with the other, we feel it as something wrong with us. We do not like being "cut dead," and we call it by its right name. We have come calling, but the other/self is not at home. Freud finds such transactions uncanny: "that class of the frightening which leads back to what is known of old and long familiar."[4] Humans know nothing longer, and with less interruption, than responsive faces. When a face fails to respond, the known and familiar have been made strange, and the unexpected, mysterious subtraction of presence and fullness frightens and dismays. The uncanny head disrupts the cognitive process of sympathetic identification fundamental to social identity. Failing to perform its usual work of defining the self through interaction, the other calls the self into question. A severed head is always the same, disturbing.

It remains disturbing until it is naturalized within a system of meanings. Then the disturbance subsides as constructed meaning replaces the natural social horror of the severed head. In Peirce's terms, the severed head shifts from icon to symbol, from a sign indicating death to a sign promising any meaning but death.[5] Death's fleshed face, a severed head is always iconic of death. As symbol, however, the severed head evokes meanings beyond itself, unrelated to itself or its production, within a discursive system one must know to interpret the symbol.[6] Who would suspect without being told that Dante's Bertran de Born holds his severed head before his body like a lantern to signify schism? The hideous, pathetic object that is a severed head dissolves into a realm of signification that simultaneously erases/re-cognizes the object and justifies its contemplation. The iconic head provokes disturbance that symbolism neutralizes and appropriates as vitality. In an intricate antithesis, in head cults the head iconic of death holds life. Collecting heads, headhunters appropriate the life of their human prey. Turning heads into signs enables modern critics to consider heaps of human heads with the equanimity of Tamerlane.

Traditional Beheadings

Preceding language and art, cherishing the head coincides with recognizing death. Neanderthals, our speechless cousins, preserved crania and scattered flower petals over bodies in graves.[7] The earliest ancestral human skulls, discovered in 2003, lack lower jaws and other skeletal parts. They also show marks of cuts, suggesting they were removed for symbolic purposes.[8] Separating the head from the body, the ancestors created a thing, a severed head, to use as a sign. Without language, their sign is for us, as perhaps for them, only partial, a signifier lacking an articulable signified. Atoning for the silences of the Neanderthals and *homo sapiens idaltu,* human cultures have elaborated five principal types of traditional, authorized beheadings: the ancestral head, removed after death, not taken by violence; the trophy head, taken in warfare or raid; the sacrificial head, taken from a living person by decapitation in the performance of a religious rite; the presentation head, taken in a political struggle to remove a contender or rival; the public execution, proceeding from a legal decision. By excluding violence, the first of these—a head not taken by violence but preserved for worship—marks an essential category: the venerated head, possessed of mystic powers that communicates with an invisible realm of being. Of these socially authorized decapitations, only the public execution survives, as a traditional Islamic form of humane execution, the west having abandoned capital punishment by decapitation in the 1970s.

Commentators tend to blur the types since distinguishing them requires looking at severed heads, objects one would prefer not to see. Jean-Louis Voisin, assimilating the Romans to what Fernand Benoît calls "the Mediterranean air of the severed head," demonstrates the prodigious variety within Roman practices, yet designates his Romans simply "chasseurs de têtes," headhunters.[9] The types matter, however, if their surviving traces are to become visible.

The ancestral head, collected and venerated within the group, may be the oldest type, if *homo sapiens idaltu* and Neanderthal skull rings exemplify it. Reported by Herodotus as a seemingly anomalous variation on the trophy head, the Issedonians preserved their fathers' heads as skull cups for use at the annual festival of the fathers. The protective head is neither the head of an enemy, nor a head taken in a hostile action. The fathers seem to have died naturally, since Herodotus does not characterize the nation as parricidal. "In other respects [the Issedonians] observe justice," he affirms. At Entremont in southern France, a Celtic head-cult site, six skulls were found belonging to men over forty-five "perhaps suggesting ancestor-worship."[10] Through the nineteenth century in Brittany, families kept skulls in boxes, ark-shaped coffers with openings that made visible the contents, inscribed "Here lies the head of . . ."[11]

Such peaceably secured heads persist in the religious relic, which may be secured by natural death or recovered after an enemy's violence. When

Margaret Roper rescued and preserved the head of her father Sir Thomas More, she simultaneously resisted tyranny and honored the father, an individual acting within a patriarchal community.[12] Religious relics occasionally pose a problem of canny opportunism. Among the Issedonians, the wise son doubtless knew his father, and the finger of St. Theresa of Avila is probably hers. The churches of medieval Europe, however, brimmed with desirable heads: John the Baptist, James the brother of Christ, Matthew the Evangelist, St. Philip—prestigious saints associated with Christ a millennium earlier. From what bodies those heads were taken, and their identity, the Lord—or the head taker—only knows.[13]

The most recent form assumed by the venerated head is the shrine commemorating atrocity. In Rwanda and Cambodia, skulls are heaped in remembrance of violence suffered. The head still protects and heals the survivors, restored and reconnected with the dead through contemplation and meditation. Severing the head once prevented the dead from coming back; these shrines collect heads to prevent the killers from coming back. Memory replaces magic. Such radically different cultural constructions share only the evocation of mystical power, appealing to a realm beyond immediate sense experience, through the presence of a sacred head.

Venerated heads share access to mystical power with the trophy head —a complex, ancient, enduring, and irrepressible icon of death, emblem of war, sign of the warrior, symbol of life. Exuberant, triumphant violence makes the trophy head at once invigorating (to takers) and horrifying (to their neighbors). A social sign of individual martial prowess, the trophy head is an always ritualized, widely distributed, terror-inducing sign of victory. Reaffirming and strengthening group bonds against outsiders whose heads are taken during the group's activity, whether war or raid, the trophy head gestures toward a transcendent realm that the head in no way resembles: life, not death, power, not impotence. The head is hunted for the sake of a power the head confers and continues to possess even after it is severed, a power that can be appropriated, possessed, and transferred to the taker. Yet the head is also hunted for power over the head as a sign of the warrior's success relative to other warriors. That power is real (indexical, in Peircean terminology), not symbolic. The head marks a difference between the dead and the not-dead, the loser and the victor.

The symbolic component of headhunting is usually invisible to outsiders. Non-participants shrink from the visible horror of the spiked, shrunken head or assimilate the practice to systems they do understand, for example as a sign of the warrior's personal prowess within the group or as evolutionary advantage. The Mundurucú of northwestern Brazil, who still make their neighbors very nervous, used to collect human heads for their contribution to animal hunts and gave a special title to the successful headhunter: *Dajeboisi,* mother of the peccary. Trophy heads, carried into the forest on hunts for game, influenced the spirit protectors ("mothers") and improved the availability and supply of peccary, the most desirable game.[14] To ensure the heads were working, the Dajeboisi refrained from sexual intercourse for three rainy seasons. In a Mundurucú myth of the origin of the peccary, collected by Claude Lévi-Strauss, the peccary were originally human, transformed into wild pig while copulating and grunting like pigs. An alternate form of the myth emphasizes that antisocial behavior by the humans warranted their transformation into peccary.[15] The myths make the pair, "human head/peccary spirit mother" metonymic, elucidating the human head's effect on the invisible realm of peccary spirit mothers, abutting the visible material world. For outsiders, the connection between human heads and peccary is not obvious, and the myths suggest the Mundurucú also want an explanation.

The trophy head is the warrior's work, a sacrificial head the community's. The sacrificial head is removed and offered with peaceable, formal, premeditated violence. Sacrificed were captives taken in war, children, virgins, slaves, retainers, the marginal members of society, expendable as materials of human sacrifice. In René Girard's account, marginal persons replace the reproducing members of a society, since the householders, the core of the social group, cannot be sacrificed without destroying the social bonds the sacrifice preserves and protects.[16] Heads taken ritually sustained the state at celebrations of triumphs (Rome), at burials of an emperor (China), in memory of fathers (Rome), upon the succession of a new ruler (Dahomey), and for the safety of bridges and cities in foundation sacrifices from Rome (Remus) to London and Borneo. In 1989 in Borneo, a spokesman for an engineering institute assured the public that heads had not been used to construct bridge foundations.[17] "Skull racks," the skulls lacking lower jaws, in the great central square at Tenochtitlan scandalized sixteenth-century Spaniards and secured the life of the sun.[18] Unlike the ancestral or trophy head, but like the execution, the sacrificial head depends upon the human willingness to proceed to certain death without resistance.

A presentation head looks like a trophy head, but isn't. Presented, a head is reduced from symbol to sign. No special power inheres in the head or accrues to the taker from it. The taker expects reward or recognition from the person to whom he presents the head. That reward is expected because the head, sign of a particular person, is dead. There is no life in it. Single, individuated, the presentation head evokes no symbolic realm, but marks the end of a succession struggle. The trophy head, rationalized, is no longer a trophy head. Two stories of David illustrate the difference.

When David cuts off Goliath's head and returns to the city rejoicing, he has taken a trophy for himself and the Lord. The head spreads dismay among the Philistine ranks but principally symbolizes the Lord's mighty power in David, who cuts off Goliath's head with Goliath's sword (I Sam. 17:51–54). When Ishbosheth's head is presented to David, the murderers, Rechab and Baanah, unsung, unsinging heroes, expect reward for securing David's kingdom from the son of Saul (2 Sam. 4:5–8). Mediated, demystified, instrumentalized, and rationalized, the presentation head is taken off by an underling and secures someone else's power. Rather than glorifying the taker, the head-taking shames him.

Who presented Pompey's head to Caesar in Egypt? The names are recorded, but not remembered. Different accounts give different names to the centurion who sawed off Cicero's head and hand to deliver them to Marc Antony.[19] No one makes any mistake, however, as to whose head was presented to whom in these notorious cases. Mediated and made instrumental to the secular transfer of power, the head is dead, demystified. No magic radiates from it. Caesar weeps when he sees the head of Pompey. He does not attach it to his person, not even to his shield. The presentation head recognizes and subordinates the individual within an incipient formal structure of state power as it signals the instability of power. It makes no gestures beyond its own efficacy.

Sam Peckinpah's *Bring Me the Head of Alfredo García* (1974) seems at first to refer to a trophy head, but inspection exposes the *in*formal execution that marks the presentation head. What could be a trophy head, were Alfredo García and I locked in combat, is inserted in a sign system in which the head marks not the prowess of the person who takes the head, but the power of the person to whom the head is presented, Me, waiting for Alfredo García's head.

The formal execution advertises stability and seems at first to belong to the sign, like the presentation head. The despised executioner or *carnifex* takes a head not for himself but on the command of others. A vestige of the violence excluded from the city by the sovereign's monopoly of violence, the head, on Michel Foucault's analysis, warns of the consequences of violating the sovereign's order or peace.[20] Held up by the hair and presented to the people, the decollated head models the sovereign's power over the living, warned, terrorized. Yet that head held up also gestures towards the realm "justice," a symbolic order shared by people and sovereign, absent from Foucault's analysis. That head fulfills the sovereign's responsibility for order and peace to the people, and it belongs to them as much as to him. The claim on the symbolic preserves behaviors that would otherwise be condemned. When heads-on-bridges suggest "justice" as little as heads-on-sticks suggest "peccary spirit mothers," the symbol has shrunk to a sign of power, shrinking again to the sign of an individual death, from index to icon. The power of the head to suggest something other than itself makes it vulnerable. Taken for a symbol, a head may be taken indeed.

Of these types, the modern reader is likely to dismiss trophy and sacrificial heads as "primitive" and non-European; to blink the analogy between ancestral skull cups and Christian saints; to regard the presentation head as rational and utilitarian, though a sign of political instability; and to regard capital punishment by decollation with more interest and distaste than other modes of capital punishment, whether he favors or opposes capital punishment. The reader may (or may not) have heard of the Celtic head cult, providing a European site for headhunting. She will know that the Romans privileged decapitation as punishment for Roman citizens and attended somewhat unsavory games, but certainly were not headhunters, and she will believe that the Greeks, pure, whole, never touched the body to mar it. Everyone in Athens died like Socrates, by hemlock, as Michael Arnush characterizes an attitude still widespread among classicists. Such views have been unsettled for the Greeks by Emily Vermeule and for the Romans by Jean-Louis Voisin, producing three headhunting peoples rather than one among Greeks, Romans, and Celts. Celtic scholars occasionally mutter that Celts "retained archaic practices . . . long outmoded" in Greece and Rome, but leave it to their readers to know what those practices were and what traces appear in Greece and Rome.[21] The following précis of European headhunting intends to bring the practice home to our favorite intellectual ancestors, rather than abandoning it to Melanesia and the Amazon. Briefly put, the Greeks masked, the Romans codified, and the Celts still mystify.

Traditional Types: Greeks, Romans, and Celts

In pre-Christian Europe, Greeks, Romans, and Celts shared many beliefs about heads, took many heads off, and differed fundamentally over severed heads. For all, the head was the life, and in it resided the procreative force. The hair on the head was linked with pubic hair as index of sexual power. The secretions of genitals, breasts, and eyes seemed analogous. Animal horns were regarded as outcroppings of sexual potency, and thus unfaithful wives made horns "for" their spouses, who lacked potency.[22] All considered the head of the highest symbolic significance. All engaged steadily in warfare, Greeks and Romans systematically and imperially, Celts persistently, exuberantly, and defensively after Rome's expansion reciprocated the Gauls' fourth-century sack of Rome.

The Greeks knew the trophy head so well that they disguised it as Athena's aegis, setting on Jove's shield the severed head that protects and terrifies. Underground, the Gorgon head protected Persephone's realm: an image of death materializing between the dead and the living. Professedly horrified by these vestiges of trophy heads, the Greeks had given them to the gods by the time of Homer and Hesiod, but kept them close at hand masked—literally—as culturally central images.

Openly, exultantly, and terrifyingly, the Celts celebrated the trophy head that the Greeks assigned to the gods. Unmistakably "cut heads" (*têtes coupées*) adorn their coins, sculptures, sanctuaries, confirming in their material remains practices recounted around 90 B.C.E. by Poseidonius (ca. 135–50 B.C.E.) in his travels through Celtic regions. His lost work, cited by Strabo and Diodorus Siculus, remains the principal literary evidence for the beliefs and practices of the Celts, who cannot speak for themselves.

Confronting the Celts as living opponents, destroying their sanctuaries (Entremont, 124 B.C.E.), the Romans condemned Celtic practices as barbaric even as they specialized in the presentation head and the legal execution.[23] Producing decapitation as the mark distinguishing civilization from barbarism, the Romans thematized aversion to decollation, perhaps the first people to do so, and practiced it proficiently. In conquered regions, they tolerated practices of which they ostensibly disapproved and often adopted those practices. They deheroicized, demystified, and instrumentalized decollation, but simultaneously elevated it as the sign of a citizen no longer invulnerable to physical punishment. That paradoxical dialectic is what the progress of civilization means.

Celts: Heads and Horses

To idealized Greeks and Romans, the Celts of Gaul present an eerie antithesis with severed heads neither monstrous nor apotropaic, and sometimes female. Pre-Roman remains in Provence attest the Celtic practice of setting heads in niches and on door lintels, often linked with horses.[24] At Roquepertuse, the niches of the sanctuary portal contain heads, now skulls. A lintel features four schematic, graven horses' heads. The lintel at Nîmes alternates galloping horses and heads. At Entremont numerous sculptures feature a hand gripping a head, its eyes bulging, yet shrunken to slits, mouth rigid (fig. 1.2). Sometimes the heads are piled up, as in an ensemble of four heads—originally six—found at Aubergue.[25] Gallic coins often represent a mounted warrior bearing a severed head in his hand.[26] Celtic burials repeat the association with horses, for horses and warriors have been found buried together, most recently eight warriors and their horses at Clermont Ferrand, dating perhaps from the first century B.C.E.[27]

That the heads were more than sculptural, Greco-Roman historians report. Poseidonius, continuing Polybius's history, condemns as disgusting the Celtic habit of preserving and displaying enemies' heads, especially on the doors of houses.[28] A century later, Diodorus Siculus, a contemporary of Vergil, still reports that heads are being nailed to house fronts. The Celts struck off heads of enemies, hung the heads over their horses' necks, sang a victory song, and finally nailed the heads to their house fronts, as if, says Diodorus, they were animals taken in a hunt.[29] Important heads were embalmed in cedar oil and kept in chests in the house, where the host showed them to visitors and boasted of their value. Livy reports that the Boii turned the head of the consul Postumus into a gold-mounted cup for use in a principal temple. More sympathetic to the Celts than Diodorus, Barry Cunliffe suggests that "evidently the skill of such a distinguished enemy was a gift appropriate to a god."[30]

Decollating conquered enemies is attested throughout the Celtic region, which for Herodotus in the fifth century extended from the Danube to the Iberian peninsula.[31] The practice of mounting heads on houses appears also east of Greece and Rome. Herodotus reports the Tauri, a people who lived entirely by war and plunder, protected their houses with heads conquered in war, elevating them on poles over the chimney, so the whole house came under the protection of the head.[32]

Fig. 1.2. Celtic stone sculpture. Hand resting on severed human head, from the oppidum of Entremont. Height about 23 cm. Musée Granet, Aix-en-Provence. (Photo Credit: Erich Lessing, Art Resource, NY)

Heads supported the foundations of the house and the prosperity of the population. Throughout the Roman period, Celts in Gaul and Britain deposited heads in house foundations and in springs. Sacrificing a head secured the fertility and safety of the house by imparting its life to it, sharing its magic, and reinforcing its power.[33] The heads were occasionally those of children, gender unspecified. In Britain, female skulls, outnumbered four to one by males, have been found in wells, in the foundations of pottery shops, and in conventional decapitated burials.[34] At Entremont's inner sanctuary, among the heads of those aged over forty-five was a woman's head.[35]

Where a head was found, power accrued. An Etrurian seer tried to steal from Rome the blessing imparted when the Romans unearthed a head where they meant to set their capitol. Unable to divine the head's meaning by themselves, the Romans sought interpretive assistance beyond their own borders. The seer Olenus of Cales drew a circle on the ground in front of him and relocated the found head "here." Warned by the seer's son of a potential trick against the headship conferred by the head, the canny Romans prevented him from relocating the head's power by saying, "Not exactly, it was at Rome."[36] Heads in springs returned life to the source of life. In the nineteenth century, numerous skulls excavated from a stream near London seemed to corroborate Geoffrey of Monmouth's story that the Venedoti decapitated an entire surrendered Roman legion and heaped the heads beside the Walbrook. Now the heads are interpreted as offerings that perhaps inspired Geoffrey's story, turning up in his century.[37]

The Celts represented their gods as heads without bodies, the part containing the power of the whole. Reproducing and multiplying the head's power, they sculpted herms with two heads and gods with three. Polytheistic cultures often multiply heads—or snakes—to signify power. Brahma has three heads; Buddha often has eleven. Peruvian Christ-the-King on the cross has three. The familiar psychoanalytic view that multiplicity signifies absence, lack, or castration descends from the Old Testament's monotheistic mockery of the many gods of wood and stone that are not gods at all.[38] For Celts, as later for Christians, three was a number of peculiar potency. Celts multiplied the names, siblings, and aspects of female and male gods in triads.[39] Cernunnos's three heads with three flowing beards and mustaches mark his wisdom, while the Gallic torque round his neck marks his riches.[40]

In later Celtic folklore, the head still retains its magic. The legend of Cuchulainn suggests that taking a head was a rite of passage, signifying a young man's new status as warrior.[41] Medieval Celts propose the Beheading Game, and Sir Gawain comes of age by risking decapitation. Bendigeidfran's head talks and eats for more than eighty years before he requires burying, at London, his face toward France.[42] Unlike other virgin martyrs, whose beheadings finally silence them,[43] the Welsh St. Winifred, decapitated by a lustful pagan, returns to life when the priest puts her head back on her neck. Saint Denis, the first bishop of Paris, shows his Celtic origins in his third-century martyrdom at Montmartre. His head having been struck off, he picked up his martyred head and ran with it. Dropping it, he picked it up again and ran some more, dropping and picking up until finally the body fell, five kilometers from Montmartre. There the faithful built the Abbey St. Denis. In the Pantheon's *Last Hope of the Martyr,* Jean-Léon Gérôme's saint extends his sinewy arms to pick up his bearded head. Such lively heads are the life itself, and they continue to live with or without the body.

Sometimes life springs from death. Cut off the head of an ogre or animal, and a whole, beautiful hero leaps from the corpse, freed. George Lyman Kittredge considers beheading "only a special means of putting to death; the main point is to kill the enchanted body" or shed its blood, but he collects three times as many decapitations as simple deaths, wounds, and bloodshed in tales Swedish, Norwegian, Lettish, Highland, Irish, Welsh, Tyrolese, German, French, and Zulu.[44] Such tales appropriate as narrative the powers symbolized in ancient Celtic practices of placing heads in springs, foundations, or lintels. The heads of medieval Celtic folklore have a protective function and remain alive when they ought, by rights (or our lights), to be dead.

In the absence of written records, the ideology associated with the niches of Roquepertuse remains elusive. As Livy's account of the consul's golden skull cup suggests, however, for Celts the skill lingered in the skull. For Romans it did not. For Romans the skull signified absence where there had been presence, not continuing presence. So Lucretius argued for the soul's mortality from the evidence supplied by watching a severed head die. Soldiers, he observed, continue to fight, unaware their arms or feet are missing. "The head too when cut off from the warm and living trunk retains on the ground the expression of life and open eyes, until it has delivered up all the remnants of soul."[45] The head emptied of soul is also empty of transcendent meaning. Yet Romans bought back the heads of their dead for burial: the head was the person.

Collectors of heads experience a magical or supernatural power passing between decapitator and decapitated. That power establishes either a continuing relationship desirable to preserve (so the head is conserved, as by the Mundurucú) or a potentially dangerous connection severed by severing the head from the body (so the head is collected, but not kept, as by the Ilongot).[46] The head's value as offering propitiates a deity or ensures fertility. To accumulate or multiply heads is to accumulate power, passing from the head to its possessor. Severing heads in battle or after requires and demonstrates considerable power—physical strength to perform the action and psychic steel to overcome the innate aversiveness of handling the dead. So these beliefs are not altogether irrational.

Masking Medusa

The most famous—and invisible—of trophy heads is Medusa's, mounted on the aegis of Athena or the shield of Jove. Of all ancient peoples, the Greeks seem most remote from headhunting practices or trophy heads. Nor is that an accident: they worked very deftly to achieve that illusion. Plato's cosmic analogy in *Timaeus* trades the traditional Indo-European imagery of the world formed from a dismembered god for an original sphere. In turn, the head is modeled on "the round shape of the universe," and the body is given it "for its service." As form and order, divine and dominant, the perfect round head is sacred without horror. Nothing could be farther from a severed head or from Medusa's snaky locks.

Yet nothing more closely resembles one possible fate of a severed head than Plato's account of the service the body offers: "Accordingly, *that the head might not roll upon the ground with its heights and hollows of all sorts, and have no means to surmount the one or to climb out of the other,* they gave it the body as a vehicle for ease of travel" (emphasis added).[47] Plato's body, four elongated, bending, clinging limbs, keeps his perfect sphere from the humiliations suffered by heads in Homer and on vases. On a fifth-century, Attic black-figured lekythos, three dancing warriors carry in their hands severed heads resembling their own in beard, nose, and helm.[48] Insofar as Plato's singular round head embodies an ideal of perfection and unitary wholeness, it masks what Greek mythology and art knew, and had already turned into a mask. Monstrous, terrifying trophy heads come first, and great heroes cut off heads in their anger. As Hans van Wees puts it, "'Anger is to heroic what sex is to Victorian morality.' In the epics, anger, not sex, is the dangerous, uncontrollable drive that rules men's lives."[49] The *Iliad* could not be more frank about its subject: it sings the "wrath" of Achilles.

Amid the *Iliad*'s flying limbs, severed neck bones, eviscerated guts, shattered thighs, eye sockets spilling their apples, heads seem to assume no special prominence. When heads are severed by the hero's powerful arm, in the *Iliad* as in the *Odyssey,* the precisely detailed episodes resemble executions. A man kneeling, supplicating, pleading for his life, loses his head to a single blow.[50] So Dolon falls to Diomede, and Hippolochus, son of Antimachus, to Agamemnon. Such heads may be thrown into the battle press, like balls, without much attention paid. Yet heads lifted up have a different effect.

When a head is cut off, raised, and made the object of a boast, the gesture stills the battlefield. So Penelaus severs Ilioneus's head, lofts the head on his lance, piercing the eye-socket, and boasts Ilioneus's name and their fate to the Trojans. The Trojans freeze:

> This said, and seene, pale feare possest, all those of *Ilion*;
> And eu'ry man cast round his eye, to see where Death was not,
> That he might flee him.
> (XIV, 506–7; Chapman, XIV, 434–36)[51]

The severed head is where death is. The sight stuns and immobilizes the warriors, reduced to gazes looking anywhere to escape what they see—destruction. Caught in that moment between fight and flight, they occupy an instant of perfect stillness that may last forever.

Nor are such displays always temporary or merely incidental. The pivotal conflict over Patroclus turns on the fate of his head. As the Greeks struggle with Hector over Patroclus's body, Iris warns Achilles what Hector is thinking—he intends to mount Patroclus's head on the walls of Troy:

> To drag him back to *Troy* the Foe contends;
> Nor with his Death the Rage of *Hector* ends:
> A Prey to Dogs he dooms the Corse to lye,
> And marks the Place to fix his Head on high.
> Rise, and prevent (if yet thou think of Fame)
> Thy Friend's Disgrace, thy own eternal Shame!
> (XVIII, 176–78; Pope, XVIII, 213–18)

"And marks the Place to fix his Head on high": Hector was last seen intending to cut off Patroclus's head after having stripped the body (XVII, 125–27). The threat brings Achilles back to the field. Reciprocating Hector's intent, Achilles promises Patroclus's shade the severed head of Hector and the lives of twelve Trojan children (XVIII, 334–36). Euphorbus also fantasies taking Menelaos's head home to give to his parents (XVII, 37–40). The structure of threats focuses on privileged heads without excluding the anonymous sacrificial heads of children.

Presiding over these severed human heads is the Gorgon head on Jove's aegis, carried by Athena through the camp, imitated in effigy on Agamemnon's shield (V, 733ff., XI, 36–37). Lofted by Athena, the aegis rouses a camp to battle fury. It creates warriors, disconnecting the men from homely attachments and arousing battle's burning desire. Forgetful of domestic, sympathetic claims, warriors catch the contagion of battle lust that hand-to-hand killing demands. As Chapman's aegis spreads fury, however, the Gorgon head does not appear:

> the gray-eyed Maide
> Great Ægis (Ioues bright shield) sustain'd, that can be never old;
> Never corrupted, fring'd about, with serpents forg'd of gold. . . .
> Through the host, with this the Godesse ranne
> In furie, casting round her eyes; and furnisht euerie man
> With strength; exciting all to armes, and fight incessant. None
> Now lik'd their lou'd homes like the warres. And as fire vpon
> A huge wood, on the heights of hills, that farre off hurles his light;
> So the diuine brasse shin'd on these, thus thrusting on for fight. . . .
> (II, 446–56; Chapman, II, 394f.)

Although the aegis works, the Gorgon head is not unveiled until three books later. Thrust forward, the Gorgon head obtrudes war's peculiar horrors, itself the emblem. In Chapman's translation, all the elements are abstract, except the entirely physical head "held out to view":

> About her brode-spred shoulders hung, his huge and horrid shield,
> Fring'd round with euer-fighting Snakes; through it, was drawn to
> life
> The miseries, and deaths of fight; in it frownd bloodie *Strife*;
> In it shin'd sacred *Fortitude*; in it fell *Pursuit* flew;
> In it the monster *Gorgons* head, in which (held out to view)
> Were all the dire ostents of Ioue.
> (V, 738–42; Chapman, V, 754–59)

A trophy head, obtained by violence, incites to violence, and its distinctive, internal mark is the rage necessary to sever a head. So as Hector drives, destroying Greeks, "The eyes of *Gorgon* burnt in him, and warres vermilion God" (VIII, 348–49; Chapman, VIII, 312–13). The terrifying eyes entering Hector make him a monster equivalent to the war god himself.

The *Odyssey* reverses these relationships: fury is still expressed by the urge to decapitate, but the prospect of seeing Gorgon's head terrifies.

Challenged by his kinsman Eurylochus, Odysseus wants to strike off his head: only that action matches his fury. At home in Ithaca, the massacre of the suitors ends with the epic's only decapitation. The challenge to Odysseus's head and wife ends when the augur's head, still stuttering, rolls across the floor.

> Full through his neck the weighty faulchion sped:
> Along the pavement roll'd the mutt'ring head.
> (XXII, 326–29; Pope, XXII, 365–66)

The actor's fury is the observer's terror. When Odysseus begins to feel too comfortable in Persephone's realm, longing to see Theseus and other heroes, he suddenly thinks that Persephone might send up from lower Hades a Gorgon's head, *kephalon gorgeion*. Nothing frightens Odysseus, yet after a momentary stillness, he flees, propelled by terror.

Jean-Pierre Vernant identifies the Gorgon as guardian of the underworld and emblem of the most "other" of all, the dead.[52] Functionally, the Gorgon that Odysseus fears is a trophy head rising on its own. Metonymically, it vents the fury expressed when a head is severed: the head comes back, armed with Earth's creatures. In Latin, *terra* terrifies, *terrere*.

Yet Homer is already playing "now you see it, now you don't" with the trophy head. Carried by Athena through the camp, it does its work without naming Gorgon or the Gorgon's head. Only when the shield is described in Book V does the head appear. So the Gorgon head is and is not the madness-working aegis. Ilioneus's head is held up but not fixed. Patroclus's is threatened with being fixed, but not with being held up, and his body is rescued. Achilles does not sever Hector's head once he controls the body, and the twelve slaughtered Trojan children probably had their throats slit and heads removed, but Homer does not describe the sacrifice. Yet when a head is treated like a trophy head, lifted up on a lance and displayed to opposing warriors in a vigorous, powerful boast, the real head on a spear produces the same effect as the Gorgon head Odysseus imagines. In the middle of carnage, the single head, lofted on a spear, stills tumult and, for a moment, turns everyone's heart to stone.

So ends the Medusa myth, when Perseus pulls from his pouch the Gorgon's head and petrifies his enemies, turning them to stone. Yet as Freud and Ferenczi noticed, something very odd has happened to this head: it is female, punished by a goddess. In Hesiod, the Gorgon Medusa is an aboriginal trophy head—stolen by ambush, raised aloft to terrify opponents, and then hung up or displayed on the person to identify the hero as a taker of heads. According to Jean-Pierre Vernant, Perseus "decapitat[es] Medusa and appropriat[es] her head" with "the *harpe* and *kibisis*, the sickle and pouch, implements for headhunting."[53] Once used, the horrid head is passed on to the gods to inspire the terror head-taking produces and the rage it requires.

Identifying Medusa is an ancient game.[54] Vernant evokes beautifully what the head means—the ultimate alterity, death—while Stephen Wilk solves the puzzle. Jane Harrison identified Medusa as a myth explaining the pre-existing mask called *gorgoneion*. That mask features bulging eyes, thrust-out tongue, round cheeks, and a fringe of snakes. A common image among the Greeks, it also occurs in Asia, the Pacific, the Americas, and Africa. Modern forensics enabled Wilk to establish the mask's referent. "Gorgon" represents the head of a dead man who has lain at least forty-eight hours unburied. Putrefying gases build up in the body, causing internal swelling, blackening the skin, pushing the tongue from the mouth and the eyes from their sockets. Sometimes the lips recede from the teeth, and the hair detaches from the scalp. The eye sockets and skin ooze. For skeptics, Wilk provides photographs from Keith Simpson's textbook on forensic medicine.[55]

The bloated face, protruding tongue, and round staring eyes are completely convincing—go look—and the sight would not have been unfamiliar to any ancient people after battles. Losers often went deliberately unburied, furnishing the tables of the birds in the great "supper of God" remarked in Job and Revelation and depicted in Greek and Assyrian sculpture. In Aeschylus, the Furies stink and ooze, repellent carriers of decay and putrefaction, like flies settling on meat. In the Gorgon head, Plato's perfect sphere rots.

Turned into a gorgoneion, the Gorgon head does for a Greek everything a trophy head does for a Celt. He puts it in the same places where it serves the same purposes. The Celtic link between heads and horses recurs in a persistent association Vernant finds between the term *gorgos* and horses. In numerous compounds, *gorgos* describes horses, pawing the ground, flaring their nostrils, snuffing the wind, mustering for battle; the word "takes on a quasi-technical meaning."[56]

A puzzling detail of the Perseus legend falls into place. The monstrous birth that Jenny Strauss Clay calls "merely an unnatural sideshow" becomes a main event.[57] When Medusa's head is cut off, there spring, born from her neck, a warrior and a horse, Chrysaor and Pegasus. The winged horse and warrior are twins. The pair renowned for severing heads, the warrior buried with his swift horse, are born from a severed head. Cause becomes consequence, and in the next generation three-headed creatures appear. Hesiod's Chrysaor, born with a horse from a severed head, has a three-headed son, Geryon, whose cattle Hercules, commuter of human sacrifice, steals. In Latin legends, the three-bodied Geryon's cattle are stolen in turn from Hercules by Cacus, a three-headed, head-displaying monster.

Unlike Celts, Scythians, and Tauri, Greeks never put heads on their lintels or on poles above their houses. Those, however, are among the conspicuous places they put the gorgoneion. The Greeks "multiplied [the gorgoneion] over and over—on pediments of temples, on their roofs as *akroteria* and antefixes, in private homes, on fabrics, gems, seals, coins, the feet of mirrors, the belly of vases, and the base of cups." They appear first, from the archaic period, "on the facades of temples or as *acroteria* and antefixes," precisely where a Celt puts his heads. Then they spread, banalized by reproduction, to coins and decoration, where the Celt also put heads.[58]

Celts put severed heads in springs. In springs, J. H. Croon finds the gorgoneion: where a hot springs exists, a gorgoneion is usually found. Of twenty-nine ancient cities whose coins bear the Gorgon, at least eleven have a spring nearby.[59] Praxidike, the goddess whose images were heads, had sacrifices that were "the same." An Orphic hymn names Persephone, goddess of the dead, summoner of the *kephalon gorgeion, Praxidice.* Praxidike's epithet "Executress of Vengeance" links her to the furies.[60] The Boeotian Praxidikai, or goddess heads, are associated with the Styx and the deadly spring Tilphousa.[61] Poseidon, the sea god, impregnates Medusa with the horse and warrior. Several temples roofed with skulls were dedicated to Ares, the god of war, and Poseidon, the sea god.[62]

Yet if Gorgon is a trophy head, the gorgoneion is an image, a representation, not the thing itself. It is not a skull found in the springs, on the coins, on the roofs and gutters, but a gorgoneion.

So too if the Gorgon is a trophy head, how can Medusa the gorgon be female? When Celts made a Medusa mask, she turned into a he: the face was male.[63] Hunted, buried, or sacrificed heads, in the spring or in the potter's foundations, may be female, but most evidence for actual female severed heads comes from Britain, in times more recent than Hesiod. From Homer to Aristophanes, "war is men's business." Trophy heads taken in battle ought to be men's. Although Medusa engages only with men, as one would expect from a battlefield trophy head, feminizing Medusa breaks the link between the head and the battlefield. As Froma Zeitlin observes from a psychoanalytic standpoint, "the petrifying effect of the Gorgon seems reserved for men, in a tête-à-tête between a male and the deadly gaze of the female. I know of no case in which Medusa engages with a female figure."[64] The problem does not arise for Homer, whose gorgon is unsexed. Hesiod's equally ancient account, however, genders the gorgons, feminizing the head on Jove's aegis, which becomes in turn Athena's aegis.

Breaking the link with the battlefield, feminizing Medusa identifies death and female fertility. Persephone links the female to death; the *Praxidikai* specifically link female heads with human sacrifice and water. Most curious of all, at the Art Institute of Chicago, a black Etruscan water pitcher, dated 550/500 B.C.E., combines water, dance, gorgoneia, and cut heads. On the bulging body of the vessel, naked dancers prance above a ring of grinning Gorgon heads, linking severed heads and the dance as in the Greek *lekythos*. The pouring spout bears three heads, one at the handle, the other two 90 degrees from the handle. The heads resemble a Celtic *tête coupée*: oval face, eyes closed, slit mouth. On tombs, the "vegetation gorgoneion" surrounds the head with living foliage and snakes emblematizing immortality, as in *Gilgamesh*.[65] On fourth-century Greek funerary vessels from Apulia, Italy, a lovely Medusa appears as bosses on the handles.[66] Medusa speaks the double character of head sacrifices, life giving and life destroying, protecting and terrifying, calming and enraging.

The contest between Medusa and a woman that Zeitlin never sees is a contest that often occurs when Greeks go headhunting: women take heads, or women's heads are taken. Female severed heads and female decapitators become a peculiarly Greek obsession. Far from Plato's forms, heroes living dangerously must cut off monstrously female or monstrously fecund heads, while monstrous females tear off heroic male heads. So Perseus decapitates Medusa, who produces twins. Hercules beheads the hydra, from whose decapitated stumps more heads grow, resembling Medusa's snaky locks. De-authorized decapitations reverse the motif in the legends of Pentheus and Orpheus. There the female decapitates the male, a sign of female madness, power, and moral monstrosity specifically associated with Dionysos, an eastern, mystery cult. Agave, possessed by the god, impales her son Pentheus's head and flaunts it until her madness fades and she sees what she has done. Ripped apart by other Maenads, Orpheus is dismembered, his head flung into water. Having floated and sung, the head of the hero who sought Persephone is buried by the Muses, Maenads in "their Apollonian right minds."[67]

Such decapitating mothers, like the decapitated gorgon and hydra, figure the disorder threatened by the irrational (female) relative to rational (masculine) control of the social order.[68] Like Freud, Ferenczi, and Lacan, the Greeks made imperfections female, initiating that theme for western culture.[69] A constant shadow, the severed head marks the fundamental mutilation that to be Greek (alive, adult, male, and citizen) is to evade and to inflict on women with a will.[70] In Hesiod, woman is *kakon kalon*, the "beautiful evil," while "beautiful death" awaits Homer's greatest warriors. In *Timaeus*, women come into existence only when evil men die and are reborn.[71] Mortal, the (bad) head turns female.

At the same time, disorder is powerful, a source of divination, insight, and mysterious fecundity. In a play about a woman's burying the dead, Sophocles affirms that "For every ill [man] hath found its remedy / Save only death" (*Antigone*, Ode 1).[72] Even the fundamental rule that death has no remedy is violated by mythic, monstrous female fertility. As Medusa's head is cut off, Pegasus and Chrysaor leap out, live births from a dead woman. When the hydra's head is cut off, it grows two more from the stumps, like dandelions in the garden. If the Gorgon begins as an ungendered trophy head, a sign of violent death, it twists and burgeons into terror of the other, twining with birth, its origins in death not quite forgotten, and not quite remembered, like skulls at Halloween or on the Day of the Dead.

Of Freud's account of Medusa's head, Elisabeth Bronfen observes that Medusa's head consoles the man threatened with castration: the mother is castrated, but he is not. Medusa castrates castration by transferring castration to the woman and stiffening the man, possessed of his erection.[73] So in the classic version, Medusa frees men from death by transferring death to the woman and empowering the man. The dead face that protects the city and moves it to war is not a warrior's, but a woman's.

From the fifth century, Medusa becomes beautiful, supplementing the monstrous gorgoneion, re-inscribing the beautiful death of the warrior, already eroticized in Homer, as the dangerous seductiveness of sex. "Come closer and die quicker," Achilles had murmured to Hector.[74] In Hesiod, Medusa had once been a beautiful woman; in Plato's time, she remains so. The uncanny face of death twists free of its referent and returns as generative, sensual beauty. The battlefield trophy head, the origin of the sign, is erased. Its simulacrum, never what it represents, always inauthentic, always in masquerade, the woman always other, changes its face to challenge representation and reinterpretation. As Jean Baudrillard might put it, beautiful Medusas, concealing "nothing at all . . . [are] actually perfect simulacra forever radiant with their own fascination."[75]

Roman Codes

The Romans are something else again. What horrified the Greeks and exhilarated the Celts, the Romans institutionalized and codified. Romans gloried in taking the heads of barbarians, a practice Jean-Louis Voisin shows modeled by Romulus himself, devolving into a banalized heads-for-pay of the civil wars and empire. Designating as barbarous and sickening the Celtic appropriation of heads, priding themselves on abolishing religious human sacrifices, the Romans specialized in presentation heads, developed decapitation as a socially marked form of public execution, and attempted to limit decapitation to the battlefield and sites of public execution. For the Romans, decollation marked differences between conqueror and conquered, citizen and non-citizen, civilized and barbaric. They developed a well-defined system of cuts that separated selves from others, and they worked both sides of the divide. The Romans codified, and what they disallowed as outside their codes, they found recurring in ways they could not control. In this, as in so much else, the Romans make visible the incipient contours of the modern.

Roman mythology records numerous attempts to control the sacrifice of heads, transforming earlier practices reminiscent of the Celts. An October festival in honor of Jupiter sent teams scrimmaging against one another to capture the head of a sacrificed horse.[76] At the *Compitalia* in January, Tarquinius Superbus allegedly restored an ancient sacrifice of boys to Mania; when Tarquinius was overthrown, heads of garlic and poppies replaced the boys.[77] From Numa, Jupiter had demanded heads. The legendary lawgiver tricked Jupiter out of that demand by giving him what he asked for—an onion.[78] Calling the tale wildly fabulous, Plutarch pluralizes the heads and has Jupiter reject the onion. He demands "the heads of living—" and Numa supplies "pilchards." Law replaces human with vegetable or animal heads; rules circumscribe violence. As Alison Futrell observes, the Romans set human sacrifices back in their own remotest history. They banned religious human sacrifice in 97 B.C.E. and attributed revivals of the practice to foreign influence. When sacrificing captives at tombs came to seem "cruel," gladiatorial games replaced sacrifices for religious purposes.[79] Nor did Romans understand how to read a severed head in a foundation: they required foreign aid and sent to the Etrurians.

As we have seen, Roman and Greco-Roman travelers and historians including Oseidonius, Polybius, Livy, and Diodorus Siculus expressed distaste for Celtic head-taking practices. Cicero singled out the Gauls for "savage and barbaric" practices.[80] Vergil condemned Celtic head displays in Italy's indigenous, three-headed monster, Cacus, defeated by Hercules. Tacitus recorded the "awful spectacle" found in Germanic groves where "human sculls were seen upon the trunks of trees" six years after the massacre of Varus' legions.[81] According to Strabo, Romans forbade the "barbarous custom" of allowing warriors to take the heads of conquered enemies.[82] Averse to its practice by others, Romans associated head-taking with Roman antiquity and contemporary barbarism. Recognizing the incompatibility between personal trophy heads and their own disciplined warfare, Romans demystified the warrior's trophy head and abjured religious sacrifices, confining decollation to utilitarian ends: terrifying opposing armies, terminating political rivals, and legally executing convicted criminals.

Roman soldiers staked heads and collected heads for pay or for their freedom (under T. Sempronius Gracchus). Roman artists sculpted severed heads presented to generals on columns and triumphal arches. Roman families bought back heads for burials. When Romans surrounded a besieged town or camp with heads on stakes, as Caesar did while warring against the Pompeians at Munda and as Trajan represents himself on his column against the Dacians, they intended to terrorize their opponents with what Appian calls a "ghastly wall."[83] Trajan's monument celebrates the presentation of numerous bearded heads to the beardless victors, a contrast repeated in the monument celebrating the conquest of Jerusalem. At the end of the Via Sacra on the triumphal route, the principal captives were beheaded or strangled before animals and booty were offered.[84] Amy Richlin describes heads in the civil wars as "exchanged like letters: from Praeneste, C. Marius sends word to Brutus Damasippus to kill Scaevola and others; Sulla responds by sending Damasippus's head (with that of Marius Gratidianus) to Praeneste; when Praeneste is captured, C. Marius's head is sent to Sulla. These heads were . . . perhaps the ultimate personal message."[85]

Romans used "head" to signify free persons, as distinct from slaves, who had no heads capable of diminution.[86] Reserved for citizens, who had heads to remove, decollation was a privileged form of execution, as the Christian tradition remembers in the contrast between Paul's martyrdom by decollation as Roman citizen, and Jesus' slavish death by crucifixion. In the early years of the republic, the bodies of citizens had been inviolable. Neither tortured nor executed, civilian citizens suffered voluntary exile or deportation.[87] The civil wars broke in upon those boundaries, and by the fourth century C.E., legal manuals specified class distinctions in capital punishment. Members of the upper classes were decapitated or exiled, while those belonging to the lower orders were crucified, burned, or thrown to beasts.[88] So Marcus Aurelius ordered the citizen beheaded, the rest crucified when the governor of Lyon asked what to do with a Christian group that included one citizen. As "an indulgence to the crowd," the governor sent them all to the beasts.[89]

Standard in warfare and executions, decapitation's casual use by authorities was discountenanced outside the appropriate framework. Among the boundaries that the Romans were interested in defining was that between "personal pleasure and public obligation," the private and the public exercise of decollation.[90] Violations of this attempted social control were regarded as scandalous. In 193 B.C.E. a proconsul was "severely punished" for having decapitated a Gallic prisoner of war when his mistress complained that she had never seen a man die. He was expelled from the Senate house at Cato's behest, deprived of his seat at the theater, moralized by Cicero and Plutarch, and turned, according to Seneca, into a school rhetoric exercise. (A variant has a young man as the lover, and the episode has been thought a source for Mark's tale of Salome, Herod, and John the Baptist.)[91] Seneca condemned as "cruel" any decollations performed at night, when surrounded by women, while in sandals, or at dinner parties.[92] Suetonius chides Caligula with keeping a headsman at hand during his meals to decapitate prisoners brought from jail. Once codified, decollation became the locus of erotic fantasy and apocalyptic politics, anticipating the nineteenth and twentieth centuries. Thus Caligula wished Rome had a single neck, the better to decapitate all the city at once. So too he fantasied ordering cut through the neck he was kissing.[93]

Drawing boundaries against violence, the second-century historians Tacitus, Suetonius, and Appian confidently designate unauthorized decapitations the work of "ruffians," "barbarians," or monsters. Hanging up Antony and the Romans for displaying Cicero's head on the rostrum at the Forum, the Alexandrian Appian reports that more people came to *see* Cicero than had ever come to hear him.[94] Suetonius and Tacitus contest Otho's succession to Galba with heads. To favor Otho, Suetonius distances him from Galba's severed head, taken by anonymous, unauthorized intermediaries and made a sign of justice. So a nameless private soldier decapitates Galba's already dead body, Galba's head is paraded by "servants and campboys," the head is hurled to the ground where Galba had ordered a murder—a sign of justice—and the imperial steward lays head and body to rest.[95]

In Tacitus, heads condemn Otho. Heads and assassins multiply, the emperor shares the blood lust, the legion parades three heads as a public act, and the soldiers claim "the honour of an atrocious deed." Three different "ruffians thirsting for blood" may have cut the throat of the living Galba and left him a "headless trunk." A "horrible tragedy," this "general massacre" takes three more named heads, on which Otho "gazed with such ardent eyes." "The three heads were fixed on poles, and carried, amidst the ensigns of the cohorts, with the eagle of the legion, through the streets of Rome." The heads are sold back to the families by "murderers."[96] Marking a shared aversion to the display of heads, the violence that Suetonius softens by attribution to anonymous members of the lower orders, Tacitus characterizes as official criminality, belonging to the emperor and the legion.

Romans recognized the pathos and the horror of a severed head and used heads as rhetoric, but their codification left a large scope for violence. As Michel Foucault observes, modern humanitarianism is not "a new sensibility."[97] The sensibility horrified by decapitation is very old: it is born together with the sensibility that horrifies by decapitating. Roman theory favored peace, but mandated violence as the only way to it: "Roman, remember, / these are your arts—to impose peace and custom, / to spare the subjugated and overturn the proud"; "Romane, memento / (hae tibi erunt artes) pacique imponere morem, / parcere subiectis et debellare superbos" (Vergil, *Aeneid*, VI, 851–53). There is no clearer sign that the proud have been overturned than when their heads are served up.

The Romans founded rights on status, not the body, and in their games modeled their warfare. John Keegan marvels at the Romans' combining "extreme ferocity in war [with] a high level of political culture." Donald R. Dudley describes Roman spectators as enabled "to glut by proxy their sadistic instincts." Others have found the ideology that justifies the practice. "[T]he moral order [is reaffirmed] through the sacrifice of criminal victims," or "the cult of Roman statehood [is mythically reenacted in a] politicized temple . . . the amphitheatre."[98]

Yet "extreme ferocity" and continuous training through sport are useful for massive, sustained conquests. Cicero and Pliny the Younger defended the games as instructing in "courage and, above all, self control." They excited men "to bear noble wounds and scorn death and to make the very slaves and criminals give proof of a love of glory and desire for victory."[99] The games implicated the spectators, who learned to share an already broad cultural support for violence by identifying with the bodies of those they watched. Even the abject participants, the slaves and criminals who were the gladiators, transcended their condition by embracing violence and pain.

The army and the arena reinforce each other. In the absence of depersonalizing technologies that mediate damage invisibly, such reinforcement is useful. Conrad's gun ships fire into the forest, enabling the warrior not to see the consequences of his actions or to imagine the effect on his own or others' bodies. When he sees at last, he often sickens. By contrast, Roman spectators, seeing the effects of violence on bodies, learned to admire them and invested the scar and the wound with desire. The Romans conquered the world, after all, by hand.

Beheadings among the Moderns: The Way We Live Now

In spite of official disapproval and private repugnance, unauthorized decollations continue to occur among us, and fantasied (or virtual) decollations proliferate unconscionably. Heads have gone missing, as in *The Missing Head of Damasceno Monteiro*. "Headless bodies are a great opener for a novel," the reviewer assures us.[100] Or heads have become anonymous, as cheerfully summed up in Edward Gorey's grisly little verse:

> From Number Nine, Penwiper Mews,
> There is really abominable news:
>   They've discovered a head
>   In the box for the bread,
> But nobody seems to know whose.[101]

Crime, anonymity, horror: the progress of civilization means, paradoxically, that heads disappear and then turn up in the wrong places, taken by wrong persons for wrong reasons. Having removed all the right reasons for the practice, we are left only with wrong ones.

The trophy head and the presentation head disappear early in the process of modern western state formation, with some of their functions appropriated by the formal public execution. Throughout nineteenth-century Europe, heads were taken to secure justice and held up in public to show that justice had been served. Decollation by axe and guillotine continued in both Germanys into the 1960s, and the last authorized European decollation occurred in 1977. France last decollated a criminal (a serial killer) in public in 1939, in private in 1977, and abolished the death penalty in 1981 during the socialist government of François Mitterand. In non-fundamentalist western countries, capital punishment has followed the public execution into extinction.

The "rights of man" first proposed abolishing the death penalty in the eighteenth century. The death penalty was abolished in Tuscany in 1786, and Maximilien Robespierre repeatedly proposed its abolition to the National Assembly at the outset of the French Revolution in 1789–90.[102] "Human rights" have effected abolition in the civilized world in the twentieth. Where capital punishment survives, other ideologies prevail, principally Koranic and Christian fundamentalisms, militarist formations, or traditional procedures not yet called into question. Utah once had beheading on the books among its options for capital punishment; no one ever chose it. Yet had France defeated Britain in the Seven Years War, before its own revolution, the red guillotine of Texas might trellis its yellow rose.

Unauthorized decapitations continue in warfare and crime, last frontiers of the heroic. Third World tribal and ad hoc popular decollations contest the authority of modern states or supplement their perceived inadequacies. U.S. soldiers profit from their photographs of Japanese and Iraqi heads, and Muslim militants videotape the decapitation of a U.S. reporter, not for profit but for politics. Such heads still function as signs, specific to their contexts, endangered by the civilizing discipline Foucault describes. When a Congolese officer requires a soldier to give up his trophy head and bury it, we see a contest between two systems of meaning at the beginning of a new millennium, a Foucauldian fable.

According to the *New York Times*, a soldier "hacked off [the head of] a young man who was quite small, witnesses said; [the head was] skewered on the tip of a spear and paraded on the back of a white pickup truck. . . . Soldiers on the truck sang a soccer anthem. . . . Finally, a Congolese commander told the soldier with the spear it was time to bury the head. 'In any family—say of 10 children—one or two will be a little odd,' said the commander, Sion Malekera, fumbling to account for his soldier's behavior. 'I was horrified. I have never seen anything like that.'"[103]

To the soldier who puts the head on a stick, the head means victory, solidarity, celebration, just triumphal rejoicing. The soccer anthem links war and sport. To his officer, the head is the sign of an individual whose humanity he shares, with whose body he identifies and sympathizes, and whose rights he defends. Regarding himself as obliged to understand the behavior he rejects, the officer hypothesizes an idiosyncratic, individual "oddity" that, however inexplicable and irrational, exists. He quantifies it at ten or twenty percent, one or two in a family of ten. The commander does not give up his obligation to control the behavior in his failed attempt to understand it. The soldier is anonymous. The reporter names only him who disapproves and stops the display, negating the negation of the human. Sion Malekera is the modern hero of the story.

Like Sion Malekera, modern Americans do not understand the decapitators. As Karen Halttunen argues, the enlightenment liberalism that took hold in the mid-eighteenth century, by replacing religious doctrines of innate human depravity, rendered human evil incomprehensible. Human nature defined as "essentially good, rational, and capable of self-government" made violence puzzling and alien, although necessary to control the irrational violence of others.[104] By its own self-estimate, human nature became innately sympathetic and "irresistibly compassionate."[105] Human society was redefined as an escape from violence, left outside at the margins. Now demanding special studies—anthropological, criminological, neurological, pathological—violence has become cultural abroad, biological at home.

Yet as the progress of civilization circumscribes violence, it produces fascination with its own violation. Sober studies of criminals abut glorification of crime. Theories of violent behavior seek to control or extirpate violence, while artists and philosophers fantasy liberation through violence, gratifying our well-bred, well-fed passion for all things subversive. Our decapitators remain peculiarly our own.

Consider Jeffrey Dahmer. In an age of mechanical reproduction, Jeffrey Dahmer collects boys and keeps his collection of heads in an icebox. Designated "pathological," Dahmer's behavior remains unexplained and unpreventable by any theory currently available to us. Not for want of trying: in depth psychology, neurophysiology, genetic "abnormality," the psyche, or self-formation, we seek the explanations we have not found.[106] Sion Malakera hypothesizes a "genetic variety," culturally expressed, that we do not question when its effects are benign, but are uncomfortable with when they are not. Dahmer articulates a complete set of American cultural values within the free anonymity of the city. Baudelaire first hymned a nameless Dahmer in "Une martyre: dessin d'un maître in-connu," but unlike Baudelaire's, the values Dahmer embodies are not artistic, aesthetic, romantic, or French, but scientific, racial, sexual, and American.

An individualist, Dahmer's appropriation of heads was not sanctioned by forms and institutions that made his actions acceptable or laudable. Although common elsewhere, decapitation has not been used as a form of public execution in the United States. Dahmer acted without cultural support and against cultural norms. He followed "a different drummer" and took a path "less traveled by." Investing his collecting with meaning, he claimed to be engaged in scientific experiments, attempting to create a zombie-servant, a sex-slave. Through it, he affirmed his sense of self and sexuality, race and gender. Living what Blake only fantasied, "Better to murder an infant in its cradle than to nurse unacted desires," he acted freely, in full accord with his desire. His victims were boys, often Asians, often black. Keeping the heads by him, empowered through them, he continued a spiritual (in American culture, sexual) connection with them, in a mode fictionalized by Will Self.

In sum, Dahmer belongs within a particular cultural framework that affirms white, male superiority, makes sexuality central to individual identity, genders physical power masculine, and prefers individual self-expression to the claims of the community. In Japan, by contrast, serial killers pretend to be women, serial killing is attributed to westernization, and films such as Takashi Miike's *Audition* (1999) reveal Japanese suspicion of women's potential for vengeful violence.[107] Sex and violence having both been made secret and forbidden, Dahmer frees himself from "the prison of the body" and reasserts man's fundamental freedoms, evading the panoptic gaze. His is the discourse of the alienated individual exerting power, at the margin, transgressing boundaries, challenging conventions, and subverting norms. If as Jacques Derrida suggests after Philippe Sollers, "the operation of reading/writing goes by way of the blade of a red knife," and quotation is "the regular cadence or fall of a severed head," Dahmer wields Sollers's and Derrida's knife *hors texte*.[108] He deconstructs the hierarchical tradition of presence and undoes "man" as unified subject. Son of Sade, Nietzsche, Bataille, he is the real toad in their imaginary gardens.

If Dahmer literalizes our imaginings, other semioticians prefer the paradoxically headed headless corpse. "Julia Kristeva's novel *Possessions'* Part I is entitled 'A Beheading,' and the very first sentence of the book is 'Gloria was lying in a pool of blood with her head cut off.'"[109] "Gloria" remains "Gloria" with her head cut off, and her head is still "with" her. Defining a crisis in ideology, the suddenly headless "humanist subject" institutionalized in the enlightenment finds that he has begun taking himself apart. We now occupy, always a little uneasily, a headless system that requires heads to use it. Beheadings used to provide dramatic endings. They are now where we begin.

2

Bouncing Heads and
Scaffold Dramas

The *body*, the *body*. They keep on saying the body and after a while
you realize what they mean is the soul.
—Carol Kay, in David Bromwich,
"Carol Kay: The Princeton Years,"
Annals of Scholarship 14.3 and 15.1 (2001), 75

I have such a lyttel neck.
—Anne Boleyn, 1536, anticipating Henry VIII's
excellent French headsman

There was a time when severed heads were at the center of things. Then
heads were head, and the head of state took off others' heads in state.
Under the Tudors, the ad hoc battlefield decollations of the Middle Ages
were restaged as great public scaffold dramas. Coinciding with administrative centralization, formal staging projected the power of the state and
the authority of its head, eliminating dynastic contenders, rival claimants,
religious disputants, ambitious men skeptical of female rule, and common criminals disruptive of the sovereign's peace.[1] The heads removed
were set up in central places: on the Parliament house, on London Bridge,
before Lambeth Palace. Continental visitors marveled at London Bridge
festooned with thirty heads. Ending the civil war it waged against Charles
I in 1649, Parliament appropriated the traditional Tudor staging to take
off the king's head and affirm its own sovereignty. One hundred years
later, the last traditional decollation staged with block and axe took place
in 1747. In the 1770s, the last head mounted at Temple Bar blew down
in a storm, and no further heads were mounted in England.[2] Heads had

been de-centered along with British sovereignty, shared among prince, House of Lords, and the increasingly dominant Commons.

The disappearance of severed human heads from public places seems indisputably progressive, a sign of improved manners, increased humanitarianism, heightened sensibility or sensitivity, and responsiveness to public opinion in an enlarging public sphere. Described as "the development of manners" (Elias), "the breakthrough of individualism" (Gittings), "increasing interhuman identification" (Spierenburg and Garland), "new sensibilities" (Thomas), "surveillance" (Foucault), or a complex "change of mentalities" (Gatrell), the change marks, as McGowen suggests, the emerging ideological primacy of the body.[3] Mounted heads had served in their horror as a sign of the horrid crime imagined by the head, their mutilation symbolizing the mutilation they had proposed to inflict on the body politic. A man's head and quarters were erected, in an early seventeenth-century account, "to the view and detestation of men . . . that the eyes of men may behold, and their hearts condemn him."[4] The hideousness of the ruptured body was accepted, even embraced, for its service to the social order. During the eighteenth century it came to seem inappropriate to use bodies in this fashion, parsed for permanent display as signs.

Yet in a paradox Jörg Fisch termed "dear limbs, cheap lives," as the English abandoned mutilation of their criminals they killed them in increasing numbers.[5] Modern paradox was eighteenth-century reform. William Blackstone (1766) regarded as signs of the progress of English law since the reign of Charles II both "the annihilation of the terrible judgment of *peine forte et dure* [pressing to death those who refused to plead to felony]" and "the vast increase of capital punishment."[6] In a dialectical contest between the claims of the body and the demands of the social order, capital crimes and executions by hanging increased side by side with an actual decline in social levels of violence and the mitigation of pain for traitors condemned to disemboweling.

After the Black Act of 1723, capital offences multiplied until more Londoners hanged in 1785 than the years between 1701 and 1780 together. The number of death sentences handed down and persons hanged continued to increase into the nineteenth century, when the reforms of 1832 reduced the number of capital crimes; death sentences fell from about 1500 to under 200 between 1831 and 1838, executions from 152 to 6.[7] Whole bodies dangled, rotting in chains in the English countryside until the practice was prohibited by statute in 1834. Criminal corpses underwent anatomical dissection, mandated for willful murderers by statute in 1752, until 1832.[8] Administrative ideology makes a difference: the Whigs of 1832 who made the first, partial reform of the franchise also moved to protect bodies still mostly excluded from the franchise. A similar dynamic obtains in the eighteenth century. Man's political rights and his body are linked by a Whig-inspired ideology intent on defending property. As lethality increases (in defense of property and person), the visible signs of violence diminish. The whole body hanging is not as grisly as the mutilated members in pieces.

At the eighteenth century's end, decollation revived spectacularly in France with the invention of the guillotine (1792), and the first two decades of the nineteenth century saw a spasm of uncelebrated English and Scottish decollations of commoners who had first been hanged. The last British public, governmental decollations occurred in 1820, seventy-three years later than the date always given for the last decapitation in Britain (1747). The block and an axe of 1747 are on view in the Tower of London, postcard available.[9] There is no sign of the surgeon's knife used in 1820 or of the noose, tightened so often before and after. An ideological watershed, the date 1747 celebrates the end of contests over the divine or hereditary right of kings and relegates decapitation to an earlier, antiquated political era.

Two questions suggest themselves: Why did decapitation, having almost disappeared in the enlightened eighteenth century, revive so dramatically at century's end? That question has an historically specific answer: the English resurrected the knife and axe to counter the guillotine and its politics by reasserting England's ancient traditions. To fit a new ideology of the rights of man, the French had invented a new machine (see "Power to the People," below). To rebut that ideology, the British raised up the axe, absolutism's ancient sign, twined in the eighteenth century with the defense of English liberties in the Protestant succession. Yet when decapitation returned under the aegis of new ideologies, the heads were spiked in neither Britain nor France. The display of heads ceased even when decapitation revived.

Michel Foucault observed that the body ceases to be the place penality marks itself: "A few decades saw the disappearance of the tortured, dismembered, amputated body, symbolically branded on face or shoulder, exposed alive or dead to public view." Foucault dismissed "humanitarianism" or "a new sensibility" as explanation, proposing "another policy," the disciplinary force of intersecting gazes, institutionalized in army, prison, madhouse, and, as T. R. Haskell proposes, capitalist enterprise.[10] Certainly the sensibility was not "new": the horror of mutilation is very old, or mutilation would not be practiced. What was new was the body as ideology, a natural sign of property in the self, supplementing and ultimately displacing other religious and heroic ideologies that justify the body's suffering and display.

Between 1650 and 1690, new theories of the state, both absolutist and contractual, took the isolated body as origin and "othered" violence. In both Hobbes and Locke, man withdraws from the state of nature in order to be protected from violence, directed against the person in Hobbes, against property in Locke.[11] Violence has often been "othered." In the version of Noah dating from the fifth century B.C.E., God floods the world because of human violence. The Greco-Roman golden age lapses into iron as autonomous violence increases. Augustine regarded violence as "an original sin"; Machiavelli saw increasing violence as a sign of a breakdown in legitimacy.[12] Locke is so hostile to violence that he denies it characterizes the state of nature: "however much some Men have confounded [them, the states of nature and war] are as distant, as a State of Peace, Good Will, Mutual Assistance, and Preservation, and a State of Enmity, Malice, Violence, and Mutual Destruction are from one another."[13] The seventeenth-century difference common to both Hobbes and Locke was conceiving that society originated in men's will to control violence and succeeded in doing so.

By 1690, Locke had summed up a century's work by making the body the starting point for multiple discourses—psychological, educational, political, economic. Property begins in the body, for "every man has a *Property* in his own *Person*."[14] Education begins with the child's body, and knowledge with physiological sensation.[15] The "inclination" that makes man sociable is bodied, that is, sexual.[16] *Self*, originating in the concept *same*, is bodied. "[O]ur very Bodies . . . are a part of our *selves*: *i.e.* of our thinking conscious *self*."[17] The eighteenth century proper saw the development of sympathy, cementing the isolated individuals of the social contract, grounding a "theory of moral sentiments" in Adam Smith (1759), and finally mooting the social contract in Adam Ferguson's *History of Civil Society* (1767).[18]

One clue to the body's new pretensions is an odd spate of bouncing heads suddenly appearing in major and minor literary works in the second and third decades of the English eighteenth century. John Gay sends three heads singing and bouncing into eternity. Jonathan Swift's severed head gushes blood sixty feet into the air as the head bounces on the ground like a thunderclap. Even Alexander Pope puts a spin on a rolling, muttering Homeric head in his translation of *The Odyssey*, and beheaded shoulders "spout" in his *Iliad*. Anne Finch, the Countess of Winchelsea, threatens Pope's head with rolling down the stream, like Orpheus's, and Lady Margaret Pennyman narrates at length the curious incident of Saint Denis's bouncing head on her trip to Paris. These heads are odd because they appear to have no purpose.

Severed heads in the eighteenth century evoked civil wars, martyred kings, and Catholic, republican, Protestant, or Jacobite plots and insurgencies. Yet these heads very conspicuously seem to mean nothing at all. Calling attention to the body's mutilation for no evident symbolic or political purpose, they puzzle a reader whom they make somewhat uncomfortable. Moving heads are not usually so difficult to read (as we will see in some earlier Renaissance examples).

Observed without sympathy, these heads violate the rules for representing scaffold dramas that secure the execution's solemnity and the spectators' acquiescence through pathos or awe. These rules, evident in Sir Thomas More's accounts of executions in his biography of Richard III, were well developed in the eighteenth century and are still observed in most verbal and visual accounts of executions: (1) Multiply preliminaries. Describe the site, the progress, the scaffold, the officers. Enhancing authority's aura of power and terror, the grandeur of the staging fills the scene and dominates attention. (2) Focus on the demeanor of the person to be executed. Recount gestures and last words; create a character fulfilling itself in its final moment. Supplementing or replacing the state's spectacle, sentimental attention to the living subject fills the scene. (3) Occlude the actual separation of the head from the body so as not to depersonalize the character just created. Shift from the body to be decapitated to the executioner when the action begins. (4) Transform the axe into an invisible or an irresistible mechanism, thus depersonalizing the executioner. (5) Stop with the axe or leap to the head held up: never mess with Mr. In-between. This is the place the sympathetic imagination does not want to go; this is where morbid curiosity lodges. (6) Be sparing of blood. It may run in the streets, or be sopped up onto people's handkerchiefs, but separate it from its source, spouting from the arteries of the neck. (7) Let the audience's demeanor support the political or rhetorical purpose of the representation: solemn for order confirmed, joyful for new order coming in, sorrowful for accepted rupture in old order, hostile to justify reform (late eighteenth and nineteenth centuries). Violating rules 5 and 6, messing with Mr. In-between, is the prerogative of Romans at their games (carnival pleasure) or satirists, subversives, and critics jabbing at the sensitive Lockean body. With powerful rules, what signifies is breaking them.

These heads bounce between 1715 and 1730, demonstrating either a depraved indifference to human suffering or something else. That something else is the claim of the body as body, in itself. These bounces resist the use of the head as a sign in a period when heads are being mounted against articulate public opposition, but there is no ideological basis for resisting their mounting. Marking the second principal period when English liberties entwined themselves with the axe, they make visible a part of the pre-history of the body's emergence as foundational after 1750.[19] While bouncing obtrudes the body's violation, actual English decapitations moved to diminish pain to the body and, a little later, to cover up the violence inflicted on the body.

An Argument of Heads

In the mid-seventeenth century, the English conducted a political argument via decollation that led both to the retirement of the block and axe after 1747 and to decollation's brief recrudescence in the nineteenth century. When the civil-war Parliament cut off the king's head to affirm its sovereignty, decollation underwent a fundamental shift in signification that differentiated England from the rest of Europe. Decollation became riveted to the concept of sovereignty in the modern sense and detached itself from the rest of the penal system that preserved the sovereign's peace and declared his responsibility for order.

As in many other parts of Europe, in England prior to the execution of Charles I, common criminals were occasionally executed by decollation or decollated after hanging, and their heads were set up. So the heads of thieves and murderers abutted the heads of "traitors," Catholics, counterfeiters, and plotters. In other parts of Europe, including Rome, Belgium, Denmark, Sweden, and Germany, decollation with sword, axe, or guillotine remained part of the ordinary repertoire of capital punishments and persisted until capital punishment was abolished or the technology of punishment shifted in the late nineteenth or twentieth century.[20]

In England, Charles I's struggles with Parliament had played out partly as a battle over who controlled decollation. Every four years, Parliament impeached another of Charles's ministers and took off his head, until finally they struck off Charles's own: 1641, Strafford; 1645, Laud; 1649, Charles. Taking off the king's head, Parliament adopted the sovereign's procedures. The king was marched, as his subjects had been, to a special location, his own palace at Whitehall, and there the masked executioner "did his office," holding up the head, but failing to name it "the head of a traitor."[21] The king's head was not spiked, but his blood was sopped up at the scaffold "by some as trophies of their slain enemy, and by others as precious reliques of their beloved prince."[22] Royalist accounts of the king's death obscured the details and emphasized the heavenly reception of the martyr. Dissimilar to artwork from the French Revolution, contemporary prints sympathetic to the king do not show his dead body.

While royalists such as Clarendon and Hobbes decline any description of the king's "murder," committed regicides "cut off" or "strike off" the king's head. In *Eikonoklastes* John Milton grieved that "the head was not struck off to the best advantage and commodity of them that held it by the hair." In his *Ode upon Cromwell's Return from Ireland*, Andrew Marvell thrust out a head to terrify and inspire, but not the king's. Trimming, he left the king's head "as on a bed" and displayed in its place a Roman head, the terrifying one found during the construction of the capitol.[23]

An unintended consequence of the king's execution was that henceforth in England only armed or verbal threats to sovereignty, the king's person or the succession, cost a man his head. In Scotland on 5 September 1716, Patrick Hamilton was beheaded at the Grass Market in Edinburgh for having murdered a vintner, and the Scottish decapitating machine, the Maiden, executed its last commoner in 1710.[24] In Ireland, insurrectionary Whiteboys were hanged and decapitated in the 1760s. But in England the only exception was the execution in 1781 of two spies, David Tyrie and the Frenchman Francis Henry de la Motte, for selling information to the French about the movement of English vessels in time of war. Theirs were also the last hearts cut out and thrown into the fire.[25] Other, traditional grounds for decollation abruptly fell out of use.

Two years after the king's death, the Halifax gibbet was abandoned. For hundreds of years, it had executed livestock and cloth thieves near Wakefield. Mak, the diabolical sheep stealer in the Wakefield Master's *Second Shepherds' Play*, feared for his head, not just his neck (hanging), if he were caught with the fat sheep he stole on Christmas Eve sometime before 1500. In 1651, three kersey-cloth and colt thieves, Abraham and John Wilkinson and Anthony Mitchell, gave their heads to the gibbet. Thereafter, decollation suddenly seemed "too severe" to inflict on thieves.[26] The machine was never used again. Class-based demands to be decapitated were rejected when the crime did not measure up. In 1760, Earl Ferrers, condemned to death for murdering his steward, claimed a right as an aristocrat to be decapitated like his ancestor Essex. The claim denied, he was hanged. His status warranted decapitation, but his offense did not.

Confining decapitation to threats to sovereignty did not make it infrequent. The political contests of the late seventeenth and early eighteenth centuries played out as a game of musical heads. After Charles I's execution, his supporters who continued in arms lost their heads to parliamentary courts.[27] The gallant Montrose, condemned to ungentlemanly quartering and display, declared "that he was so far from being troubled that his four limbs were to be hanged in four cities of the kingdom, that he heartily wished that he had flesh enough to be sent to every city in Christendom, as a testimony of the cause for which he suffered." Sir John Owen, condemned along with the duke of Hamilton and the earls of Holland and Norwich, thanked the court that sentenced him to lose his head: "[I]t was a very great honour to a poor gentleman of Wales to lose his head with such noble lords . . . he was afraid they would have hanged him."[28]

After the restoration of Charles II, parliamentary regicides were drawn, quartered, and decapitated, or dug up, like Cromwell, to be decapitated. Popish plots and Rye House plots felled Catholic and Whig republican heads. A by-blow of the Popish plot, a goldsmith lost his head after saying in a tavern that he could kill a king.[29] Hundreds of his followers lost their heads with the duke of Monmouth in 1685, as Protestants rose in arms against the accession of the Catholic James II. Monmouth's head was sewed back on for burial. His followers' heads were boiled and tarred and raised high across the west country, until on a progress the next year, James II found the display disturbing enough to order the "heads and quarters removed and buried," a new response for an English king.[30]

After James II was deposed in 1689, his adherents' dissatisfaction with the Hanoverian succession in 1714 produced martyred heads until 1753. Decapitated after the Jacobite risings of 1715 and 1745 were five Scottish lords (two in 1716, three in 1746–47), attended by 34 hanged and dismembered commoners in 1715–16 and 120 in 1746.[31] Hanged and then decapitated were feckless fantasists who dreamed of assassinating George I in 1718 (James Sheppard) and 1723 (Christopher Layer), and a pamphleteer who impugned George's right in 1721 (John Matthews the printer for *Vox populi, vox dei*).[32] The last aristocrats executed with block and axe were Kilmarnock and Balmerino in 1746, and Simon, Lord Lovat, in 1747. Lovat's block is the one in the Tower. Ratcliffe, brother of Lord Derwentwater, executed in 1716, was also beheaded in 1746. The last commoner hanged and disemboweled for taking part in the '45 was the physician Archibald Cameron in 1753. Some thought clemency in order when eight years had elapsed since the insurrection. When Hogarth, "a warm partisan of George II," insisted "there must have been some very unfavourable circumstances discovered in this particular case," as the execution so long after the rebellion looked like "putting a man to death in cold blood," Samuel Johnson attacked George II as "unrelenting and barbarous."[33]

Over the same period, several small changes mark bodily sympathy's mollifying the claims of law. From the 1720s, disemboweling was performed only on the dead, a sign of aversion to pain in the sympathetic body.[34] In 1715, a bribe determined whether one was cut into alive or dead. Bruce Lenman sneers that Walpole's idea of mercy in 1723 was that Layer was dead before he was dismembered.[35] Lenman would not, perhaps, have sneered had he considered seriously the alternative. The eight men hanged at Kennington Common in 1746 were cut down after five minutes and beheaded with a cleaver. Only then were they disemboweled, their hearts cut out and put in the fire. They were spared pain, though not humiliation. The head of Francis Townley was to be set up in Carlisle, of Thomas Siddal in Manchester, and David Morgan at Temple Bar.[36] In 1753, the last participant condemned in the '45 was hanged thirty minutes, until dead, and only then cut down, decapitated and disemboweled.[37] In 1781, de la Motte was hanged for fifty-seven minutes before his head was severed and his heart removed.[38] In such decapitations, a cleaver was used, not an axe, facilitating control over the head as it was severed.[39] These innovations enhanced control over the trajectory of the head, reduced pain for the sufferer, and diminished certain spectacular effects.

Aristocrats' decapitations diminished not pain, but humiliation, the visible loss of control over one's head intrinsic to decollation. When the Scottish lords were decapitated in 1746, their heads were not held up. When Lovat asked if his would be, the sheriff assured him that "as it had not been customary of late Years to expose the Head at the four Corners of the Scaffold, he really thought he might indulge his Lordship with a Promise as to that Point, for he did not think he could expose the Head (though it was desired, and indeed ordered by a Message) without being liable to Censure."[40] Silently renounced was the climax of the sovereign's assertion of power over the heads of aristocratic subjects, a power re-claimed over commoners in 1817. No order came to expose the head, and the sheriff implies that in a contest between an order and the censure of public opinion, he would prefer the public voice.

Nor were aristocratic heads any longer allowed to bounce or roll on the scaffold. Instead, they were caught in red baize cloths, held by four men. Responsible for initiating that change was Lord Kilmarnock, whose concern about his head's trajectory suggested these innovations to the sheriff. Although having his head held up he called a matter of "no mo-ment," Kilmarnock was disturbed at the prospect "that his head might roll about the stage," and he suggested means to avoid it.[41] After Kil-marnock's request, Ratcliffe's head was also caught in baize.[42] The pro-cedure was sufficiently novel that Lovat requested that his head "might be received in a cloth and put into the coffin," as it was. The cloth ob-scured the head, its red color the blood. Occluding the ultimate signs of subjection and power, authorities veiled the violence that a rolling head exposes and that an exposed head thrusts at those passing by.

After 1753 and the interruption in 1781 for wartime spies, there was a hiatus until the 1790s when post-hanging decapitation revived at the margins—Scotland in 1794, Quebec in 1797, Ireland in 1798—and flowed to the center, England, in 1803, 1817, and 1820, where it stopped, except in India. There the English decapitated Indian subjects intermit-tently from the 1770s to 1857 and later. Hanged and then decapitated for treason, but not disemboweled, were Robert Emmet (in Dublin) and Colonel Despard and his co-conspirators in 1803; the men of the Derby rising in 1817; and the five Cato Street conspirators in London, two weavers of the Bonnymuir rising in Stirling, and a third weaver, James Wilson, in Glasgow in 1820.[43] In Stirling, a masked Glasgow medical stu-dent performed the decollations; in Glasgow, a masked coalminer used an axe, assisted by a man with a knife.[44]

Jacobinism having displaced Jacobitism, these decapitations re-sponded to the new shape of revolution: popular risings and conspiracies directed against Britain's unreformed parliamentary sovereignty, not at-tempted regicide. By the end of the eighteenth century, attacks on the king's person sent the perpetrators to madhouses, not the block. In 1786, a woman went after George III with a knife, and in 1800 a man fired a gun at him in Drury Lane Theatre. The king survived, uninjured, to watch the play. In both episodes, the perpetrators were tried, found not guilty by reason of insanity, and confined to Bedlam, where they outlived the king himself.[45]

In 1813, reformers attempting to abolish the axe as the penalty for treason were answered by new Burkean arguments on behalf of the old. Having "the sanction of centuries," decapitation should not be tampered with. Opposing the bill to change the punishment for high treason, Sir William Garrow, as attorney general, said he would not vote for it if it were "to be enacted now, but since it had the sanction of centuries, he was against changing it."[46] Beheading preserved ancient custom. Having failed to change the punishment itself, the reformers succeeded in 1814 in legislating that the hanged be dead before beheading and quartering.[47]

Debate having made the symbolism self-conscious, London authorities in 1817 insisted that the axe be used on the men of the Derby rising. The high sheriff had proposed the knife, but instead both were used: the men were struck with the axe and finished with a knife.[48] Inadvertently, but appropriately, the authorities elevated the common man in his taking off when they traded the base butcher's knife for the aristocrat's axe.

So too authorities restored the custom of holding out the head before increasingly hostile but disciplined audiences. Eighteenth-century crowds had rioted, stoning a hangman in 1768 and almost lynching one in 1769.[49] In 1803 the crowd hissed when Colonel Despard's head was exhibited: "While the heads were exhibiting, the people took off their hats."[50] In 1817, Jeremiah Brandreth was the first of the three men hanged and decapitated for the Derby rising, along with Isaac Ludlam and William Turner. When Brandreth's head was held up at the scaffold's corners and proclaimed "the head of a traitor," the crowd, startled and frightened, retreated. They moved as one body to remove their bodies from contact with the head:

> From the manner of this functionary the mob were apprehensive that the head was to be flung in the midst of them, and they rushed back in great precipitation. . . . [T]he same course being pursued with regard to Turner and Ludlam, they . . . regained their confidence.[51]

The more modern crowd is moved, literally, by the head.

By 1820, when the last head was held up on an English scaffold, the *Gentleman's Magazine* termed the decollations of the five Cato Street conspirators "the revolting ceremony," a bodied, visceral oxymoron as averse as the crowd. The spectators hissed, gave a universal groan, and applied "atrocious expressions" to the "operator" when the masked executioner's assistant took the knife to Thistlewood's throat. The *Morning Chronicle* reported an "exclamation of horror and reproach" and "the hootings of the mob." Théodore Géricault's sketch of an English hanging is usually held to be the Cato Street conspirators, but it is not usually noted that those hanged men were also decapitated.[52] On the last man, the executioner's assistant fumbled and dropped the head. As Brunt's head bounced, a perhaps apocryphal voice from the crowd cried, "Ah, butterfingers!"[53]

A bouncing head that exposes the executioner's incompetence and an executioner mocked by the spectators he means to awe make an apt ending for a capsule history of British decapitations. Whether or not it occurred, tradition delivers it to us. In this anecdote, authority's pretensions are undercut. Authority masters the body, but breaking rules 3, 4, 5, and 7, it becomes ridiculous. The executioner loses control of the head, and a voice from the crowd, from among the people, passes a judgment showing not terror or fear, but contempt. The voice from the crowd knows that authority is supposed to subject the rebellious head to its own irresistible authority, on the model of Foucault's fantasied executions. Power is supposed to stop the movement of the head forever. Heads that move, whether slipping from authority's fingers or leaping from shoulders, elude control in death as they attempted in life. In Renaissance images and writings, such heads figure resistance, defying both control and pathos and increasingly calling upon the body to protest its own violation.

Moving Heads and Speaking Bodies

> Like the wild Irish, I'll not think thee dead
> Till I can play at football with thy head.
> —Francisco de Medici on his brother-in-law,
> Bracciano; in John Webster, *The White Devil*, 1612

Duke Francisco fries his brother-in-law's brains with a poisoned helmet rather than kicking his head across stage, as he imagines. Yet playing ball with the severed head is the most gratifying image his rage can summon. In English Renaissance drama, moving heads encode resistance, rebellion, insurrection, and defiance. Heads are thrown, flung, kicked, or swung in rage, fury, or triumph. Most of the violence is verbal, but *The Revenger's*

Tragedy (1606) swings an actual severed head like a bludgeon, beating an officer off stage with it. Authority puts a stop to movement, stilling heads on spikes, whether the Fawkes conspirators in reality or Macbeth's in the play. Whose head is up and whose head is still on separates the losers from the winners.

Ad hoc medieval decollations and Renaissance theory of headship are nowhere better represented than in Christopher Marlowe's *Edward II* (ca. 1592). No scaffold dramas dignify death. The "base minion" Gaveston's head is struck off in a ditch (III, ii, 122–23); the earls of Warwick and Lancaster are carried from the field for beheading (III, iii, 61–63). Kent, the king's brother, asserts the fixed, motionless head against the rebellious barons' defiant motion:

> *Kent*: Yet dare you brave the king unto his face?
> Brother, revenge it, and let these their heads
> Preach upon poles for trespass of their tongues.
> *Warwick*: O, our heads! . . .
> *Lancaster*: Adieu, my lord, and either change your mind,
> Or look to see the throne, where you should sit,
> To float in blood, and at thy wanton head
> The glozing head of thy base minion thrown.
> (I, i 116–19, 130–34)

Heads fly back and forth until Edward III, resting Mortimer's head on his father's coffin, offers a detested, unpitied head to his father's spirit as satisfaction. In the end of the head's movement, rightful order is restored, and the severed head signifies a just triumph.

Yet fixed severed heads served both sides as atrocity propaganda in Reformation quarrels. Protestants and Catholics alike deplore the decapitators. The forest of traitorous Catholic heads on London Bridge, fifteen in all, becomes in a Catholic print "English cruelty killing Catholic Christians," *Crudelitas in Catholicis Matandis*.[54] The execution of Mary, Queen of Scots, closes Richard Verstegan's Catholic martyrology *Theatrvm Crudelitatum Haereticorum Nostri Temporis* (Theater of the Cruelties of the Heretics of Our Times; Antwerp, 1587). For the Huguenot Amboise conspirators, their heads spiked on the city walls in 1560, Agrippa D'Aubigné demanded in *Les Fers* vengeance for the "hot, smoking blood / of the beheaded" (le sang fumant et chaud / Des premiers etestés).[55] Only the caption differentiates the martyr from the criminal.

Under these conditions, defiant movement becomes just resistance. The startling *Haerlem 1573* represents the mass executions imposed on that city when it fell to the Spanish after a long siege, the year before the Dutch finally expelled Spain (fig. 2.1). Gallows dangle with bodies; men stand in line waiting to be executed. The foreground fills with decapitations in progress. Fallen, headless bodies lie about; heads are scattered here and there, and one head still leaping from its body stops in mid-air. Crude, but riveting, the head's kinesis climaxes defiance. The head in stopped motion resists the fall intended for it, as the printmaker resists the decollating power. So long as the head remains in the air, it is unsubdued and uncontrolled.

By the seventeenth century, the suffering body had supported Christian ideology for almost a millennium. While sixth-century representations of the crucified Christ show him triumphant, like a Roman emperor, over death, images of a suffering, dying Christ had appeared in western Europe in the eleventh century (the ninth in Byzantium) and were everywhere by the twelfth century.[56] In the Renaissance, sympathy was taught by suffering martyrs, detestation by the suffering damned and tortured criminal bodies, represented with increasing precision and realism, as Edgerton and Merback show. That long training in sympathetic identification was transferred to the most unlikely secular political figures. In Locke's time, Dutch printmakers turned the spectacularly botched decapitation of the duke of Monmouth in 1685 into a contest between authority and the suffering body, whose suffering accused. Authority asserting its right minimizes the show of violence, while the suffering body trains sympathy in the tradition of Christian iconography, making the grandson of the royal martyr, Charles I, a secular, tortured saint.

Favorite of the Whigs who were opposed to a Catholic succession after Charles II, the duke of Monmouth, the beautiful Absalom of John Dryden's *Absalom and Achitophel* (1681), was the king's Protestant bastard and the lover of Lady Harriet Wentworth, for whom he deserted his wife. When Parliament attempted to control the succession by excluding the king's Catholic brother James, duke of York (the "Exclusion Crisis" of the early 1680s), Monmouth had been favored over James's legitimate Protestant daughters. After his father's death in 1685, Monmouth sailed from Holland to take arms in the west country against his Catholic uncle, now James II, but was soon defeated, condemned for treason, and executed. Behind him in Holland, Monmouth had left numerous Whigs, including John Locke, waiting out the reign of James II, wishing success to Monmouth's Protestant rising, and finding their vindication three years

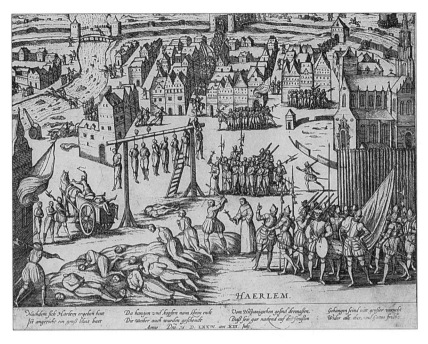

Fig. 2.1. Haerlem 1573. (Bibliothèque nationale de France, Paris [BN R154369])

later in the revolution of 1688–89.[57] Monmouth had also left behind James's legitimate Protestant heir, his cousin Mary, wife to William of Orange, whose claim would have been mooted by his success.

On the scaffold, Monmouth conducted himself like a Restoration hero, defending his adulterous liaison with Lady Harriet as true marriage. Denied the sacraments by disapproving clergymen, he had prayed earnestly to God that if his connection with Lady Harriet were wrong or displeasing, God should tell him so by making his affection for her cease. Since his affection continued undiminished, he knew his connection with Lady Harriet pleased God. To the chagrin of Puritans and bishops, he defended Lady Harriet's virtue and pleaded the inner light of love as religiously as Luther himself.[58] What happened next commentators did not attribute to God's verdict on adultery. According to contemporary accounts, the first blow with the axe was too light. Monmouth turned to stare at the executioner. The silent reproach seems to have been unhelpful. After two more failed blows, the executioner gave up. He threw down the axe and went at Monmouth's neck with a knife.[59]

Warhaffte Abbildung der Execution / welche an

Hertzog JACOB Von Montmuth.

den 15. Julij 1685. volzogen worden.

Er nicht glauben wolte / daß des Höchsten Gerechtigkeit die Aufruhr jederzeit mit den nen Schäuffesten Straffen heimgesucht / und verfolget / auch noch jetziger Zeit das scharff-schneidene Oberkeitlich Gerechtigkeits-Schwerd / ernsthafft wider selbe zucke / selbiger dörffte nur dieses erbärmlich hingerichteten Hertzogs Exempel behertzigen / dann daran wird er genugsam sehen / wie eiligst die Straffe solchen Verbrechern auf dem Fu nachfolge.

Fig. 2.2. Execution of the Duke of Monmouth, 15 July 1685. (Bibliothèque nationale de France, Paris [BN 151044])

Monmouth's fate was of great interest in Holland, and Dutch printmakers executed prints for two audiences: one content to see in the execution a lawful exertion of authority, and the other eager to see in Monmouth's mangling a judgment not on Monmouth, but on James and his court. For the first audience, a wide-angle print represents a crowd, a scaffold, and the executioner holding up the head. All at a distance compose a quiet, disciplined scene. The focal executioner and prize make one related object of what were two persons, as authority holds defiance "by the hair" (fig. 2.2). The mastered head, the massive, orderly crowd second the solemn justice of the act, and violence vanishes. Such images pick up after the messy part of the business. Their written equivalents end just before it. The quasi-official *Account of What Passed at the Execution of the Late Duke of Monmouth* concludes with the phrase "the executioner proceeded to do his office."[60] State and people are one, order has been restored. These are executions as Foucault expects executions to be, and as the execution of Monmouth was not.

For the second audience, artists represented the horrid contingency and mutilated body the first image erases. One image links Monmouth's fate iconographically with the execution of his grandfather, Charles I. The other replaces such iconographic references with the kinetic body, whose suffering accuses.

In the first, the executioner has gone to work with the knife on the half-naked Monmouth crouched awkwardly at the block (fig. 2.3). On the scaffold, Protestant clerics manifest their dismay, their helpless hands outstretched, their bodies gracefully swayed, against the strong vertical of the bewigged courtier standing squarely and cruelly behind the executioner. The emptiness at the right front of the scaffold opens a space above the emotions of the crowd, in turmoil below. Modeled on images of the execution of Charles I, the spectators turn away, flee, or stand riveted in helpless apprehension. Only one gentleman, waving his bright white hat just below the scaffold, seems pleased. The design rebukes and overshadows him with the darker, looming multi-generational, multi-class, masculine trinity at the left. An apostolic figure, Pauline in quasi-classical drape like the smaller clergymen above, raises a hand almost in benediction over a gentleman whose contorted body expresses horror and helplessness, while a curious, lower-class boy climbs atop the boxes for a better view.

The bilingual image by Schoonebeek is designed to seem to allow the body to speak for itself (fig. 2.4). The print manipulates the position of the viewer and the movement of the gaze to elicit—and politicize—sympathy with the suffering body. Rather than choosing the moment when the executioner has regained control and taken up the knife, Schoonebeek chooses the moment when the executioner throws down the axe. The axe itself is still in motion. Around the body on one side, common clergy, executioner, soldiers, and one gentleman express horror, while another gentleman turns away at the front of the image, bracketing the viewer's position. The reader of the print, directly before the body, positioned among the gentlemen on the scaffold, aligned with the horrified, looks out on a sea of helpless, bobbing, unhappy heads and directly across at the responsible courtiers. Of these bewigged gentlemen, one is amused, one points judgmentally and self-righteously toward the contorted body, a

Fig. 2.3. Execution of the Duke of Monmouth. (Bibliothèque nationale de France, Paris [R 151046])

third, with a round, unthinking, unblinking, cheerful face, looks in another direction, toward two impassive friends. Between the reader and the courtiers lies the body, still moving, beautiful though contorted and mutilated. Blood spurts from the neck; eyes and mouth are open. The graceful back, well-muscled leg, strong buttocks suggest the elegance of classical forms, violated by courtly artifice and its hidden bodies. The elegant hand impossibly cut off indicates with long fingers those responsible. The body itself, in its mutilation, accuses.

Bouncing Along

> Wherever sympathy (fellow-suffering) is preached nowadays—and if I gather rightly, no other religion is any longer preached.
> —Friedrich Nietzsche, *Beyond Good and Evil*, #222

In *Haerlem 1573* the head in motion defies the intention of the executioner, as Marlowe's barons defy their king by threatening to pelt him with Gaveston's head. Animated, the bouncing head asserts in its independent motion the continuing presence of a self that may or may not be present to itself and vanishes from itself in twenty-five to thirty seconds.[61] The self ironized, bouncing also ironizes the political project decapitation intends. The bouncing head escapes the control of the executioner and nullifies for the duration of its escape the political and social purpose of the execution. Before he can hold it up, the executioner has to catch the bouncing head. Yet the irony does no one any good, for the bouncing head has also escaped the control of its departing occupant or erstwhile owner. In this less-than-zero-sum game, control has been lost by both parties, but no usable freedom has been gained.

The spate of bounces in the early eighteenth century coincides precisely with a controversy over decollations after the accession of the Hanoverians in 1714. The decollations between 1716 and 1723 presented a paradox: a German king, regarded by some as a usurper, was cutting off the heads of English and Scottish subjects whose crime was their loyalty to their "natural" monarch. Yet the "usurper" was king by virtue of an act of Parliament, making him the choice of the people in whom sovereignty ultimately resided. He cut off those heads only to assure the sovereignty of king-in-Parliament that Parliament had chosen him to secure.[62] How could anyone complain?

Fig. 2.4. Adr. Schoonebeek, Execution of the Duke of Monmouth, 25 July 1685. (Bibliothèque nationale de France, Paris [R 151045])

In fact, many people did, and the Hanoverian propaganda machine, from Joseph Addison to Daniel Defoe, went to work to prove that relatively few persons had been executed, that George I was not a German brute lacking compassion, honor, and fairness, and that the executions were justified to preserve the (Protestant) social order from (Catholic) tyranny. Addison's *Freeholder* accused George's detractors of "calumnies" and charged that those showing "the greatest tenderness for the persons of the rebels" also "extenuate the heinousness of the rebellion." Addison outraged Swift by observing that there were few more than forty dead. Swift jabbed "A trifle!" in the margin eleven years later in 1727.[63] A pamphlet attributed to Defoe (1716) attacks Lord Derwentwater's last words for defamation and ingratitude: Derwentwater should be grateful he was only beheaded and not disemboweled alive. *Colonel Jack* (1722) praises George's clemency in issuing a general pardon.

Those executed "became a sign," one zealous preacher insisted, "and a monument to everlasting justice."[64] An assize preacher acknowledged that "holding out the terrors of the law" was the necessary but "harsh and unpleasing business of the dispensers of distributive justice."[65] Decapitation had begun to have to justify itself even though no one disputed the right to decapitate.

At such arguments, bouncing heads whistle. Like Uncle Toby, they cannot argue back, but they do not defer. They insert themselves in a political context in which the abstract right of the sovereign to take heads is not questioned, but the application is revolted against, and the sign of revolt is to call upon the body as complainant. These bounces make the reader look at the head, bereft of meaning or symbolism. Refraining from argument, articulating no polemic religious or secular, abjuring any political position, they foreground the body as body alone.

In 1716, Gay reduces tales of tragic love to a comic tale of tragic merchandising, contrasting a brutalized modern body with a sentimental antique one. In *Trivia, or the Art of Walking the Streets of London* (1716), the Thames is frozen, steers roast on spits, boys play at dice in the encampment risen on the river—a Brueghelian winter scene. At its center the matronly Doll hawks her round, red, desirable apples as she strolls across the ice. The ice breaking abbreviates her and her song:

> Her neck grew warpt beneath autumnal loads
> Of various fruit; she now a basket bore,
> That head, alas! shall basket bear no more.
> Each booth she frequent past, in quest of gain
> And boys with pleasure heard her shrilling strain.
> Ah *Doll!* all mortals must resign their breath,
> And industry it self submit to death!
> The cracking crystal yields, she sinks, she dyes,
> Her head, chopt off, from her lost shoulders flies;
> Pippins she cry'd, but death her voice confounds,
> And pip-pip-pip along the ice resounds.
> (*Trivia*, II, ll. 381–92)

As Doll's head bounces cheerily and vocally along the ice, most modern critics cringe.[66] They remain untroubled by the classic pathos of the Orpheus simile that follows:

> So when the *Thracian* furies *Orpheus* tore,
> And left his bleeding trunk deform'd with gore,

His sever'd head floats down the silver tide,
His yet warm tongue for his lost consort cry'd;
Eurydice with quiv'ring voice he mourn'd,
And *Heber's* banks *Eurydice* return'd.
(II, ll. 393–98)

Sympathizing with Orpheus's body, attuned to crying, quivering, mourning, the reader elevated by compassion does not observe that Gay is much
grislier and more bodied than his Ovidian and Vergilian sources. The mutilated torso is deformed, gory, bleeding, the tongue "yet warm." Yet the
reader accepts the death, murmuring "Eurydice." The bounce disturbs,
challenging acquiescence. "Chopt" and flying, Doll is more kinetic than
Orpheus, floating, quivering. Compared to Orpheus's distant Thracian
fate, his head delicately "severed," Doll's loss is immediate and modern.
"Pip-pip-pip" sounds like the cheer of a crowd. Her head "chopt off," it
"flies" from her "lost shoulders." That is what happens to a head severed
with an axe in a single blow.

Although Gay's poem is not at all political, it fingers decollation at a
sensitive time. *Trivia* appeared in January 1716, the month preceding the
February executions of the Scottish lords and their followers. Many of
Gay's close friends were under suspicion or imprisoned for Jacobite activities. Of Queen Anne's last ministers Robert Harley, Earl of Oxford,
was in the Tower awaiting trial. Henry St. John, Viscount Bolingbroke,
had fled to France and would be attainted for treason. James Butler, duke
of Ormonde, had followed him. The poet Matthew Prior was under arrest. Jonathan Swift had removed to Ireland, where he had been warned
to hide his papers. Reading *Trivia, or the Art of Walking the Streets of
London* later in 1716, one might have remembered other separated,
rolling heads, wrapped in black baize, near the wintry Thames.

In 1726, Swift, more aggressively, thrusts blood and bounce in the
reader's eye and ear, without explanation. Swift waited ten years—and
several more decollations (James Shepheard or Sheppard, 1718; John
Matthews, 1721; Christopher Layer, 1723)—to represent a beheading. In
Gulliver's Travels (1726), Swift borrowed Gay's bounce to produce the
largest, loudest, and most explosive decapitation yet on record. Visiting
Brobdignag, whose inhabitants are sixty feet tall, Lemuel Gulliver, the
surgeon hero, is invited to attend an execution, not for treason, but for
murder. Like Gay's, the decollation in Brobdignag is deliberately apoliti-
cal. Swift had alluded to the trials of his friends Oxford and Bolingbroke

in Gulliver's voyage to Lilliput, but he separates his decapitation from English politics in both motive and style. Familiar with Dutch decollations from editing the *Memoirs* of Sir William Temple, Swift knew that as envoy to Holland Temple had seen, and been deeply disturbed by, the public decapitations, for the crime of fraud, of men of good family. Such executions, Temple thought, should at least have been private.[67] Swift's account is more democratic.

Criminal, not political, Dutch, not English, the execution supplies no interesting victim, with touching last words, not "Eurydice" or even "pip, pip, pip." An anonymous "Malefactor" is fixed in a chair, Dutch style, rather than kneeling or lying at the English block. Gone is the kneeling, prayerful posture visible in *Haerlem 1573* that requires the hero or martyr not to flinch. Using not the English axe but the Dutch and German sword, a highly skilled executioner takes off the head in "one Blow," and then disappears with his forty-foot sword. By the ordinary rules of scaffold dramas, the executioner should hold up the head, or the spectators should applaud, or the account should end with the blow. Instead, in an almost unprecedented movement, Gulliver's eye follows the blood, and he recoils when he hears the bounce of the head. Gulliver has not followed the head's trajectory; it has imposed itself upon him. Moral evaluation has been replaced by a physical shock, to the spectator as well as to the decapitated:

> The Malefactor was fixed in a Chair upon a Scaffold erected for the Purpose; and his Head cut off at one Blow with a Sword of about forty Foot long. The Veins and Arteries spouted up such a prodigious Quantity of Blood, and so high in the Air, that the great *Jet d'Eau* at *Versailles* was not equal for the Time it lasted; and the Head when it fell on the Scaffold Floor, gave such a Bounce, as made me start, although I were at least an *English* Mile distant.[68]

Such a bouncing head is curiously liminal. Like Doll's, it serves no purpose.

Although Swift analyzes the motives for attending or avoiding an execution, Plato's and Montaigne's justification for having public executions —deterrence—is inconspicuously absent. Favoring attendance are sympathy with the criminal's victim and curiosity; opposing it are compassion and detestation of such sights in themselves. "Tender-hearted" Glumdalclitch, Gulliver's ten-year-old nurse, prefers not to attend. A young gentleman, an intimate friend of the murdered man, "urges" her to do so and "prevails." Gulliver "abhors such spectacles," but is curious about an event that must be "extraordinary." "Humanitarian sensibility," feminized and infantilized by attribution to a girl child, is overcome by an "urgent" young man and in tiny Gulliver by curiosity. Swift understands, as Adam Smith will later, that sympathy with the victim is itself a provocation to violence.[69] Swift's account neither defends nor attacks any human actions, but presumes and exploits a response in and through the body produced by seeing and hearing another body's violent disruption. Elsewhere, Swift attacks warfare and colonialism by figuring them as spectacles of mutilation.[70] The bouncing head forms part of a critique that invokes the body, though the body is not yet a ground on which one can base an argument.

Bouncing more benignly, other heads mark new forms of devotion, as in Lady Margaret Pennyman's curious tale of St. Denis's bouncing head. As a severed head may be the object of religious devotion, so may its bounce. An altar may be built where the head was cut off, where it first bounced, and where it stopped moving, as at the Basilica of St. Paul, Rome.[71] So Montmartre and the Abbey of St. Denis mark the start and stop of St. Denis's head. Justifying her repetition of the story, Lady Margaret replaces religious with architectural devotion. Her "fabulous" story brackets the start and stop of the saint's head with architectural excellence—"the finest Gate in the City," "this noble Abby":

> When St *Dennis* lost his Head (which was at a Place not far from the Gate of that Name, which is a most beautiful Structure, and by much the finest Gate in the City of *Paris* . . .) . . . where his Body dropped, and stirred no more, is this noble Abby built.[72]

Unlike the disgruntled political purposefulness of Gay and Swift, Lady Margaret is fascinated by an interest in the body that dares not speak its name, parenthesizing and deferring until St. Denis's hands take hold of his head, dropping and picking up every half-mile for precisely five miles. Then she runs with it, but decorously ends with another edifice.

Across the channel, in Amsterdam in 1730, the French printmaker Bernard Picart produced an image of the execution of Charles I that showed the executioner's assistant poised to catch the head, bent over, his legs spread, his hands wide apart, like a ball receiver[73] (fig. 2.5). Evidently an invention, Picart's image knows that the king's block was low, but not

Fig. 2.5. Bernard Picart, Execution of Charles I. (Bibliothèque nationale de France, Paris [R 150984])

that the executioners were masked. Yet it is the executioner's assistant who focuses the scene, as Gay's "chopt" focuses Doll. He crouches, like a rugby player, to catch the head when it flies in his direction. Like Gay's flying head, Picart knows—and makes his viewers know—that what happens in the next few instants after the axe comes down is uncontrollable and unpredictable. Making in itself no argument for or against the execution of the king, Picart's assistant "catches" the contingency of the execution, the next unsentimental moment, the brutal carnival leap of the head that is about to take place. Below, the text condemns "hypocrite Cromwell," and this "tragic," "unique and incredible" event.

Eighteenth-century authorities mitigated that response through the body by removing certain physical features of decapitation from sight in the 1740s. Authorities covered up—and so protected sensibilities from—the effects of an action few opposed on theoretical grounds but some had begun to consider too disturbing to be seen. Bouncing is an in-between, disorderly, unstable state, equally at odds with authority's purposes and the crowd's sympathetic identification. Its jaunty defiance of authority's control has more in common with the irreverent, scapegoated crowd, jesting about the gallows and heroicizing the condemned, than with sentimental solemnities or indignant reform. Bounces make visible the violation of the body, as violation, that scaffold dramas, official or sentimental, scurry to cover up. As part of a high-culture carnival, they mark a not-yet-articulable resistance to absolutism's principal sign, attacking not through argument but through the body.

In the 1720s, opposition to the Hanoverians could cost a man his head. By the 1730s, however, the English opposition had re-appropriated the sovereign's sign. With the rise of Walpole, decollation returns to satirical prints with 1640s vigor. Cutting off heads once again means resistance to tyranny, whether Walpole's or Jowler the dog's in *Roderick Random* (1748). Henry Fielding's Tom Thumb carried old Grizzle's head in triumph in *The Tragedy of Tragedies, Tom Thumb the Great* (1731). A print showing a meeting of the scandalous Calves' Head Club titillated London in 1735, the saintly martyr Charles I reduced to a calf's head on a platter. Kathleen Wilson remarks on the extensiveness of regicide imagery in the Wilkes and Liberty crisis of the 1760s.[74] Hogarth portrayed Wilkes in a posture similar to his famous portrait of Lovat, a hint as to the correct disposition of Wilkes and Liberty. The execution of the queen of Denmark's favorite, Struensee, in 1772 inspired anti-Bute prints. A headless corpse floating toward Bute, its head in its hands, was titled "Struensee's Ghost, Or Lord B-TE & M-N-D [Mansfield] in the Horrors," followed by "The Fate of Favourites."[75] The 1780 print *The Heads of the Nation in a Right State* set three ministers' heads on pikes above Temple Bar to general acclaim, above a placard for [Stephens's] Lecture on Heads.

Over the course of the eighteenth century, satire, sentiment, and the sovereignty of the people contrived in turn to expose, repress, and restore decapitation as a political sign. Satirists exposed the carnival brutality of decapitations, and newspapers reported the demeanor of the spectators. Theorists of sentiment and shared feeling, the sympathy that binds the individuals of a contractual polity, repudiated carnival and brutality but affirmed the social order that decapitation and other capital punishments existed to enforce. If satire exposed and sentiment and social order tended to repress bouncing heads, the affirmation of popular sovereignty in the French Revolution enabled the revival of decapitation as an expression of the power of the people.

3

Power to the People
His Pike and Her Guillotine

The French Revolution saw two kinds of beheadings. Through the little national window of the guillotine, one kind looked toward our own time and the technological perfection of impersonal violence. Aloft on pikes, the other looked back a much longer way. Heads speared on pikes, posted on bridges, gates, and walls, or heaped beside a tent, are far more ancient than the guillotine and far more widespread in their geographic dispersal. But the guillotine, like other works of human art, has accrued meanings more complex than the simpler work of human hands that severs a head and impales it on a phallic pike. A machine to sever heads, the guillotine makes the severed head disappear twice. When the guillotine cuts off a head, the head falls out of sight into a basket. When the guillotine becomes the capital instrument of the revolution, it breaks the pike.

For contemporaries, both the guillotine and the pike symbolized the revolution, but they occupied distinct though overlapping semantic spaces. Heads on pikes were the product of primitive, popular violence (or justice). The guillotine was the mechanism of revolutionary, institutional violence (or justice). Pike and guillotine shared the multiple, culturally determined meanings that belong to the public display of severed heads. Both evoked contradictory responses—horror in some quarters, relish in others—and the continuum in between: fascinated horror, queasy relish, and the shrug of indifference. But the guillotine was new. It was an instrument of public order, and almost at once it acquired a spectacular history that knotted it inextricably to the most controversial period of the Revolution. As Tristram Shandy might have said, it was a new whim-wham inserted into reality. One way or another, every observer had to accommodate it, and reality had to be reshaped to fit it in, precisely because the guillotine was an instrument of order that generated (what seemed to many) disorder.

The first beheadings of the Revolution took place on 14 July 1789 when the heads of Flesselles and de Launay were promenaded on pikes in the gardens of the Palais Royale.[1] As Bertier and Foulon followed, an observer across the channel remarked that "the old Parisian ferocity has broken out in a shocking manner."[2] To Edmund Burke there was nothing new or surprising in the capacity of crowds for murder, and he would be the first in a long line of authors and artists to exploit such capacity for violence in order to denigrate the revolution and its ideologies.

For the better part of a century, men of Burke's class had been congratulating themselves on the improvement of modern manners relative both to violence and to sexuality. Pope historicizes Homer's brutality; Garrick lops off Wycherley's obscenity and turns *The Country Wife* into a *Girl*. Johnson recounts that in his mother's time, men quarreled as to who took and who gave the wall, while in his time it had become settled by convention. Circumscribed ever more narrowly, the legitimate uses of violence had visibly diminished. What such changes meant, Montesquieu, Adam Smith, and Adam Ferguson were prepared to explain: commerce civilized. The exigencies of exchange softened the manners of men and improved the treatment of women. The late eighteenth century was no peaceable kingdom, but by the time the Bastille fell, violence had become what it remains in modern western sociology: an aberration to be accounted for.[3]

Whatever view of human nature one held, whether one followed Hobbes, Locke, or Rousseau, whether one preferred culture or nature, violence required explanation. For the advocate of culture, the progress of society had rescued mankind from Hobbes's state of nature where the war of all against all raged on. For the advocate of nature, society had corrupted and deformed the innocence of peaceable, cooperative, equal man. It was not nature, but "the new-born state of society" that plunged mankind into the same "horrible state of war."[4] Whether one preferred society and progress or nature and simplicity, violence belonged to the Other. Man as machine potentially occluded violence altogether.

In the *Reflections*, Burke deprives the crowd of any motivation—ideological, political, or economic—for its violence. The violence stands alone, isolated, irreducible, and incomprehensible. Like the other bodily functions and vices, this violence squats at the Augustinian base of human nature, grotesque, sordid, and inseparable from the column. It can be hidden by draperies, or it can be chained up, but it is always there: "The *old* Parisian ferocity has *broken out*" (emphasis added). When Burke describes the activities of the crowd during the October days, his metaphoric categories label the crowd's violence as they remove that violence from sympathetic understanding. His similitudes identify the crowd's behavior as part of the human repertoire, but relegate it to ancient history and contemporary barbarism.

The march from Versailles, with the royal family led by the Garde Nationale and the women of Paris, is likened to "a procession of *American savages*, entering into *Onondaga*, after some of their *murders called victories*, and leading into *hovels hung round with scalps*, their captives."[5] As so often with Burke, the judgment is proleptic: the metaphor precedes the event that justifies talk of scalps and murders. Pages later, two gentlemen of the king's bodyguard are "cruelly and publickly dragged to the block, and beheaded in the great court of the palace. Their heads were stuck upon *spears* and *led the procession*; whilst the royal captives who followed in the train were slowly moved along, amidst the *horrid yells*, and *shrilling screams*, and *frantic dances* . . . of the *furies of hell*, in the abused shape of the vilest of women."[6] "Spears" brandished by "American savages" replace the pikes of a European army. Yells, screams, and dances of natives on the warpath challenge the ordered ranks of Europeans. For us, such scenes are very remote. They belong to Grade B movies, and the cavalry always arrives in time. In Burke's day, such scenes were remote geographically, but not temporally. In the 1770s, the propriety of scalp-taking as a policy in America had been discussed in a session of British Parliament (Burke attacked the policy as barbarous), and Captain Cook's fate reminded contemporaries that the natives were not always friendly.

To sum up the horrors of those days, Burke snatches at classical references: "the furies of hell" and "Theban and Thracian Orgies." Such sanctified, classical, religious debauch is also violent, sexual, and specifically female. At Thebes, Agave, first of the maenads, mother of Pentheus, thrilled as she carried "Pitcht on a Poale the grisly head of him that was her Sonne."[7] Led by severed heads and surrounded by shrilling women, this procession parodies a civilized triumph, the celebration of a victory. Monstrous, every element is out of nature, out of place, out of time, out of order. But Burke, whose affinities with radicalism have often been pointed out, catches an element of the scene that most apologists for the revolution have chosen to ignore these two hundred years. Although he would have his depiction revolt us, Burke shapes the exuberance and the uncanny pleasure of those who cut off the heads and put them on pikes.

Friends to the revolution of Burke's class, then and now, have evaded the violence of the revolution by restoring the ideology Burke excises. They provide the people with a respectable motivation for acts of violence, usually retaliation against oppression, and they attribute the people's excesses to a culpable but comprehensible fury at release from oppression. Entirely absent is any sense of the pleasure of violence. If the fact of violence is acknowledged, the horrid details are dropped. For Paine, the mob's cutting off the head of the baker François and presenting it on a pike to his wife becomes only "the affair of the unfortunate baker."[8] An unfortunate baker indeed, and one would not know from Paine the form his misfortune took. Philip Francis speaks in generalities of "the fury of the populace," "the crimes of individuals," "the loss of a *single* life, in a popular tumult," but he describes more specifically the scourgings, dragoonings, and galleys of the ancien regime.[9] Or Anacharsis Cloots, the cheerful atheist, reminds us early in 1790 that there have also been not so very many heads lost: only "dix ou douze têtes," when the people have "douze ou quinze siècles d'oppression à venger" (ten or twelve heads; twelve or fifteen centuries of oppression to avenge).[10] The oppression takes up where the heads leave off—at twelve, less than a head per century.

Modern historians are equally predictable in their choices. Alfred Cobban, who would prefer that there should have been no revolution, deploys violence as rhetorical decoration, artfully, wittily, and horribly. Albert Soboul, Georges Lefebvre, R. B. Rose, and Lynn Hunt ignore it almost entirely, while popular historians, such as Christopher Hibbert, wring all they can from pathetic and shocking events. More interesting is the tact of George Rudé. In *The Crowd in the French Revolution*, Rudé does not obscure the fact of murder, and he names many of the victims: de Launay, Bertier, Foulon, François, the two *gardes du corps* at Versailles. But only de Launay and the two *gardes* have their heads cut off. The rest are merely murdered. That is a little odd, but more interesting is what Rudé does with the heads when they are cut off. Nothing. Nothing more is done with them or to them. The pikes are excised. There is no promenade. One might well wonder why anyone went to the considerable trouble of sawing through bone.[11] Removing the promenade removes the celebration and denies the perpetrators of violence their pleasure. It also removes the threat explicit in the action.

When the people cut off and displayed the head of a "traitor," they made the "sovereignty of the people" more than a pretty compliment. They enacted that sovereignty by exercising a traditional prerogative of the sovereign. Cutting off the heads of the king's officers, the rabble have re-defined themselves as the sovereign people. Instead of learning the old lesson of the heads, they teach a new one. Disturbing to those identified with the old order, the act invigorates those who identify with the new. As for those identified with the old order who believe they identify with the new, they ignore the lesson or palliate it. Many supporters of the revolution desired to see no changes beyond their own admission, and that of their class ("the best," as Wordsworth described them), to power, prestige, influence, and participation. The lesson of the heads is that there has been a fundamental change in social hierarchies and the distribution of power. Article Three of the Declaration of the Rights of Man and Citizen declared that the people were "the source of sovereignty." Taking a head transforms the *menu peuple* from the passive "source of sovereignty" to the active executor of sovereign power.

Here and there, beyond such transparent acts as taking the Bastille or storming the Tuileries, burning a manor or demanding the heads of the Gironde, there are traces of the people's awareness of their subversion and their appropriation of sovereignty. After the first paroxysm of excitement, the man who hacked through de Launay's neck with his cook's knife was frightened. Dénot feared punishment, and he justified the act as self-defence: de Launay had hurt him in the fray that led to de Launay's death. The crowd, offering him the knife, represented the decapitation as an act of justice: "It was you he hurt," they told him. Then, as time passed and customs changed, he decided he should put in for a medal and made the act his boast: "He believed it a patriotic act and one that deserved a medal" (Que s'il en a agi ainsi, il a cru faire un acte patriotique, et mériter une medaille).[12] He had not committed a shameless mutilation for which he should be punished, but a patriotic act for which he should be rewarded. Neither self-defense nor simple justice, but his service to his sovereign, the medal-awarding people, finally justified Dénot to himself and others.

The people's subversion and appropriation of power appear in numerous prints that stress the exuberance of popular decapitations. These were, in spite of Cloots and Paine, not decapitations to be hidden, but decapitations to be flourished, to be brandished under the nose of power. Among the more popular subjects of revolutionary prints was the double decapitation of Bertier de Sauvigny and his father-in-law, Foulon. Thrusting the head of Foulon on its pike into Bertier's face, the crowd had chanted, "Baise papa, baise papa" (Kiss papa, kiss papa), and anonymous printmakers loved the joke. In one version, "C'est ainsi qu'on se venge des traiteurs" (So we take vengeance on traitors), the crowd hoist Bertier in a chair above their heads, among the pikes. Looming above them, his position of authority is suddenly ambiguous. In helpless horror, Bertier gazes into the face of Foulon, his "papa." Behind and above are the heads of Flesselles and de Launay, taken off a few weeks earlier. The authority of position is as precarious as the authority of Foulon's title, "papa." Bertier is higher than the people, and will be higher still, yet the people are sovereign. So much the title tells us, for only against a sovereign can treason be committed.

The presence of Flesselles and de Launay as supernumeraries in this oddly oedipal drama suggests a certain anxiety to accumulate evidence for that sovereignty. Child Bertier will in moments become like papa, with a pole of his own, and "baise papa," that affectionate command from an adult to a child, may be spoken by a papa, a mama, or a nurse. Those asserting the new sovereignty have not replaced the old authority in the position at the top; they are still below, and they are still in the act. The print argues subversion and re-appropriation of authority, but the re-appropriation is not complete. There was another father whose head still had to be appropriated.

The principal head taken during the revolution was the king's. No active, insurrectionary pike figured in that grand moment of subversion. The most commonly reproduced "historical" image of the king's execution emphasizes the new authority to which the power of the head has been transferred. Off-center, a tiny *bourreau* holds up a tiny king's head to massed troops and people. Like the *Execution of the Duke of Monmouth, 15 July 1685,* similar in design as in ethos, the image is dated: *Journée du 21 Janvier 1793,* subjecting death to the objectivity of calendar and history. Such wide-angle representations interpret the French revolution from a liberal perspective as orderly and controlled, rather than radical and violent.[13]

Unlike seventeenth-century images of the martyrdom of Charles I, prints sympathetic to Louis XVI expose his bleeding head and body, as in James Gillray's *Blood of the Murdered Crying for Vengeance* or Isaac Cruikshank's *Martyr of Equality.* The body of the king, now a body like that of other men, engages sympathy in its violation. In Gillray, the king's head is not handled; in Cruikshank, the king's kinsman, the duc d'Orleans, now Philippe Egalité, doffs his plumed hat to the severed head he holds.

More radical prints emphasize the people's direct manipulation of the king's head (fig. 3.1). In profile, like the head on a coin, Louis' head is held

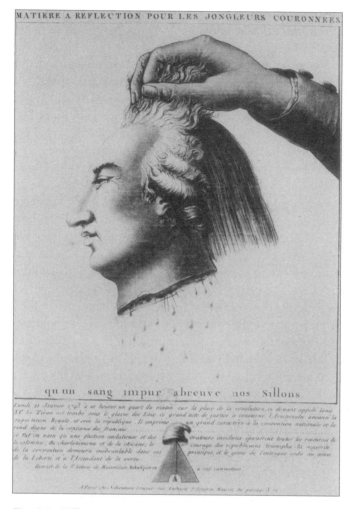

Fig. 3.1. Villeneuve, Matter for Crowned Jugglers to Reflect Upon. (Bibliothèque nationale de France, Paris)

by a graceful hand and forearm with plebeian buttons on the cuffs. The hand dominates the head easily, holding the top curls of the hair without gripping them. The neck drips blood, and the title is a warning: "Matière à reflection pour les jongleurs couronnées" (Subject of reflection for crowned jugglers). Villeneuve's model is Cellini's Perseus holding the head of Medusa.[14] As from Medusa's blood sprang a warrior and a miraculous horse, so the king's impure blood will water France's furrows, in the words of the *Marseillaise* below his bleeding neck: "qu'un sang impur abreuve nos sillons" (may an impure blood water our furrows).

The message is unmistakable: the people have power over this head. The affect is equally clear: the heroic people have triumphed over their enemy and display this head in sign of triumphs past and triumphs to come. Although this head, like other "portraits de guillotinés," was neither severed by hand nor put on a pike, nothing in the image precludes such a disposition in the next, unrepresented moment.

The discourse of the pike is fundamentally a simple one. The pike had been the weapon of the common foot soldier, of the "poor bugger who possesses only a pike," as *Père Duchesne* put it.[15] In the eighteenth century it was being superseded by the bayonet, the instrument carried in revolutionary prints by smart, up-to-date National Guardsmen. Old-fashioned, primitive, common, simple, and cheap, the pike was an apt instrument for the people to use when they sought to show their old masters that the mastery had changed hands. The pike that once upheld the old order now held the dead old order up to its still-living face in the promenade, a simple, gruesome paradox. For counter-revolutionaries, it was equally well adapted to represent the horrors of that transfer of mastery.

Since pikes have to be held up if they are to display heads, graphic representations are committed to showing someone holding the pike, and the argument of any print can usually be inferred from who is doing the holding. The delights of overturning the repressive old order emerge in the exuberant revolutionary prints that show a particular, albeit anonymous, sansculotte shaking his Foulon at Bertier. Far less unsettling are the popular revolutionary prints that show the heads rising from a sea of pikes and bayonets, the individuals who actually hold the pikes submerged in "the people." Distributed in orderly ranks, the people display the heads their justice has exacted, but they are not actively questing for more. As in traditional prints of the head held up, the orderliness of the people endorses their justice aligned with their power. The pikes are present, but they are, for the moment, still.

The discourse of the pikes is the discourse of the people's insurgency. "Resurrect the pikes" was the cry of expiring Jacobinism in 1799, when it was too late. The pikes had been broken by the guillotine, the new machine that not only cut off the heads of the leaders of the sansculottes, but also replaced their pikes as emblem of the revolution among revolutionaries and counter-revolutionaries alike.

The guillotine originated as a technical solution to a practical problem. The practical problem, however, was not simple: it had been created by an intersection of egalitarian and humanitarian ideals and promoted by a powerful desire for public order. In the new criminal code of 1791, the Constituent Assembly decreed that decollation would henceforward be the punishment in all capital crimes. The *bourreau,* Henri Sanson, protested that present technology, the sword, was inadequate to meet the projected demand. Each decollation would require one or two swords, and any number of successive decollations would put a severe strain on the headsman. The Assembly appointed Dr. Antoine Louis to pursue the suggestion of a decapitating machine made by Dr. Joseph Ignace Guillotin in 1789. After meticulous experiments at home and extensive research abroad into such decollating machines as the Maiden at Edinburgh and the Halifax gibbet, Dr. Louis and Sanson produced a machine that was first used on a thief in April 1792.

Nicknamed at first "Louisette" and "La Petite Louison" for Dr. Louis, the machine soon took its name from the voice that had suggested it rather than from the hands that had designed it. "Louisette" and "Louison" evoked the king before the doctor, inadvertently erasing the member of the Third Estate whom the name meant to honor. The neologism "guillotine" reminded men only of the member of the National Assembly, and the state's implement of justice became popular, rather than monarchical. Calling the new machine "guillotine" placed the fatherhood of the machine firmly in the Assembly and prevented the people's authority and the people's justice from being mistaken for that of the king.

The Constituent Assembly's motives for decreeing decollation the punishment in all capital cases were egalitarian and humanitarian. Early in the discussions of reform of the criminal code, it had been determined that along with other privileges and exclusions, differential sentencing based on the rank or quality of the criminal was to be eliminated. All crimes of the same kind should be punished by the same sentence. For crimes for which the penalty was death, it was proposed that the punishment be decapitation.[16] The effect was not only to eliminate social differences in dying, but also to level upwards. Although Enlightenment Europe practiced both aristocratic and common decollations, only aristocratic decollations had a genealogy reaching back to Rome, reinvented in the Renaissance. Now all citizens would be treated to an equal and honorable death.

Paralleling the egalitarian argument was a humanitarian one. When Guillotin presented the projected reforms in the criminal code to the assembly, he proposed at the same time "un simple mécanisme" (a simple mechanism) to effect the decapitations. Such a mechanism, he argued, would permit a punishment less cruel and less painful than hanging, hitherto the commonest mode of execution. With his death delivered to him more efficiently, the victim would struggle less and endure less agony. Such a machine would enable the state to kill citizens without hurting them. Foucault manifests a lingering admiration for the machine, not the frequently incompetent headsman, when he describes decapitation as reducing "all pain to a single gesture, performed in a single moment—the zero degree of torture."[17] For many, the guillotine embodied the best of the Enlightenment in capital punishment. The condemned were spared pain to their bodies, the executioners pain to their sensibilities.

Seconding the egalitarian and humanitarian arguments was a powerful desire for public order. In the debates on decapitation, both those who opposed and those who favored it argued from its effects on the populace at large. Those opposed, such as the Abbé Maury, argued that decapitation was too bloody a mode of execution, that it would accustom the people to effusions of blood and render them *féroce* (ferocious). Against the negative effect on character, those who favored decapitation argued that decapitation would have a positive effect on the people's actions. Performed at any lamppost, irregular hangings had often preceded the equally irregular promenade of the pikes. A decapitating machine would control the exercise of popular violence and restore control over violence to more conventional custodians. As the duc de Liancourt put it, a decapitating machine would lend itself less easily to popular vengeance and irregular application than bloodless hangings.[18] His observation was greeted with applause by his fellow deputies. With a decapitating machine, the monopoly of violence would be restored to the state, re-institutionalized, and immobilized.

Unspoken but clear to all were the various ways in which formal decapitation would contribute to public order. A machine restored control of public punishments to the established authorities. Removed from their role as actors, the people would be returned to their traditional position as spectators, while the authorities tended the mechanism and managed the delivery of victims from trial to prison to place of execution. Developed by the Constituent Assembly, the machine would represent the people's justice, but that justice would not be exerted directly by the people. Fundamental to these good effects was the immobility of the machine. Unlike pikes, decapitating machines are stationary. They do not perambulate palaces and streets. They cannot surge threateningly and randomly through the ways and still do their work. The days the guillotine walked, forced by a crowd to remove to the Place du Carrousel or the Champs de Mars, the work was delayed.[19] Nor did these implications of the guillotine's fixity pass unnoticed. From radical quarters, there came persistent, unanswered demands for portable guillotines and multiple stations.

Finally, crowning the project was the technological magic of the machine *qua* machine. Egalitarian, humanitarian, and still, "un bienfait pour l'humanité" (a benefit to humanity), the machine had the peculiar virtue that it effaced the headsman. When the *Ancien Moniteur* praised the humanity of Dr. Guillotin in making his proposal, the impersonality of a machine was singled out for admiration. Displaced from persons to a machine, the act of death became the product of justice itself: "comme la loi" (like the law).

L'innovation de mettre la *mécanique* à la place d'un *executeur* qui, comme la loi, sépare la sentence du juge, est digne du siècle où nous allons vivre, et du nouvel ordre politique dans lequel nous entrons. [Substituting a *mechanism* for an *executioner* that, like the law, separates the sentence from the judge, is an innovation worthy of the century in which we are going to live and the new political order on which we are entering.][20]

In this new age, the machine, like the law, disguised human agency, responsibility, and violence.

Converging to create the guillotine were the best hopes and the highest ideals of the liberal (or bourgeois) revolution. Equality, humanity, stability, and the impersonal majesty of the law: few human inventions have ever had such sponsors. The only discordant note was that the idea of a beheading machine made some people laugh. The same article in the *Ancien Moniteur* that praised Guillotin's project also chided the people for making such a machine the subject of jokes, "trivialités indecentes" (indecent vulgarities). A free people, it was hoped, would overcome its low habits, among which the most disgraceful was that of "plaisanter sur les supplices" (joking about public punishments). Carnival laughter recognizes the discrepancy between the pretentious sponsors and the actual function performed by the machine. Rejecting the solemn order proposed by authority, it insinuates an alternate subject position, death-defying and impudent. It also dissipates anxiety about a machine that, it was promised, would take off your head before you knew it.[21]

At first, the guillotine lived up to expectations. The people nicknamed it, flocked to see its initial use, and registered disappointment at the spectacle. It was too quick; there was nothing to see. The blade fell, and the head disappeared, without bouncing or rolling, into the basket. Equal, humane, stable, legal, and boring: the guillotine was, for the Assembly, a complete success. As the Revolution lurched toward violence in the summer of 1792, the guillotine soothed sensibilities exacerbated by other horrors. Although the fact is often forgotten, the guillotine was innocent of the worst atrocities of the Revolution, from the September Massacres at Paris to the drownings at Nantes and the shootings of Lyon. In 1794 the *Annual Register* promised that

> posterity will learn with astonishment and horror, that for the space of several months a tribunal existed in the large and populous city of Nantz, legally commissioned by public authority to [destroy] whole tribes and districts of their fellow-citizens.[22]

The guillotine at least preserved the individuality of the victim, the dignity of death inflicted one at a time.

Soon, however, the people began to make the guillotine their own. Although the neighbors complained about inadequate drainage, others were not troubled by the puddling of blood, and the guillotine became a place of popular resort. More importantly, radical elements, from the sections up to Danton and Robespierre, began to direct the guillotine's use for their own political ends. From the fall of the Gironde to Robespierre's last speech, the radicals' means included intimidating, or attempting to intimidate, the Convention.[23] When they turned on Robespierre in the year 2 (1794), the deputies turned on the guillotine as well.

Claims on the instrument from outside the Convention made the deputies uneasy, as in an incident of 7 April 1794. Two days after the execution of Danton and his supporters, a stranger appeared at the bar of the Convention to "offre une somme qu'il destine, dit-il, aux frais d'entretien et de réparation de la guillotine. Les plus violents murmures interrompent le pétitionnaire" (offer a sum of money that he intended, he said, for the expense of maintaining and repairing the guillotine. The most violent murmurs interrupted the petitioner). The bar cleared, the Committee of General Security was ordered to look into the conduct of this too charitable citizen.[24] The meaning of his gesture remains obscure, and its lack of clarity was deeply disturbing at the time. Did the citizen mean indeed that the guillotine needed repair so that more blood should flow? Did he accuse the deputies of neglect? Or did he mean slyly to suggest that they had already done too much? The gesture represented a danger to those who took him to be sincere, to those who took him to be ironic, and to those who hoped he was only mad. Rejecting the "patriotic donation" on behalf of the guillotine, the deputies recognized that the guillotine's significance had passed beyond their control.

When the deputies turned against the Robespierrist Terror, they also turned against its instrument. In January 1795, six months after Robespierre's fall, one deputy sought to erase the guillotine itself. Already the painlessness of the guillotine had been called into question. Doctors disputed the cessation of sensation when the spinal column was severed. Much debated was Charlette Corday's blush when the executioner slapped her severed head.[25] The guillotine became the first victim of a law proposing to abolish the death penalty. Like other Jacobins, it was to suffer death without delay:

> II. Toutes les guillotines, avec leur échafauds, qui existent dans la république, seront détruites, brisées et brûlées, au moment même de la publication de la présente loi, par les exécuteurs des jugements criminels. [II. All guillotines, with their scaffolds, existing in the republic, will be destroyed, broken and burned, the very instant this law is published, by those who execute criminal judgments.][26]

"Broken and burned" like a traitor or murderous wife, the guillotine was to be destroyed by those who had used it.

While the deputies saved their guillotine (the order of the day was moved on the resolutions), they shared the desire to separate themselves from it. In July 1795 there was considerable discussion as to how to celebrate the anniversary of Robespierre's fall on 9 thermidor. While controversy swirled over speeches and places, one proposal of the organizing committee found immediate acceptance: the Convention ordered that there should be no more executions in the place de la Revolution.[27] That order removed the guillotine from its place at the heart of the Revolution and consigned it to the periphery. In that gesture of removal, the guillotine was riveted to the Terror, that period of great hopes and great disappointments when the guillotine had been at the center of the (place de la) Revolution.

Once fastened to the Terror, the guillotine increased in significance and, in representations, in size. Before then, however, the guillotine belonged to the people. By those who lived with it, the socially egalitarian guillotine was domesticated, miniaturized, familiarized, familialized, feminized, and sanctified, as "our holy mother" or "the patriotic razor." It was the little national *window* of the national *domus*. Those who saw their neighbors at the window reduced whatever terrors it held by fitting it into the order of things in a subordinate and controllable position, associated by nicknaming with houses, barbers, women, children, and religion.

For a brief, halcyon period between the execution of the king and the acceleration of the Terror later in 1793, the guillotine was a neutral implement, as the *Annual Register* suggests in its horror of Lyon and Nantes, or a playful adjunct. Early, innocent, charming, and small representations of the guillotine do exist. Among them, the *Réception de Louis Capet aux enfers par grand nombres de brigands ci-devant couronnées* (fig. 3.2) shows Louis XVI arriving in hell, his head smiling under his arm, to be greeted by his illustrious ancestors and many friends who carry their own heads on pikes. It is a cheerful scene. The elegant headless ones are, it appears, responsible for the well-coiffed heads entrusted to their care. The sons and daughters of liberty, who might have been blamed or congratulated for taking those heads, dance in the distance. In sunlit Elysian Fields, they circle a pole crowned with a Phrygian cap and cockade that resemble, but are not, a head. Still in the world of the living, above a medieval castle, across the Styx, high in the left corner of the sky, flies a tiny guillotine. Its wings are batlike, but it is a most unthreatening little creature.

The miniature guillotine was a pet. It served as a paperweight or a child's toy or, smaller still, women's hair ornaments and earrings. Children have long been given toy swords, guns, and lasers to play with, and women have worn their bodkins and ornamental swords as brooches. But neither have been often supplied with miniature gallows, blocks and axes, or electric chairs. The practice has been attributed to a gruesome levity that is peculiarly French, but it is more probable that the intricacy of the mechanism fascinated and that the identification of the machine with the people's justice, not the king's, made it less alien. Revolutionary ideology proposed the people's sovereignty as active, and the guillotine came to signify the people's protection from the Revolution's enemies. As a talisman protecting the Revolution and oneself from aristocrats and tyrants, a mini-guillotine replaces the cross, also a sign of (judicial) death and victory. It wears equally well as an emblem sporting hostility to aristocrats and tyrants, like a Mao button.

Fig. 3.2. Villeneuve, Reception of Louis Capet in Hell by Great Numbers of Once Crowned Bandits. (Bibliothèque nationale de France, Paris)

Certainly the oddest and most unexpected miniaturization of the guillotine is Wordsworth's. Leaving France at the end of 1792, the first year of the guillotine's operation, Wordsworth could have seen the guillotine before his departure. He could scarcely have avoided hearing talk of it. In *The Prelude,* Wordsworth excises the machine from his account of the Terror when "Domestic carnage . . . filled the whole year." "Head after head and never heads enough / For those that bade them fall": heads fall to voices, magically. A child's toy, a windmill, replaces the guillotine exercised by the terrorists:

> They found their joy,
> They made it proudly, eager as a child
> (If light desires of innocent little ones

May with such heinous appetites be compared),
Pleased in some open field to exercise
A toy that mimics with revolving wings
The motion of a wind-mill; though the air
Do of itself blow fresh, and makes the vanes
Spin in his eyesight, *that* contents him not,
But with the plaything at arm's length, he sets
His front against the blast, and runs amain,
That it may whirl the faster.
(*Prelude*, X, ll. 363–73)

In his account of this passage, Ronald Paulson speaks of "the monstrous child playing with a guillotine."[28] Dissolving what is perhaps Wordsworth's most perfect epic simile, Paulson preserves a dangerously reckless child, but translates the toy into its tenor. There are two problems with this procedure. The first is logical: a child playing with a guillotine cannot run, and the point of Wordsworth's image disappears. In the heedless celerity and determination of the Terror, the mechanism's speed is created by resistance. The terrorists were like children, dissatisfied with the slow workings of nature. The second problem is more instructive: Paulson makes the image grotesque, a grinning deformity out of Goya. Seeing the image through the Terror, Paulson overlays it with a scum of horror, whereas Wordsworth asks us to see the Terror through the image. Wordsworth refuses to allow the Terror to dominate his sense of the Revolution, and he refuses to dismiss his earlier hopes as foolish naiveté. Paulson's translation of Wordsworth's image reflects our inability to do anything else.

Among the most fruitful and familiar of the guillotine's domestications is her feminization. Like her elder sister, the gallows, the guillotine also bore the nickname "la veuve" (the widow) as long as she was in use, and she was always female: Louisette, La Petite Louison, La Guillotine. Although a French *machine* [f.] will conventionally take grammatically feminine gender, English writers, lacking grammatical gender, still insist on feminization. Lemuel Hopkins in 1796 called his American democratic dirge "The Guillotina," carrying the femininity into English as far as he could. Thomas Carlyle sputtered at the impropriety of naming a beheading machine "la guillotine" as if it were M. Guillotin's daughter.[29] He could have spared his outrage: his fellow Scots had anticipated the French with their own beheading machine, called "the Maiden." John Wilson

Croker thought strange a sobriquet that now seems inevitable. The last aristocrat to die by the Maiden, the Earl of Argyle in 1685, declared "as he pressed his lips on the block, that it was the sweetest maiden he had ever kissed."[30] Whether Guillotine or Louisette, the new machine always took a female name from a male progenitor, and through the mid-nineteenth century, *guillotine* was usually capitalized. Since the male progenitors were not anxious so to bestow their names, Arasse calls the guillotine a "fille naturel" (natural daughter) whom no father wished to acknowledge.[31]

Behind "la veuve," who has consummated her affair, and "the Maiden," who sheds her first blood, is the guillotine as a gaping, single-toothed vagina dentata. The man who flirts with her attempts to retain his dominance, asserted as sexual. The elegant innuendo or crude joke insists on amorous foreplay before the opportunity for play is foreclosed. (Desire for domination and insistence on self-assertion underlie both of Danton's famed last remarks: "You will not be able to prevent our heads from kissing in the basket"; "Show my head to the people, it will be worthwhile." By contrast, famous guillotined women assimilate themselves to higher powers: Mme. Roland to liberty, the Carmelite nuns to God.)

On the scaffold, decapitation is real, "gallantry" a fantasy. Coping with the threat to the head, decapitation anxiety restructures the encounter as sexual, displacing anxiety from the primary narcissism of the head to the secondary narcissism of the genitals. "Castration anxiety" turns on its head. Instead of fantasying decapitation to mask a threat to the genitals, the man facing decapitation asserts his manhood as sexual, obtruding his secure possession of genitalia to mask the threat to his head. The machine that would be feared and fled, were that choice available, is dominated by being wooed. Feminized, death may be mastered like other women. Cooing to a mistress is, under such circumstances, more comforting than crying out for mama.

While other capital implements have been feminized and thence slipped into a dynamic of sexual interaction, only the guillotine has been so explicitly eroticized. The *tricoteuses* knitting around the guillotine domesticated it: they turned the scaffold into the family hearth. Those women who wore guillotine earrings or guillotine hair ornaments eroticized the guillotine by associating it with female sexual display. But if the guillotine could be used by women as an erotic adjunct, it was also turned against them.

Fig. 3.3. Isaac Cruikshank, Republican Belle. (Bibliothèque nationale de France, Paris)

Just as the guillotine replaced the carnival of the people's violence with the immobile, institutional violence of established authority, so its representations acted to repress disorderly feminine sexuality. Cruikshank's hideous Republican belle with her guillotine earrings is familiar (fig. 3.3), as are his counter-revolutionary Mariannes, drunken, blowsy "furies of hell."[32] But other explicit eroticizations of the guillotine remind us that in the family drama taking place on the scaffold, the authority masked by feminization and dominated by eroticization is in fact both dominant and masculine. Although grammatically feminine, "guillotine," more obviously male-derived than "Louisette," cannot be confused with any real female. The surname evokes the male as a Christian name cannot and carries a reminder of male authority. It is not mother up there, going chop, chop, chop, but father. It is the state.

In a few explicit eroticizations of the guillotine, a sensuous female body, such as Dickens's Mme. Defarge, replaces the guillotine.[33] More usually, the guillotine is linked with a sexually inviting female body. Such depictions emphasize the parallels between female anatomy and guillotine geometry and set up a tense oscillation between desire and destruction. Sex and violence, both repressed, both tempting, occupy a single space and offer a gendered choice—castration or decapitation? If the desiring male reaches for the body, he chooses his own castration. More wisely, he chooses decapitation for the desirable female whose body is obtruded. His threatened castration becomes her decapitation, if he is to save himself.

One of the few images of this kind to emerge in the revolutionary period assaults Marie Antoinette (fig. 3.4). The queen stands high bosomed and seductive, her right hand turned invitingly on her hip, her fingers making a crude gesture. Below her is a guillotine acting as cinch or stomacher for a very explicit piece of female anatomy, breasts, hole, pot. The image is in the tradition of obscene depictions of the queen, and its caption, "Ah! ça ira" ("how it will go," the refrain of the revolutionary song and dance, the Carmagnole), rejoices at the prospect of the fate the image proposes for her. The upside-down inscription demands that the handler-possessor of the print turn it head down. Doing so reveals what lies under the queen's skirts, in a receptive posture. The breasts offer themselves as buttocks in an invitation to sodomy, mounted by the basket-turned-Phrygian cap. With the hole above, the guillotine blade covers the hole below. No hostility is directed toward the machine. Instead, the skeletal guillotine, providing the frame and supports of the pictured flesh, shows the

Fig. 3.4. Ah! Ça Ira. (Bibliothèque nationale de France, Paris)

queen what she must come to. The grinning skull beneath the proud, painted face of living beauty: this is a modern version of that favorite Jacobean image. Although the explicit subject is an eroticized guillotine, the effect is to de-eroticize the woman and to replace eros with thanatos.

A hundred years later, Adolphe Leon Willette made a parallel drawing that reflects the intervention of the Terror between the image of Marie Antoinette and his own time (fig. 3.5). On a scaffold, by night, a lamp above her inscribed "93," a strong, Phrygian-capped, entirely naked and entirely beautiful young woman leans against the guillotine, one arm akimbo, one supporting her head, with her legs arrogantly and tauntingly apart, one foot propped up. She reclines against the board to which victims are strapped, her head haloed by the guillotine's neck-hole, and she represents, shockingly, the Revolution as a young and experienced whore. On the bottom step, the artist writes his name, inscribes himself. (Reproduction obscures a certain wistful delicacy, an innocence, evident in the original.) The considerable tension of the drawing is relaxed by the caption below the image, for the caption explains what part or aspect of the Revolution is embodied by this dangerously ambivalent body. In the inscription, the woman speaks, "I am holy Democracy. I await my lovers." Although the politics of the images of 1793 and 1887 are antithetical, the images share an essential impulse: *épater les bourgeois* and upend the slut. The bourgeois obliged: when the drawing became the cover of *Le Courrier Français*, the edition was confiscated by the police.[34]

Willette repoliticizes an image of Baudelaire. Among the *Fleurs du mal*, Jeanne, the mistress-whore, is likened to the guillotine, as voracious, insatiable, and vampiric as the equally undiscriminating engine of the Terror:

> Tu mettrais l'univers entier dans ta ruelle,
> Femme impure! L'ennui rend ton âme cruelle.
> Pour exercer tes dents à ce jeu singulier,
> Il te faut chaque jour un coeur au râtelier. . . .
> Machine aveugle et sourde, en cruautés féconde!
> Salutaire instrument, buveur du sang du monde,
> Comment n'as-tu pas honte et comment n'as tu pas
> Devant tous les miroirs vu pâlir tes appas?
> (*Les Fleurs du mal*, 1861, xxv)

> [You would take the whole universe into your alleyway,

Fig. 3.5. Adolphe Leon Willette. I Am Saint Democracy, I Await
My Lovers, 1887. (Bibliothèque nationale de France, Paris)

Unclean woman! Boredom gives you a cruel soul.
To keep your teeth practiced at this singular game,
You need a heart to scrape every day. . . .
Blind and deaf machine, fecund in cruelties!
Healthful instrument, drinker of the world's blood,

How can you be so shameless and how can you not
See your looks fade before the mirrors?]

Turning the blood drinker into his mistress, Baudelaire substitutes woman for the guillotine and the Terrorists as drinkers of blood, a common image after Thermidor. In anti-Terror prints, when Robespierre was not manipulating a guillotine, he was squeezing hearts into a cup brimming with blood. Joseph Le Bon, standing between two guillotines, filled two chalices with blood and drank them off in *Les Formes Acerbes*. Jeanne's body, a blind and deaf machine, drinker of the world's blood, consumes the poet, a more fortunate Chénier.

Juxtaposing eros and thanatos, Baudelaire and Willette seem to refuse to subordinate eros. The female instrument flaunts her machinery, a devouring sexuality, threatening masculine self-control and manhood. Sufficient to destroy, she needs no *bourreau*. Yet both Baudelaire and Willette, restoring masculine authority, dismantle their machines. As blood drains from a severed head, so Baudelaire's "machine" grows pale in another of the *Fleurs du mal*.

In "Une Martyre: Dessin d'un maître inconnu," the poet explores the bedchamber of a woman decapitated by her lover. There the pale, bloodless head rests on a dressing table, before the mirror. The consummation at which Baudelaire hints in "Tu mettrais" and saves for another poem, Willette achieves by passing from the image to the tension-dissolving inscription. Impudence invites her lovers to her bed, the guillotine; and the inscription invites the reader, teased by the naked body, to make this her last bed. The wise reader, presumably male, will strap her down and put her to a final rest, before those legs, like Madame Defarge's, can carry out their purpose. "Strangle her, else she sure will strangle thee," as Una said to the Redcross Knight. If "Holy Democracy" has her way, her lovers will find not pleasure but death. Whether the whore or her lovers pass under the blade, the guillotine is the instrument that halts the copulatory activity of disorderly sexuality, with a different spasm and an ejaculation of another color.

Images of the Revolution as a young and beautiful whore do not appear during the revolutionary period itself. Marianne was virtuous, and counter-revolutionary imagery did not risk obscene or attractive representations of her. When Marianne appears as a whore in counter-revolutionary engravings, she is old, deformed, and drunken: no sober man would buy. During the revolutionary period, the shocking function of the eroticization of the guillotine seems to have been filled by the beatification of the guillotine.

At first the beatification of the guillotine seems just a bad joke of the de-christianizers at the expense of the traditional hierarchies of church and state. It was that and more. In the new religion of the Republic, the guillotine became La Sainte Guillotine to be decked in blue velvet and roses for Robespierre's Festival of the Supreme Being. In the older and simultaneous iconography, blue is the color of the virgin, the rose one of her many emblems. La Sainte Guillotine had ambitions of rising; she was also called "our holy mother."[35] J. B. Amar of the Committee of General Security confused her sex and called for the "red mass." With the guillotine replacing the Mother of God, icons overturned and broken, the altar was not left empty. Protecting the Revolution from aristocrats and bandits, the guillotine was as apt an intercessor as Mary, who protects mankind from gods above and devils below. If the guillotine herself made one uneasy, putting her in the pantheon placated and neutralized her. Safely elevated, she could be appeased by continual sacrifice and ritual attendance. While she shocked and horrified the counter-revolutionary enemy, the good revolutionary sat safe in her shade.

The Terrorist revolutionary followed Burke's counsel. He (and she) adopted the guillotine "into the bosom of our family affections; keeping inseparable, and cherishing with the warmth of all their combined and mutually reflected charities, our state, our hearths, our sepulchres, and our altars."[36] Nor did their posterity fail to look back to their ancestors. Under the Directory, Parisian workers praised Robespierre's time, when the blood always flowed and the people never lacked bread. In March 1848, at Paris, *La Guillotine, par un vieux Jacobin* appeared for a single issue. The guillotine replaced the pike as the people's emblem during the Terror. Having done so, the guillotine in counter-revolutionary imagery came to resemble the pike.

The anti-Terrorist guillotine grew enormously in size. It began to move, and it loomed farther and farther above the heads of the crowd. The relative size of the guillotine and the *bourreau* indexes the politics of a print. As the guillotine grows and the *bourreau* shrinks, rhetorical declamation replaces historicity. When the declamation is more obvious, as in Joseph LeBon's drinking blood amid corpses in *Les Formes Acerbes,* the guillotine does not need to be enlarged. It remains, however, above him. If once Catholic revolutionaries beatified their little "Sainte Guillotine," Protestant counter-revolutionaries deified it. Revolutionaries, they

Fig. 3.6. Isaac Cruikshank, Republican Beau. (Bibliothèque nationale de France, Paris)

alleged, had replaced the altar with the scaffold. Cruikshank's Republican Belle with guillotine earrings has a mate, the Republican Beau. Behind him stands a guillotine with the motto: "This is our God" (fig. 3.6). God is more powerful than our holy mother, less mediatory than the red mass, and male.

Those aspects of the guillotine that had once seemed most positive, its rationality and its mechanical self-sufficiency, became in themselves sources of revulsion. Mme. de Staël turned the guillotine into a metaphor of the revolutionary government of the Committee of Public Safety. Arguing that events were out of anyone's control, she shows law replaced by a naked blade. The impersonal efficiency of the machine so praised by the *Moniteur* in 1789 was now turned against the machine: "La machine de terreur, dont les ressorts avoient été montés par les événemens, exerçoit seule la toute-puissance. Le gouvernement ressembloit à l'affreux instrument qui donnoit la mort: on y voyoit la hache plutôt que la main qui la faisoit mouvoir" (The machine of terror, the springs of which had been prepared for action by events, exercised alone unbounded power. The government resembled the hideous instrument employed on the scaffold; the axe was seen rather than the hand that put it in motion).[37] The triumph of impersonality, a mark of technical perfection, is also deeply threatening. The independence of the machine suggests, in Paulson's memorable image, "that the machine would continue to cut off heads, as a pinmaker continues to make pins, as long as it is supplied with bodies."[38] In their first tentative steps, the liberating procedures of industrial capitalism joined in the dance of death.

Thomas Carlyle made metaphor soup of organic death and inorganic industrial processes. Mingling images organic and inorganic, mechanical, industrial, classical, and natural, he fantasied a power that requires no human operator: a realized idea of oak and iron, a cyclops ramming in grooves, the pumping heart of the circulatory system of sansculottism. The guillotine has no maker, and no one controls it: "The Guillotine, we find, gets always a quicker motion as other things are quickening. The Guillotine, by its speed of going, will give index to the general velocity of the Republic."[39] No longer the immobile representative of the people's justice, the guillotine now moves of itself. No longer an invention controlling the people's violence, the guillotine has escaped control. No longer individuating victims and dignifying the deaths of common men, the guillotine levels. It does not discriminate high, low, rich, poor, old, young, male or female. It does not respect persons. The faceless, irresponsible, shameless mob has become a faceless, irresponsible, shameless machine.

For radicals of a certain stripe, of both the left and the right, there is nothing paradoxical about the guillotine. The scientific implement of the people's power, the guillotine illustrates what must happen when the people overturn the established order. "You can't make an omelette without breaking eggs." The radical left embraces the necessity that the radical right waves as a warning. For those who regard history itself as a movement of inexorable forces, sweeping mere human actors along, the guillotine is also an apt emblem. Impersonal, indifferent, and inevitable, history is a blade that cuts whatever interposes. Nor are its cuts to be questioned. They are only to be rationalized and understood: "When *we* are lashed, *they* kiss the rod, / Resigning to the will of God."[40] For those who regard history as the continuing evidence of unintended outcomes, the guillotine is equally apt: an instrument of progress that produced great horrors, an embodiment of failed hopes and frustrated good intentions. For skeptics dismayed but not surprised by the failure of utopian projects, it defines the progress of civilization. A humanitarian, egalitarian mechanism minimizes pain, obscures death agonies, and enables enhanced, ideologically justified lethality. As a paradox of the Revolution, the guillotine is a fit figure for the paradox of revolution.

Yet the guillotine is more than a figure. In its origins and its actions, the guillotine shaped the views of history that turn to it as emblem. Its technological and mechanical efficiency provided more than a metaphor; it supplied a conception. Without the guillotine, Carlyle's Terror could never have been so implacable or so remorseless. As texts so commonly do, the guillotine redefined the historical space it entered.

The guillotine continues to mirror our revolutions. In France, the revolution remains domesticated and integrated with commerce. *Le Figaro* stretches, between a pair of domestic guillotines, a clothesline holding sansculottes T-shirts emblazoned *1789 1989* (23 mars 1989, 2). Continuing eighteenth-century practices of commemorative commerce, a mustard company made mustard pot-coffee cups with famous scenes of the Revolution. Two cups featured decapitations: the king's head held up at the guillotine, and sansculottes with a head on a pike. On the cup with the guillotine, opposite the guillotine, under the date 1789/1989, was a cannon. Opposite the pike was the Gallic cock: potent emblems of order and carnival (figs. 3.7, 3.8).

Fig. 3.7. Bornier mustard cups, cannon and pike, 1789–1989. (Photo Credit: Skidmore College Media Services)

Elsewhere, the guillotine gestures toward revolutions in progress. In Andrzej Wajda's *Danton* (1981), the guillotine glints in the dawn, dark, bright, and cold. Driven through an empty square, Danton's coach circles the scaffold as Danton himself peers up, up, up at the blade. That looming augury, the implied gigantism of the machine, has a precise political meaning as Danton and Robespierre dance through the period of pro-Soviet repression in Poland.

More suggestive is the astonishing image that opens the Cuban Alejo Carpentier's *El siglo de las luces* (1962, "Century of Lights," the usual Spanish term for the enlightenment, translated as *Explosion in a Cathedral*). In the early years of the Cuban revolution (1959), Carpentier summons the guillotine as phantom guide and warning to spectators caught in a moment of suspended animation. On a ship embarking for the new world from revolutionary France, stands in the bow an uncovered guillotine:

I saw them erect the guillotine again to-night. . . . Its naked, solitary skeleton had been newly raised above the sleeping crew, like a presence, a warning, which concerned us all equally. We had left it far astern in the

Fig. 3.8. Bornier mustard cups, cock and guillotine, 1789–1989. (Photo Credit: Skidmore College Media Services)

cold winds of April, and now it had reappeared over our very bows, going ahead of us like a guide, resembling, in the necessary precision of its parallel lines, its implacable geometry, some gigantic instrument of navigation. . . . Here the Door stood alone, facing into the night above the tutelary figurehead, its diagonal blade gleaming, its wooden uprights framing a whole panorama of stars.[41]

Carpentier's guillotine leads both to the new world and the other world. Raised by men, it dwarfs them. Through that shape in tension we glimpse the infinite while the frame marks our limits and reminds us of our finitude. As an impersonal, man-made instrument of death, the guillotine collaborates with the oblivious infinite, whose indifferent, unconscious, annihilating action the blade mimics. With its peculiar fusion of function, form, and history, the guillotine also recurs, as Carpentier's geometry suggests, because it possesses certain formal properties.

Of capital instruments in repose, only the guillotine so thoroughly reveals its threat while refraining from the actual display of violence. A gas chamber is only a room with ducts; an electric chair is only a chair with wires. The gallows' noose is flaccid, like the Phrygian cap. To produce its full effect, it must bear the burden of a body, hanging limp, doubling flaccidity. To have any effect at all, the pike must sport a head. But the geometry of the guillotine is energetic.

Between the uprights slants the blade, the sharp edge of the knife, straining to fall, promising a swift, sharp descent. In repose the guillotine is discreet. It evokes violence, but shows it only as a potential that may be actualized in an instant. The blade is always there, potentially active, and the blade requires only release from tension to execute its fell purpose. It waits ready, when needed. It makes this point by itself, without any need for human actors to intervene or even to appear. The machine thus politely, if misleadingly, erases the humanity of violence. Yet it simultaneously thrusts violence forward in the always visible edge of the knife, looking back at the head looking at it

The guillotine's persistence derives from the same source as its existence, the "improvement of manners" on which the eighteenth century so prided itself. The ancient pleasures of violence recede from view as the machine erases the human hand. The carnival of the pikes falls to the order of the machine that controls and subordinates the vehemence of popular violence. The bloodless stillness of a waiting guillotine invites rhetoric, passionate, ironic, or frenzied, to twine around it or to break against it. Inhumanly passive, the machine challenges language, and language will always rise to the occasion. For the dainty who would never make their hands wet or sticky by impaling a head on a pike, the guillotine provides a *frisson* that holds blood in reserve, mediating an ancient promise of violence and power, striking at the head.

4

At the Sign of the Baptist's Head

For Eliza Callard

These days of disinheritance, we feast
On human heads. . . .
We feast on human heads, brought in on leaves,
Crowned with the first, cold buds. On these we live,
No longer on the ancient cake of seed,
The almond and deep fruit. This bitter meat
Sustains us . . . Who, then, are they, seated here?
Is the table a mirror in which they sit and look?
Are they men eating reflections of themselves?
                    —Wallace Stevens, "Cuisine Bourgeoise"

From 1860 to 1910, there flourished in England, France, and Germany a vogue for representing decapitating ladies, focused particularly on Herodias and her daughter. No guillotines need apply; the sword had revived for a hands-on struggle over gender roles. Suddenly, every author, painter, or composer whose name one knew was producing a work on the theme of Herodias or Salome and the decollation of St. John the Baptist. Stéphane Mallarmé began his "Hérodiade" in 1864, inaugurating the deluge and leaving the poem unfinished, still open on his worktable at his death in 1898.[1] In prose there followed Gustave Flaubert (1877), Joris-Karl Huysmans (1884), Jules Laforgue (1886), and Oscar Wilde (1891, published 1893).[2] Jules Massenet (1881) and Richard Strauss (1905) wrote operas (and Strauss cut off another composer's attempt to use Wilde as libretto). Aubrey Beardsley sketched (1893, 1894), Odilon Redon charcoaled (1869/1885), and when was Gustave Moreau (1872–1885/90) ever going to paint or draw anything else?[3] This list, confined to names still well known, seems impressive but represents only the smallest fraction of works generated by the theme.[4] Between 1840 and 1920, diligence has counted 2,789 separate items.[5]

Such proliferation is a little strange. If images of dancing girls seem desirable enough, and common, to boot, why should a male painter or artist (and they were almost all male)[6] want to garnish a lovely lady with an image of his, or his brother's, severed head? Why revive a medieval and Renaissance topos with such passion in a more secular age? Where there is a head, there is a crisis. Around the figure of the dancing girl and her mother whirl explorations of gender, without interruption.[7] The Baptist's head looks elsewhere.

The nineteenth-century proliferation of Salomes coincides with unprecedented upheavals in the gender order. "The angel in the house" seemed to be taking to the streets, securing new laws relative to divorce and women's property, agitating for the franchise and birth control.[8] In France, *féminisme,* as a position favorable to women's interests and rights, appears in 1837, a *féministe* as a partisan of women's rights in 1872 (Hachette, *Dictionnaire Encyclopédique*). In England, between 1850 and 1890, "feminism" ceases to be a rare word meaning "the qualities of females" (OED, 1851) and becomes a common word referring to "advocacy of women's rights" following a French model (OED, 1895, "after *féminisme*").

Salome dancing asserts female sexuality, confines female power to the seductions of the daughter, disempowering the mother, and privileges the invisible masculine gaze that watches the dance and for whom the dance is performed. Orientalized and historicized, she figures the colonized east and the past surpassed. As Renaissance misogyny is retailored as evolutionary theory, the old "sacks of sin" become woman as biologically determined, "less evolved," trapped in natural processes.[9] As compensation, moving beyond Enlightenment's sentimental idealizations of womanhood and nineteenth-century women's activism, the topos also makes its heroine definitive of modernity, the perverse desiring body. There is, however, more to the story of Salome and the Baptist than Salome. There is the Baptist's head.

No head has undergone more vicissitudes than St. John's, from object of mystical veneration in the Middle Ages to an inn sign advertising "Good Eating" in Hogarth's *Four Times of the Day: Noon* (1737–38). As Salome and her mother have been vehicles for sexuality, so John's head traces the trajectory of transcendence, a signifier gliding across shifting signifieds. His head always differs: never valued in itself, it always points to another, greater thing. Yet, from its inception in the Gospel of Mark, on it depends the identity of the greater thing.

In the gospels, Jesus needs John in order to be (identified as) the messiah, living or dead. Throughout the Middle Ages and Renaissance, John's head indicates Christ's sacrifice, until, as Helen Zagona showed, the symbolist movement wrested St. John's head from religion to the religion of art. In the post-Freudian collapse of creative interest in the head, the transcendental signifier becomes the phallus. The head that promised liberation from the body becomes only another part of the body that, Lacan insists, is not a body part at all. Marking St. John's mutations recovers some heads we may learn once again to look at.

The topos of Salome and St. John's head originates in Mark, the earliest Christian gospel (post–70 C.E.) and source of the narrative of Jesus' life adopted by Matthew and Luke (ca. 80–90 C.E.). Matthew edits and shortens the tale; Luke omits it, probably as misogynist. From a different tradition, the gospel of John (ca. 90 C.E.) mentions the Baptist's imprisonment but omits his death, as antithetical to John's theology of eternal life. The Roman Jewish historian Flavius Josephus (37–ca. 100 C.E.) supplies the name "Salome" and confirms John's execution by Herod, but not the gospel's story.

Josephus links neither Herodias to the death of the Baptist nor the Baptist to the crucified Jesus. "Salome," a common Herodian name, appears in a genealogical account as the name of Herodias's daughter who married her uncle Philip.[10] In Mark, a "Salome" is among the women witnessing Jesus' empty tomb at the resurrection (Mk. 16:1), a coincidence exploited by some well-read nineteenth-century authors.[11] Some Greek manuscripts name the daughter "Herodias," like her mother; most call her "daughter of Herodias."

Mark's story begins when Herod, hearing of Jesus' wonder-working, exclaims (twice), "It is John, whom I beheaded: he is risen from the dead" (Mk. 6:14, 16). In the gospel's only flashback, the Baptist is imprisoned at the instigation of Herod's wife, Herodias, whose marriage to Herod, after divorcing his half-brother Philip, the Baptist had attacked as adulterous.[12] Celebrating Herod's birthday, the daughter of Herodias dances for her [step]-father and, at her mother's instigation, requests as a reward the head of the Baptist on a charger. Reluctantly the king orders the execution in the prison, and the head is brought to the girl, who delivers it to her mother. John's disciples bury his body. They "took up his corpse and laid it in a tomb," from which it does not rise (Mk. 6:29). The head is last seen scripturally in Herodias's unfriendly hands.

Mark does not invent John's execution by Herod, but he does invent Herod's answer to the gospel's great question (Who is Jesus?), as well as the dancing daughter, the malevolent Herodias and sympathetic Herod, the head delivered on a platter at a feast. These details might be regarded as (otherwise unattested) historical fact if they did not so clearly advance Mark's evangelical and theological purpose: to identify Jesus as the dying, risen lord who raises believers from the dead, preceded by a dying Elijah, who comes before and announces him. Herod's phrase "he is risen from the dead" is precisely the phrase the angel will use to announce Jesus' resurrection to frightened women at an empty tomb (Mk. 6:16, Mk. 16:6). John dies in this narrative so that Herod can declare him Jesus risen from the dead and the wiser reader smile, knowing that it is not John who has risen, but Jesus who will rise. As John serves to identify Jesus, so without John, Jesus cannot be identified.

The opening of the gospel affirms the inextricability of John's identity as prophet and Jesus' as prophesied Lord: "As it is written in the prophets, Behold, I send my messenger before thy face, which shall prepare thy way before thee" (Mk. 1:2). John appears in the narrative before Jesus does (Mk. 1:4, 1:9), and thanks to Herodias and her daughter, he also departs the narrative first. Anticipating Herod's belief that the dead rise, Jesus raises Jairus's twelve-year-old daughter (a young girl, *korasion*) from the dead, tells those who watch to "be not afraid, only believe" (Mk. 5:36), and cures a woman with a bloody issue that has lasted twelve years. The strangely specific "twelve years" links Jairus's daughter and the woman with a bloody issue as if they were mother and daughter, like the korasion and her mother Herodias in the next episode, where the mother's desires have a very bloody issue.

Herod and Herodias's hostility to John's attacks on their marriage is plausible, but to contrast resurrection and death, Mark cannot do without a dancing daughter. The girl who dances is a korasion like Jairus's twelve-year-old daughter, and her movements parallel the other korasion whom Jesus raises from the dead: the daughter came in and danced, Jairus's daughter rose and walked. The daughter danced at a feast, Jairus's daughter is fed when she rises, and Jesus feeds five thousand when the apostles return. So the platter Salome asks for is indispensable: it turns the Baptist's severed head into food on a plate, like the body and blood Jesus shares at the Last Supper (Mk. 14:22–24). In the narrative, the head of the Baptist disappears, like the body of Christ, last seen among (evil) women (Mk. 15:47).

In this account Salome once again upstages Herodias, but Herodias too has her uses. Her malevolence and her husband's interest in John (unique to Mark) parallel the Old Testament's Jezebel, who sought Elijah's death, and Ahab, who recognized and respected the Lord's prophet. Opening his gospel with the prophets and John, Mark singles out Elijah from the prophets. John wears camel's hair and "the girdle of a skin about his loins" (Mk. 1:6) that belonged to Elijah the Tishbite, a hairy man, and enabled others to identify him in his absence (2 Kings 1:7–8). In Kings, Ahab and Elijah meet with hostility, but respect; Ahab recognizes the prophet of the god of Israel. When Elijah demands the assembling of the prophets of Baal, Ahab calls them together (1 Kings 18:17–20). When Elijah predicts rain after drought, he runs before Ahab's chariot to Jezreel (1 Kings 18:46). When Elijah predicts that dogs shall eat Jezebel and the offspring of Ahab, Ahab repents, and Elijah turns the curse from him in his lifetime (I Kings 21:21–29). When Ahab tells his wife Jezebel what Elijah has done, then, and then only, is the prophet's life endangered (I Kings 19:1–3). What is narrative action in Kings the narrator asserts in Mark, insisting on a sympathetic Herod whom no one could possibly perceive in Herod's actions relative to John: arrest and beheading. Without this parallel, the only "scriptural evidence" identifying John as Elijah is the leather girdle.

Mark demonstrates he wants scriptural evidence when he invents it. Asked about Elijah's coming first, as the scribes say, Jesus replies, "Elias is indeed come, and they have done unto him whatsoever they listed, as it is written of him" (Mk. 9:13). By identifying John with Elijah, Mark has invented a dying Elijah to accompany the dying Messiah. Until Mark, it is nowhere "written of him" that Elijah, carried away in a whirlwind, should die. After Mark, it is gospel truth.

When Matthew and Luke rewrite Mark, Matthew asserts explicitly that John is Elijah and retains the story, but changes its placement. The Old Testament parallel is preserved—Matthew always insists on scriptural parallels—but Mark's argument about resurrection and fear disappears. Dropping banquet and dance, Luke, mindful of women, makes John's execution entirely Herod's fault, exonerating not only Herodias herself, but even her admittedly irregular marriage (Lk. 3:19–20). Luke identifies John as Elijah and Jesus as Messiah in the birth stories (Lk.

1:17, 32–33, 35), retaining one of Mark's purposes through the cousins Elizabeth and Mary, another pair of female relatives, one older and one virginal.

When Mark handed John's head off to Herodias and put his body in a tomb, where it remained, he appropriated for Christianity a prominent preacher whose historical relationship to Jesus remains a subject of considerable debate.[13] Subordinated within the Christian tradition, embedded in a structural antithesis with women and death, John's head embarked on an extraordinary career.

No head better illustrates plasticity of signification than his. Like Celtic severed heads, John's has been a fertility symbol and solar disk, his feast day celebrated at midsummer, June 24.[14] Like the relics of other decapitated saints, his head has cured headaches, fevers, and epilepsy, known as "St. John's evil."[15] It has served as moral warning (dancing's victim), emblem of the host (offered like Christ's body at a table), patron of condemned criminals (the San Giovanni Decollato, St. Jean Decollé, and San Juan Degollado brotherhoods), and the occasion for American Masons' annual orations and odes.[16] John's disappearing head makes the solar year prove the gospel's truth. "He must increase, but I must decrease," the Baptist announces in the Gospel of John (3:30). After John's feast day, 24 June, the days grow shorter, visibly so after 29 August, the feast of the decollation or harvested head. Born in December, Jesus makes the days grow longer—cosmic evidence, textually predetermined by Luke, that the gospels speak true.[17]

Salome first danced in a manuscript from ninth-century Chartres, her whole body moving in mosaics in twelfth-century Venice, stone in Toulouse and stained glass in Lyon.[18] From the Middle Ages through the early Renaissance, "dragged by dances to martyrdom" ("e che per salti fu tratto al martiro," Dante, *Paradiso*, 18:135), St. John's head warned against courts, dancing, seduction, feasting, and pleasure. Representations often reverse the gospel narrative, placing the execution in the foreground, like the crucifixion, as revelers prance in the background. The luxurious, corrupt courts are contemporary; neither orientalism nor historicism obscures the moral. Presented at a rich table, the head parodies demoniacally the Last Supper. In countless Feasts of Herod, the world (the courtly table), the flesh (the woman), and the devil (the executioner) unite against the saint.

In the fourteenth century, the identity between the Baptist's head, offered at a luxurious table, and the eucharistic wafer of the body of Christ, offered at a simple table and in the mass, entered theological discussions. Bread or a fish on Herod's table, as in a tenth or eleventh-century evangelary from Bamberg,[19] juxtaposes with the Baptist's head signs of the body, miracles, and acronym of Christ (Jesus Christ the Lord/*ichth*). Christ on the table of the unwitting Herod develops ironies present in the gospel: throughout, Herod speaks more truth than he understands. These parallels become more abstract and more explicit. "As the head of John was offered on a platter, so Christ is offered daily in the Mass on the paten."[20] The round head on the charger reproduces the round wafer of the host above the chalice in the mass: "*Caput Iohannis in disco: signat Corpus Christi: quo pascimur in sancto altari*" (the head of John on the dish signifies the body of Christ by which we are fed at the holy altar).[21]

Since the fourth century, the sculptural *Johannisschüssel* or St. John's head has been a reliquary representing a head and holding a fragment of the saint. From at least the twelfth century, the head becomes an independent graven, sculpted, or beaten devotional image.[22] Interest in the Baptist's head parallels devotional images of the face of Christ as *vera icon* (Veronica) or "Man of Sorrows," appearing in the thirteenth century and with renewed popularity in the fifteenth.[23] Allegorizing the round head on a round platter, the theological development stimulated interest in the head as object of devotion. As the theological symbolism of the head developed, so did the cult of the head. At Nottingham, ceramic heads were manufactured for export to central France.[24] Alabaster and marble heads on platters invited prayer in country parishes, and painters portrayed their patrons kneeling before such sculpted images. About 1450 in the Netherlands, the devotional platters became paintings.[25] Painted on round canvases replacing the charger or miraculously poised, as if they remained sculptural objects, these heads often lack any visible means of support. Marco Zoppo (or Giovanni Bellini),[26] Aelbert Bouts, Andrea Solario, Gianfrancesco Maineri, and Marco Palmezzano painted heads of the Baptist, alone, without executioner, without the Feast of Herod, without Salome.

Salome never stops dancing, then or now: recent turns include Tom Robbins's *Skinny Legs and All* (1990), Robert Altman's *Cookie's Fortune* (1999), Binnie Kirshenbaum's *Pure Poetry* (2000), and Al Pacino and Oscar Wilde's *Salome on Broadway* (2003). At the turn of the sixteenth century, however, two variations abruptly appear in the work of Andrea Solario: the painted head of St. John, serenely idealized, and the so-called "portrait of Salome."[27] Antithetical to Solario's idealization are contemporaneous, agonized St. John's heads by Zoppo and Maineri. In the second variation, Salome trades her legs for a face and head. An abbreviated narrative, in the "portrait of Salome," a half-length or bust of Salome abuts the severed head of St. John either on the platter or presented by the executioner. The modern designation "portrait of Salome," erasing the saint's head, has Renaissance precedent: catalogues listed such images as "Herodiades." In a new, empathic dialectic active in both types of image, Solario situates the viewer's self-consciousness within the image.

In Sixten Ringbom's terms, the head of St. John, alone, is an icon, constituting a cult object of worship or devotion; the portrait of Salome is a truncated narrative. On the head of St. John, one meditates, moving from the corporeal vision of the eye to spiritual and intellectual apprehension of the meanings of the physical image. To meditate is to move beyond the eye to the mind, to honor the figure represented, and to adore.[28] From the second, narrative image, one takes a moral lesson for edification's sake. Theology justified narrative as didactic, the communication of moral lessons, and the feast of Herod brims with warnings. Both the isolated head and the head with Salome add to "adoration" and "edification," an approach Ringbom calls "empathic." The objective is intensity of feeling. Attention focuses "on an attitude in the beholder which consists neither of thirst for information and guidance by means of *historiae,* nor of the revering and adoration of *imagines,* but of a deep emotional experience."[29]

Before Solario, the circular canvas of Marco Zoppo displayed a face contorted with agony, eyes open, mouth gaping, hair in medusan tangles, strangely beautiful (fig. 4.1). Light catches the eye and ear; the curves of brow, beard, and hair play against each other. The eyes open on the viewer, challenging response, asking to be closed. After Solario, Maineri obtruded the wound in the neck of his helpless, open-eyed, gaping Baptist. Dark, hairy, horrible, eyes and mouths open in death, these heads force on the viewer the pain they represent. To meditate on these images, the viewer enters the physical spasm produced in the face, moving through horror to redemptive meaning, beyond the visible. Do these staring eyes see, or are they as blank as they seem? Instancing Esther Cohen's *philopassianism,* such images seek agony's vicarious experience, mediated through the eye, felt and desired by the body.[30]

Erasing pain, Solario's influential image insinuates a new form of self-consciousness, holding a mirror to the immersive identification of

Fig. 4.1. Marco Zoppo, Head of Saint John the Baptist. (Musei Civici di Pesaro. Reproduced by permission of Museum Services, Commune of Pesaro)

philopassianism. Inviting a paradoxical serenity, like many silver and alabaster heads, this idealized, Leonardesque, yet individuated head, David Brown observes, would seem to be sleeping were it not so pale (fig. 4.2). Painted in 1507 for Cardinal Georges d'Amboise at Gaillon near Rouen, recognizing his special devotion to the Baptist, Solario's image is framed with a theological inscription inspired by Luke that harmonizes the gospels: "alvo virginis latentem christum ex utero agnovi editum indicavi lavi et lotus futurae salutis angelus cruore fidei testimonium sanxi."[31] (Christ hidden in the belly of the virgin, I knew from the womb [Luke], brought forth I showed [him] [John], I washed [him] [Mark, Matthew]

Fig. 4.2. Andrea Solario (d. 1524), Head of Saint John the Baptist, 1507. (Photo Credit: Erich Lessing / Art Resource, NY. Louvre, Paris, inscription on frame not shown)

and was washed, angel of future deliverance, in blood, witness to holy faith.)

Paralleling, yet differentiating Christ and the Baptist, different words appear for belly/womb (*alvo/utero*) and for blood ([*sanguis*]/*cruor*). Active "showing" and "washing" turn passive, from water to blood, from baptism to decapitation. The text encloses the head, reassuring the viewer about the head's meanings, leaving no doubts, securing the promise of signification and the signification promised.

At the same time, Solario encloses the viewer within the image. Inside the inscription, below the head, an observer is mirrored, twice reflected in the chalice foot. Patron or artist sees himself within but apart from what he meditates upon. The viewer is simultaneously part of the image and alienated from it. As he meditates on the Baptist's head or text, his own reflected image fades before the Baptist as the Baptist's mere physicality fades before the greater, invisible Christ. The shadowy reflection in the chalice is less visible, less "real," than the painted head or the words that reveal the truth contradicted by appearances. Activating self-consciousness, disabling a stable interpretive position, the observer's presence sends the observer back to himself, to his own body, as the inscription sends him beyond the severed head for meaning. Marco Zoppo allows no alternative to the head itself.

Although the copyists, Brown observes, overlook the reflection, the design was widely imitated. The earliest dated copy is 1508, with some fifteen others scattered through France, England, and northern Italy.[32] Solario's meaning moderated pain.

At about the same period—the dates are in dispute—Solario's three "portraits of Salome" put the Baptist's head in a radically new context (figs. 4.3, 4.4).[33] Facing Salome's breasts, the Baptist's head parodies Christ with the nursing Madonna. Intimate didactic dramas, these truncated narratives draw the viewer in to punish him through the eye. Scurrying from desire to its consequences, the eye oscillates between eros and thanatos, between Salome's sweet visage and the severed head. To escape to meaning requires resting where one least wants to look—the severed head of the Baptist—and resisting what one most desires.

Meditative, solemn, angelic, inscrutable, the young woman's face resembles the Baptist's as the Feast of Herod shrinks to a non-scriptural "close-up," to apply Ringbom's term. As she looks at the Baptist, modeling what the viewer should do, the viewer's gaze shifts, darting from the man's head to the woman's breasts, the executioner's hand, the woman's face, as she prepares to receive for the first time the man's weight.

In Turin, a cameo hangs between Salome's inviting breasts. As the gaze plunges after the invitation, it encounters on the cameo Judith, waving a long, long sword that makes the gaze hesitate, draw back, startled. What is the sword of Judith doing on the breast of Salome? In the Old Testament apocrypha, the widow Judith saved her city Bethuliah and the Lord's people by cutting off the head of the besieging Assyrian general Holofernes. Judith destroyed no prophets. The female David, she is at

Fig. 4.3. Andrea Solario (d. 1524), Salome Receiving the Head of St. John the Baptist. Galleria Sabauda, Turin. (Photo Credit: Scala/Art Resource, NY)

home without head or knife in nineteenth-century American Episcopal altar painting, or with head and knife, by Donatello, in Florence's Piazza delle Signoria.

That other Jewish heroine, evoked, guards the portals of the breast and thrusts the viewer's gaze back to the Baptist's head. Judith's sword warns of desire's consequences for the guilty, as the Baptist's head shows the consequences to the innocent. As for the viewer, he finds his desires explicitly and unmistakably threatened at the verge of enjoyment, simultaneously seduced and cut off. Like his St. John's head, Solario's Salome reveals the position of a third party, the viewer himself, in motion.

Revisiting the theme (fig. 4.4), Solario removes the moral condemnation explicit in the figure of Judith and develops the secondary sexual characteristics of his three subjects: princess, Baptist, and executioner. Meditating impenetrably on the hairy head before her, the more heavily jeweled New York Salome has a less inviting but more pronounced décolletage. More compressed by her gown, her breasts swell above the line. The Baptist's hair has grown curlier, thicker, on both head and chin. He has more beard, as she has more breast. The executioner's forearm has gone naked. The arm emerges from softly folded white fabric that resembles bedding, quite unlike Turin's crisply slashed sleeve holding an almost beardless head. The executioner's garb identifies this Salome as the source

Fig. 4.4. Andrea Solario (d. 1524), Salome with the Head of St. John the Baptist. Oil on wood. 57.2 x 47 cm. (The Metropolitan Museum of Art, The Friedsam Collection, Bequest of Michael Friedsam, 1931 [32.100.81])

Fig. 4.5. Bernardino Luini (c. 1475–1532), Salome holding the Head of St. John the Baptist. Oil on canvas, 62.5 x 55 cm. Louvre, Paris. (Photo credit: Erich Lessing/Art Resource, NY)

for Bernardino Luini's copy, purchased for the Louvre by Louis XIV in 1671 (fig. 4.5).[34] Making a moral argument similar to the traditional Feast of Herod, such images bring the dilemma more intimately home to the viewer. It is impossible to be unaware of the temptation guarding the approaches to the Baptist's head, and difficult to be superior to it.

At the turn of the sixteenth century, Solario's images—*Johannisschüssel* and "portrait"—make self-consciousness visible as the painter situates within the frame a presence outside the frame. In the next decade, Titian introduces the self-portrait *en décapité* (1517). Identified as an *Erodiade* in 1592 (since the head is on a platter), Titian's self-portrait as Baptist was re-identified as Holofernes to Judith in 1992 (since a Cupid is over the doorway and other Judiths occasionally have platters).[35] Although the early seventeenth century sees a vogue of beheaded self-portraits, including Cristofano Allori (1577–1621) and Caravaggio (ca. 1571–1610), they explore sexual guilt. The painter represents himself as Holofernes or Goliath, decapitated by his beloved Judith or David. Representing oneself as the Baptist becomes common only in the nineteenth century, as the Baptist edges out Christ.

In the seventeenth century, although representations with Salome flourish, the Baptist's solitary head becomes less frequent, as if the desire to enter the transcendent through pain were diminishing. Isabel Combes Stuebe locates only a few as the topos travels to Spain and, in the eighteenth century, Mexico and Peru.[36] Passing through horror to sublimity moves to Spain, where ravaged Christs still shock atheists to awe.[37] Solario's portraits of Salome already outnumber his solitary head of St. John three to one.

As St. John diminishes, Salome increases, not only in numbers, but also in misogyny added to self-consciousness. Salome and Herodias wax darkly erotic, self-consciously and dangerously seductive, turning into orgasmic or triumphant man eaters. When Salome danced, her body said all anyone needed to hear. When Herodias took a knife to St. John's head, she showed how dangerous she was without tempting the viewer's erotic submission. Roger van der Weyden (1400–1464) invented the anguished Salome, who turns away from the head. Solario's virgins contemplate the head solemnly, unselfconsciously, meditative as the viewer before the *Head of St. John*. Focused on the head, they show the viewer how to look.

When Luini (ca. 1483–1532) copies Solario, he turns Solario's troubled, empathic virgin into a self-satisfied seductress. Cesare da Sesto (1477–1523) makes his full-length Salome a triumphant prostitute. Lucas Cranach (1472–1553) paints a hideous serpentine Salome, whose bent neck echoes the snake, repelling the viewer who looks at her. Fascination with the erotic psychology of the taunting female body—Salome or Herodias delighting in her own bloody power—appears most spectacularly in

Francesco del Cairo (1607–1665). From the innocent Baptist, attention shifts to the terrifying triumph of the woman, who gazes at the viewer as though he will be next (da Sesto) or caresses the head, absorbed in erotic abandon (del Cairo).[38]

In such images, traditional misogyny intensifies under pressure from Renaissance reconsiderations of the nature and place of women. Fifteenth- and sixteenth-century interest in "female worthies," female education, female artists and patrons of the arts did not proceed without generating opposition as vehement as the nineteenth century's. Solario's unselfconscious Salome is potentially a more exemplary figure than the viewer who stares at her. Other artists riposted by making the new self-consciousness visible in the predatory female. The intelligent, passionate, loving virgin turns inscrutable, passionate, powerful, sympathetic, victimized, dangerous whore/wife. The contest Solario staged between the virgin and the head is over: the head loses.

No longer the object of the gaze as she dances away the man's head, these Salomes look triumphantly back at the viewer or lose themselves in their own self-contained world, upstaging the saint's head. "Behold, dear Mother, who was late our fear, / Disarmed and harmless I present you here . . . , / As lovers use, he gazes on my face, / With eyes that languish, as they sued for grace": so Salome speaks in Anne Killigrew's translation of an Italian lauda for Mary of Modena (ca. 1685). Facing such competition, the heads of St. John, grim and "gruesome," bloody and gory, might be expected to recede forever to the places where Stuebe found them, in the back galleries or storage rooms of museums and churches.

Yet the head of the Baptist reappears in the French Revolution and its aftermath, no longer as the last prophet and first martyr of Christianity, but as the last prophet and first martyr of the Jacobin revolution and the rights of man. As David modeled his *Marat assassiné* (1793) on a *Descent from the Cross,* Dominique-Vivant Denon transformed Robespierre into the Baptist. Solario's arm, by way of Luini's copy, enables the identification. Well after the Revolution, the head of St. John, shorn of identifying iconographic apparatus, appears as mere severed head. No longer a saint, no longer a revolutionary, his head is only the head of man, victim of human justice in a world where other faiths have destroyed one another. Charles Émile Callandre de Champmartin and Théodore Géricault secularize the *Johannisschüssel,* disturbing and puzzling their viewers, century after century, for what meaning can a secular *Johannisschüssel* have?

Baptizing the Revolution / Revolutionizing the Baptist

After Thermidor (July 1794), Dominique-Vivant Denon (1747–1825) put Robespierre's head in the executioner's hand, hesitating as to whether the Incorruptible was the petrifying, protective head of Medusa or the martyred head of the Baptist (figs. 4.6, 4.7). Alan Wintermute argues that Denon's guillotined Robespierre evokes Villeneuve's Louis XVI (fig. 3.1) and exults over his fall. Villeneuve modeled both his Louis XVI and *Ecce Custine* on Cellini's *Perseus with Medusa*.[39] The clue is the hand. In Villeneuve and Cellini, the hero's hand stays level relative to the head as Perseus raises Medusa's weightless head above his own. There is no tension in the hand holding the head by the hair. Relaxed, the people's power controls without contortion, exertion, or effort the coin-profile of the king or the three-quarters head of Custine, where the *bourreau*'s arm is visible to the elbow, below the head. In both images, the *Marseillaise* promises fertility through sacrifice: "May an impure blood water our furrows."

Cut off, giving birth to horse and warrior, turning the Revolution's enemies to stone, these fertile Medusa's heads protect as aegis or petrify as threat. Custine's head is a sacrificial offering to the divine souls of the dead, the manes not of fathers, but brothers, sacrificed by the traitor: "Aux manes de nos frères sacrifiez par le traître." Louis' head warns other "crowned jugglers." Jubilant dismemberments remake the world, and Robespierre's falling blood curls thickly, like snakes. Mounted as the central figure in a row of three pencil sketches, Robespierre's head as Medusa enacts an allegory of terror and protection: Robespierre faces two Hébertistes, Gobel and Chaumette, sketched with their eyes open in the charrette, going to execution, doomed by Robespierre and his allies (fig. 4.6). Behind Robespierre, protected by his head, a fragile Couthon, Robespierre's supporter on the Committee of Public Safety, guillotined with him, holds a little dog. But there is something amiss in the hand that holds the head.

Denon's naked hand grips Robespierre's hair with the force needed to hold up so heavy an object as a head. Contorted, the sinews strain as the hand struggles to lift the head. This is not Perseus's graceful, easy triumph over the monstrous, fertilizing Medusa. This is the Baptist's iconography, thematizing violence, struggle, and sacrifice of the good. Denon's second, group version of the image (fig. 4.7) enables the model to be identified specifically as Luini's copy of Solario through the garb of the executioner's arm.

Fig. 4.6. Baron Dominique-Vivant Denon, Severed Head of Robespierre. Lead pencil. 6-7/16 x 4-3/16 in. (The Metropolitan Museum of Art, Rogers Fund, 1962 [62.119.8b])

Unwilling to remember Robespierre as a hero vilified or a martyr trapped by history, Wintermute is puzzled by Denon's portrait. As he observes, Robespierre's face and jaw are unmarred by the gunshot wound inflicted at the Hôtel de Ville. In David's sketch, a bandage holds Robespierre's face together. Robespierre's broken jaw fell apart, at the guillotine. Not here. Expecting to see punitive pain, Wintermute argues that the wound was on the left side of Robespierre's face and the image is in right profile.[40] Robespierre's jaw, however, would not hold together unbandaged. As an historical image, Denon's has no standing.[41] Although the portrait is from life, the image idealizes Robespierre as guillotined, like David's Marat or Solario's Baptist, but more ironically.

Marie-Anne Dupuy-Vachey finds Denon's political position "obscure," but she relates Denon's images to his gratitude to David and the Jacobins. Expelled from Venice as a convention spy in 1793, Denon returned to Paris to find himself marked down as an émigré, his Burgundian properties confiscated. Protected by David, invited to engrave *The Oath of the Tennis Court*, entrusted with engraving images of a new official costume in 1794, Denon was removed from the list of émigrés in June 1793, his properties restored in October.[42] Years later, Denon recounted meeting Robespierre in the antechamber to the Committee of Public Safety. Robespierre asked the waiting artist in a "petrifying tone" (d'un ton à lui pétrifier) what he did there; Denon explained; Robespierre softened, invited him in, they spent the night in conversation. Years later, the episode seemed "like a dream" (comme une songe).[43] Whatever Robespierre and the Committee of Public Safety did to others, they preserved and employed Denon.

In *Victims of the Terror* (fig. 4.7) Denon gathered his sketches of figures active in promoting the Terror, condemned by the Terror. Under a garlanded, cruciform guillotine, radiating light, he grouped Couthon, Chaumette, Gobel, and others, with Robespierre again at the center. The executioner's hand, placed in front of the blade of the guillotine, forms an equilateral angle with the blade, creating a crotch, feminized by the garland of flowers. His pushed-back shirt copied from Solario-Luini is now conspicuous. Unlike the figures surrounding him, Robespierre's eyes are closed, like the Baptist's in the Solario tradition.

Conventional hostile imagery associating Robespierre with the guillotine makes him the *bourreau*, not the victim. Denon has represented the great Jacobins as martyrs to a divinity represented not by the cross—that old method of execution, Roman and slavish—but by the guillotine, the

Fig. 4.7. Dominique-Vivant Denon, Victims of the Terror. Original lost.

new method of execution, nationalist, patriotic, and egalitarian. As a form of legal execution, the guillotine is intrinsically no less divine than the cross, but Christians abolished crucifixion as capital punishment soon after they had the power to do so.[44] Ironic and oddly tender, Denon's is a curious tribute to the new faith of the rights of man. The *guillotineur* lifts man up in hope and aspiration, through blood shed for others. Yet here the hope had been in man, who destroyed others and himself in his hope. Dying for the guillotine's meanings, they also died by it. To Robespierre's Baptist, who is the Christ? If Denon is ironic, it should be remembered that irony always entails saying exactly both things one means.

Twenty years after Denon's sketches, Auguste Raffet, the young friend of Callandre de Champmartin and Géricault, played with a severed head, shifting it from pike to platter. Raffet "reportedly spent several days in morbid play with the decapitated head of a man which he painted alternatively stuck on a pike or laid out on a charger."[45] The head on the pike is the people's triumph as sovereign. The head on the charger is the people's consolation as victims of others' sovereignty. Raffet evidently saw the images as reversible, the codes as equally transparent and equally empty of meaning. The rights of man or religion: each made its claim to the sign of the severed head. The critic designating Raffet's "play" as "morbid" has a clear, if unarticulated, view of the proper way to treat human body parts, especially heads. They should be handled reverentially, not instrumentally. They should certainly not be tossed from one discursive system to another. They should not flit.

In the 1820s, disdaining Raffet's contending contexts, Callandre de Champmartin and Géricault produce severed heads that have no ostensible context at all. The heads are unidentified. They affirm nothing. Not saints, kings, political enemies, or political heroes, they are only the heads of guillotined men, produced by human justice. Beyond Solario's head, God gave meaning to injustice and provided recompense for reality's horrors. Beyond Géricault's and Callandre de Champmartin's heads lies nothing, neither God nor recompense. Man's injustice and lust severed the Baptist's head. Man's justice severs a guillotined head.

Callandre de Champmartin remains closer to the traditional iconography of the martyr's head, and his image is correspondingly easier to regard and to describe than Géricault's. Once attributed to Géricault, Callandre de Champmartin's *After Death, Study of a Severed Head* (fig. 4.8) needs only a sword, a chalice, or a new title to be a martyr's or Baptist's head, like French, Italian, and Spanish paintings at the Louvre. Most

Fig. 4.8. Charles Emile Callandre de Champmartin, After Death, Study of a Severed Head, 1818/19. Oil on canvas, 45.6 x 55.6 cm. (A. A. Munger Collection. Reproduction: The Art Institute of Chicago)

saints' heads turn somewhat toward the viewer, however they may be angled.[46] This head turns slightly away. Unidentified and unidentifiable, the man evades the viewer's intrusive gaze; the cut in the neck is obscured. The grave cloth of a pietà gently swathes the gray, blood-drained profile. The eyes do not stare, the mouth gapes only a little. Nothing visibly holds the head in place. There is no triumph of any kind in this image; this desacralized head is no one's boast. Calling up sorrow and tenderness, this head must be touched with awe, with care, with the greatest delicacy. It is a holy image, of man, alone, without God behind him.

The eyes of Géricault's guillotined man are open (fig. 4.9). The man is ugly. He has bad teeth, a slack jaw, staring, unfocused eyes, flaccid skin. The mouth gapes. The oversized ear juts.

In the preparatory sketches, the man's head is alone. The head moves, circling the paper, angling around an empty center. The eyes are open, like the mouth that can no longer speak. Two heads are in profile, the other two three-quarters, turning slightly toward the viewer. No longer self-supported, the heads lean against a cloth, or the visible edge of a wooden table. In another painting, the head rests on the table, thrusting the "ghastly wound brutally . . . to the foreground."[47] Géricault evokes the ravaged tradition of Zoppo, Palmezzano, and Maineri rather than the idealizing tradition represented by Solario, Ribera or heads with Salome.[48]

Pairing two heads, a man's and a woman's, Géricault used a live, hunchbacked model for the woman.[49] She is one of fewer than a dozen women he painted in the course of his career.[50] Parodying bourgeois domesticity, the pair give us Adam and Eve, all humanity, guillotined. No Salome, she leans toward him, eyes closed. Livelier than his mate, the dead man protects her silence as he looks out at the world, his eyes almost

Fig. 4.9. Théodore Géricault, The Severed Heads. Oil on canvas. 50 x 61 cm. (National Museum, Stockholm)

focused on the viewer regarding him. The viewer no longer knows how to respond to that gaze.

Unable otherwise to explain them, Lorenz Eitner assumed the guillotined heads were preparatory for the *Raft of the Medusa*. Nina Athanassoglou-Kallmyer insists that Géricault's severed heads "can only be understood" as part of the debates in the 1820s over the guillotine, an implement with a Terrorist past and a conservative, royalist present.[51] Citing his representations of a classical Roman decollation and a modern British hanging (probably the also decapitated Cato Street conspirators), she links Géricault to the explicitly anti-guillotine arguments made by horrid heads in Sue, Hugo, Lefèvre, and others. In Lefèvre, the severed head leaps and rolls with a familiar horror:

> Le tronc recule et meurt, le sang jaillit et coule,
> La tête convulsive bondit et roule;
> L'oeil terne agite encore un regard effacé,
> Puis la bouche se sert et la vie a cessé.

> [The trunk recoils and dies, the blood spurts and flows,
> The convulsed head leaps and rolls;
> The dull eye still flickers a vanished glance,
> Then the mouth freezes and life has stopped.][52]

Yet Géricault's images remained in his studio, not presented as argument to any public. Stripped of iconographic context, they present the severed head as body without meaning, the problem contemporaries had, Eitner shows, with *The Raft of the Medusa* itself, a heroic painting without a heroic argument.[53] The explicitly argumentative images, bouncing across page and picture, follow Géricault's by at least a decade and trouble their viewers less. The viewer knows what to feel when he looks at them, how to categorize, naturalize, and neutralize the images. Even at their most futile, reformist political arguments comfort those who make them.

Géricault's images of man unmade by men do not console. Athanassoglou-Kallmyer knows that, so she also sets his images on "the uncertain ground between empathetic social statement and delight in social horror," linking them to the canonization of the ugly, as "private but equally militant assertions of aesthetic and ideological freedom."[54] Ingres rejected the images presciently and violently, "pictures of the dissecting room which show man as a cadaver, which show only the Ugly, the

Hideous. No! I don't want them!" Delacroix admired Géricault's guillotined heads and severed limbs as "subject-less" painting, sublime,
forceful, bold, proving that no subject is hateful, making the best argument for beauty, as it should be understood.[55] Delacroix thus dissolves
the transgressivity that Ingres—and Géricault—insist upon. If the subject
were not hateful and hideous, Géricault would not have chosen it, Ingres
would not have been offended, and Delacroix would not have defended
it. The pleasures of horror remain unexplored as Delacroix shifts to
"beauty" and the critic to "freedom," escaping the subject that faces
them.

These images challenge Géricault's own masculine aesthetic, exposing
the contradictions intrinsic to glorifying man. Géricault's canons of the
heroically beautiful were antique and Napoleonic, human and animal,
but also democratic. No Ingres, he turned from the great name, built up
on the bodies of thousands, to anonymous heroes. Closer to the old Jacobin David, to whom he made a pilgrimage at Brussels, Géricault preferred David's Napoleonic horse to his ephebic Barat.[56] Painting
Napoleon crossing the alps, David had replaced Napoleon's mule with a
rearing white mount. Géricault painted the emperor's rearing white
mount without the emperor. *Tamerlan, the Emperor's Stallion,* curvets in
his full-body painting with no emperor on his back. Rather than senti-
mentalizing the feminine as David did, Géricault ignored it. No great
painter has ever been less interested in representing women, dressed or
undressed, saint or sinner.[57] Rejecting the feminine as ideal, temptation,
or obstacle, Géricault rendered heroic male and animal forms, cuirassiers
and racers, horses and lions. Rejecting famous names, he approached
grandeur through common men, the anonymous man on horseback, the
nameless racer, the muscular crowd. In the guillotined heads, Géricault
abjects the man he made his hero.

Persons violated, identities erased, the obtruded body reveals symbolism's failure. No external order makes this dismemberment meaningful.
Were these the dripping heads of Rutulians, Cacus, or Goliath, someone
would triumph. Were they the dripping head of the Baptist, passing
through pain would achieve salvation. If they bounced, they would make
a cruel self-dissolving joke. Accompanied by mourners and a blade or
identified as historical figures, Lady Jane Grey or Charles I, pathos and
progress would console the viewer, assenting to historical inevitability,
Paul Delaroche's specialty.[58] If they were given a title, "man's inhuman-
ity" or "they call this justice," then a political campaign could begin, their

eyes closing. Instead, man's unmade self stares, his eyes almost focused, on the self looking at him. Géricault looks for a long time at what should not be and should not be looked at, and he invites his viewers to do the same. The system of values to which these heads belong makes the body primary, but powerless, save for the appeal that the empty, open face makes to the other, living face that regards him.

Géricault copied numerous paintings on religious themes, but no decollations of the Baptist. Instead he and Callandre de Champmartin brought the *Johannisschüssel* into post-enlightenment modernity, where its pain and horror, acknowledged and embraced in Renaissance and medieval images, have no redemptive meaning. Here God is absent, thrown from the churches, and the rights of man lead to the scaffold and Terror. No executioner, there is only an artist, voyeur and executor, illustrating man's freedom and posing death as a question, with a face of flesh. Man, exercising his rights to paint or to dismember, appears as inscrutable and terrible as Job's God.

From this nadir, this revelation of what man is and does, there can be no redemption, but there is distraction. Change happens when the female head—that living woman set beside a dead man—opens her eyes. Picking up the man's head, she closes his eyes and walks away with the topos. Saved, the head winks. Held by Salome, the abjected head becomes the greatest head of all. As Jesus put it, "Among them that are born of women there hath not risen a greater than John the Baptist" (Matthew 11:11).

Montmartre versus the Martyr

The year was 1869; the place the stained glass of the Église Saint-Vincent, now installed in the Église Sainte-Jeanne-d'Arc, Rouen, Géricault's birth-place—a city famed for the acrobatic Salome, dancing on her hands over the cathedral's portal.[59] In 1526, the Église Saint-Vincent possessed so magnificent a window of the life of St. John, the work of Engrand le Prince, that the Église Saint-Ouen in nearby Pont-Audemer commissioned a copy in 1535. The Baptist preaches and baptizes Christ in two large panels at the upper level. Below, two equally large panels present the decollation. At the viewer's left, the executioner hands to Salome the Baptist's severed head, the face clearly visible. A hound, on its haunches between her and the Baptist's fallen body, turns its head toward her platter. At the viewer's right, in the Pont-Audemer copy, Salome brings the head, facing both the viewer and the feasting table, on a charger to Herod and Herodias. Behind Herodias stands a hideous man, lust's true face. Three hundred years later, the glass in the original at Rouen needed restoration, and Duhamel-Marette undertook the task, *con amore.*[60]

Eliminating the presentation of the Baptist's head, Duhamel-Marette concocted a dancing Salome, with swirling skirts showing leg to the knees, striped stockings à la mode Moulin Rouge, ballet slippers, a prancing shock dog, and at her mother's feet, a sweet little white pussycat. Montmartre has replaced the martyr (fig. 4.10). Inside the church Duhamel-Marette puts images Toulouse-Lautrec had saved for advertising posters and Adolphe Willette for Le Chat Noir, where his Salome wears a pink tutu.[61] As to Herodias's white pussycat, and Salome's little dog, they suggest that female genitalia, including the mother's, may be more appealing (even in the nineteenth century) than Freud's Medusa's head suggests.

The hideous man, horrid lust, has vanished, replaced behind Salome by a cross, formed architecturally by a color-contrasted intersection of transom and mullion. The cross-window is purplish, color of the passion, against the blues of the rest of the architectural scheme. Barely noticeable, the sign of patriarchal, religious power overlooks her dance. Ostensibly

Fig. 4.10. Duhamel-Marette, Salome Dancing, Église Sainte-Jeanne-d'Arc, Rouen. (Author's photo)

independent, discreetly supervised, Duhamel-Marette's dancing Salome delights the eye, an enticing spirit of contemporaneity, her dominance within the frame real as experienced, illusory as ultimate reality.

Even in the scene of his execution, the Baptist's head vanishes. Where the Baptist's head must be, there remain fragments of glass and dark leaded lines, but no recognizable visage. Nor was Duhamel-Marette merely confused or in error about what the image had been. He knew the Église Saint-Ouen in Pont Audemer, and in 1895 he "striped" again. Restoring the window of St. Nicholas in that church, he supplied a Renaissance fisherman with the striped pull of a nineteenth-century dockworker. Devout or ironic, Duhamel-Marette enabled nineteenth-century worshippers to see themselves in the stained glass, as Renaissance and medieval spectators had. As artist, defining what his times demanded, he gave them Salome dancing, not the grisly head.

When "the decollation of the Baptist" becomes "the Salome topos," as it did for all to see in the stained glass of the Église Saint-Vincent, desire is undergoing rehabilitation in the heart of nineteenth-century bourgeois sexual morality. Conventional wisdom associates the nineteenth century with sexual repression, but in its mass production of condoms, campaigns for birth control, flirtatious Salomes, and even Jane Eyre's demand for a "true," that is, sexual, marriage, it recognized the desirability of desire.[62] Man's ugly lust is erased, replaced by a woman's attractive pussycat. Preceded (and coded) by art, sexuality has set out on its way to replace religion (and politics) as a source of identity, self-definition, and self-transcendence. Not uncontested: the struggle between the severed head and the dancing damsel marks the distance to be traversed.

Alexandre Masseron abruptly halted his discussion of "St-Jean Baptiste dans l'art" at the mid-nineteenth century, for the topos now "n'a rien que faire" with religion.[63] Having nothing to do with religion, the Baptist's head marks the place where meaning was and new meanings gather. In the eclipse of meaning, the Baptist's head lifts up the abjected heads of Géricault and Callandre de Champmartin to celebrate a re-divinized manhood, a transcendent masculinity, engaging the conflict between body and spirit. The head of St. John possesses a residual prestige, an excess of signification, a presence beyond referentiality. It provides an easy *frisson* even in its absence, and it gives Salome her value. Without his head or the promise of his head, Salome is only another naked lady, anonymous, powerless, *insignifiant*.

From John's head, Salome takes her meaning as temptation, or obstacle. He does not even need to appear: Henri Regnault painted a gypsy girl with a knife and plate in her lap. He then named the painting *Salomé la danseuse, tenant le bassin et le couteau qui doivent servir à la décollation de saint Jean Baptiste* (Salome the dancer, holding the platter and knife for the decollation of St. John, 1870), and created a sensation, especially when the Metropolitan Museum in New York outbid the Louvre for it. Regnault now hangs beside a painting of a woman painter painting a society lady as Salome, with platter, no head.

In his turn, St. John needs Salome to know himself and to be recognized as yielded body or resistant spirit. Without her, as in Odilon Redon, he becomes an uneasy, unidentifiable floating head. Without her, the heads of Géricault threaten to return. Salome keeps the abyss at bay. Yet she is also the abyss she keeps away: woman's work is never done.

In Salomes that remain familiar, the Baptist first rises as the divinized, suffering artist, and then sinks slowly into the body. Unmanned, reverenced or mocked for ideological or sexual insufficiency, he remains Elijah to the coming sacred, sexual, modern, masculine body. Artists at first appropriate Christological and divine iconography for the Baptist, and the Baptist for the artist. Ascending heads, such as Moreau's and Beardsley's, take off from Christ's ascension. Mallarmé's rising head of St. John re-assimilates the Baptist to the sun worship Mallarmé argued was fundamental to all religions.[64] The kiss Salome bestows on the Baptist in Wilde and Beardsley belongs to Judas and Christ (Wilde's personal refrain in the *Ballad of Reading Gaol*). Strauss presses down a crown of thorns on the Baptist's forehead.

Not merely Christlike, the Baptist is also artistlike. In Redon and Moreau, the heads are self-portraits. Agnès Lacau St. Guily asks, Are such self-representations "un désir inconscient d'automutilation expiatoire ou une soudaine bouffée de mégalomanie délirante?" (an unconscious desire for expiatory self-mutilation or a sudden bout of delirious megalomania?).[65] They are, of course, both. The narcissist's fate: elevated and debased, he rises above and sinks below the mirror in the water. So the nineteenth-century artist negotiates the chasm between art as trivial pursuit ("automutilation") and art as transcendent calling ("mégalomanie délirante"). The Baptist's head is holy, but it is also trash.

Already in Flaubert, reacting to Moreau (as Moreau responded to *Salammbô*), the living Baptist slips toward the ridiculous. Denying transcendence to the man, Flaubert finds in the severed head seriousness that the living lack. Flaubert brings the head down, but he does not turn off its light, and he affirms its weight. Against both rising and falling heads, Redon moves athwart: he starts with the Baptist and moves to the self in disembodied, floating heads that lack referentiality but create unease. He displaces the agon of the heads by the beauty of flowers. As sexual organs of plants, flowers are homologous to heads, but anxiety free and purely beautiful. Redon's move away from the body is answered by the move into sexuality, by Strauss (1905) and Freud. Like Flaubert, Strauss found the living Baptist absurd. His music identifies the sexual longing, not initially perverse, of Salome for the Baptist with the Baptist's religious longing for the coming of Christ. Salome and the Baptist sing the same tune, in dischords.

In Freud, sexuality comes forward, and it costs the Baptist everything. When decapitation becomes castration, the body achieves a new and absolute value. Since we all have only one head, decapitation must have only one meaning, and Freud's hermeneutic swept all before it, including St. John.

The conception that set Moreau to work was Pierre Puvis de Chavannes' *Décollation de saint Jean Baptiste* (1870). Kneeling, facing the viewer, the Baptist awaits the executioner, his arms outspread, undaunted, heroic, celebratory. He should have his hands together, in the prayerful posture of those who expect decollation. Instead, his posture evokes the risen Christ as king in the last judgment. Subverting the doctrines from which the subject and its iconography derive, the purely human body replaces the divine in gesture and power. The contrast with the artist's earlier *La fille d'Hérodiade donnant le signal de la décollation de saint Jean Baptiste* (The daughter of Herodias giving the signal for the decollation of St. John, 1856) is stunning.

In the earlier painting, a dominant Salome, brilliant in yellow and white, her strong, white back to the viewer, holds the charger over her head like a castanet as she looks down into a deep dungeon where the saint is barely visible. Studies for the saint show a pitiably vulnerable naked body, bent and bound, the face hidden, the penis dangling helplessly on scrawny thighs. From this darkness, the later Baptist emerges into light. Haloed a brilliant yellow, a thick, massive tree directly behind him, this Baptist figures phallic affirmation. The artist dates the painting more specifically than usual: it is his forty-fifth birthday.[66] His adored mistress modeled the Salome in the shadows. Uniting manifestations of male power, multiple lines of force meet in the central figure, the phallic tree of life, linked to the executioner by his patterned cap, seconded by the phallic sword. Ella Ferris-Pell, representing Salome without the "masochistic head," produces a glow of light in the lower right of her frame, emanating from a source incomprehensible to Salome, but understood as the presence of the Baptist, not the Christ (1890).[67]

Gustave Moreau's *L'Apparition* (1876), perhaps the single most famous treatment of this subject, inserts St. John's head in the iconography of the risen Christ, suspended, surrounded by an aura. Moreau's head evokes a traditional iconography for the Baptist: dark haired, bearded, noble nose, tragic profile. Unlike any *Johannisschüssel*, however, the eyes are both open and focused: the head still sees. As glorified and risen, the head represents a spiritual ideal that torments and infuriates the earthly Salome. Rising undone above earthly things, divine manhood confronts woman as terrorized, terrorizing, inferior reality, fixed to the ground he leaves behind. So a furious Salome points frantically at a luminous, bleeding, haloed, horrified head that rises both serenely and in agony above her.

A perfect counterweight to Flaubert's heavy head (1877), Moreau's was made iconic by J.-K. Huysmans (1884). Later a Catholic convert, Huysmans knew an ascension when he mentioned one, though his translator obscures the theological implications of the oxymoronic "frightful ascension":

> Une mosaïque cernait la figure d'où s'échappait une auréole s'irradiant en traits de lumière sous les portiques, éclairant l'affreuse ascension de la tête, allumant le globe vitreux des prunelles attachées, en quelque sorte crispées sur la danseuse.
>
> D'un geste d'épouvante, Salomé repousse la terrifiante vision qui la cloue, immobile, sur les pointes; ses yeux se dilatent, sa main étreint convulsivement sa gorge.

> A mosaic encircled the face whence shone an aureola darting gleams of fire under the porticoes, illuminating the ghastly lifting [cf. "l'affreuse ascension"] of the head, revealing the glassy eyeballs, that seemed fixed, glued to the figure of the dancing wanton.
>
> With a gesture of horror, Salomé repulses the appalling vision that holds her nailed to the floor, balanced on her toe tips; her eyes are dilated, her hand grips her throat convulsively.[68]

Ghastly, but dead, the head produces horror rather than experiencing it. Huysmans does not see the Baptist's horror of Salome, more pronounced in later images.[69] Instead, he shares it. Of the companion watercolor to the painting Huysmans describes, a ten-year-old boy at the Moreau museum in Paris observed that the Baptist looked terrified of Salome, rather than the other way around (fig. 4.11).

Something in the image, however, is not quite right. In Renaissance images of the head of the Baptist, the head may not be supported physically, but it is not rising. It is not in the air. That position is reserved for the risen Christ or the soul heads, the winged cherubic heads of spirit essence. The Virgin never rises on her own—she is always pulled or pushed up by others. In Mallarmé's "Cantique de Saint Jean" the head speaks at the height of its arc, but it is about to fall. Moreau's head poised in mid-air is secure and self-sustaining.

The novelty of Moreau's iconography transfixed his contemporaries as it did Salome. Moreau sold *L'Apparition* Huysmans describes, but kept the other for himself, in his atelier. In that version (reproduced here), the mosaic disappears, and the aureole becomes cruciform, reproducing the conventional sunburst pattern of the pix that displays the host at the feast of Corpus Christi. The head of the Baptist, once analogous to the host in the mass, now replaces Christ, as host and as risen. By replacing the risen Christ with a risen head, Moreau appropriates religious significance while emptying its original content, as David had in his *Marat Assassiné*. A human hero replaces the divine, absorbing and transferring the affect traditionally reserved for the divine image. His head or spiritual part rebukes executioner, king, Salome, and mother. She remains in the flesh, defiant, but he goes beyond the flesh, indicative of a triumphant, higher principle, purchased at a terrible price.

Moreau's other favored subjects—Orpheus, the poet ripped apart by mad women, the Poet and the Sirens, even Sappho—also stage the contest between spirit and flesh. As Moreau's first severed head (*Orphée*, 1866), Orpheus remained competitive with the Baptist, but, torn apart by a group of women, he lacked the hostile confrontation between a single male and a single youthful female. Puvis de Chavannes seems to have led Moreau to this reinvention of the Baptist. Moreau's earliest *Décollation* (1872–73) puts an erect, kneeling Baptist in profile relative to an active executioner, with a sidelined Salome, as if Moreau were turning Puvis de Chavannes' figures around, viewing them from other angles.[70] In 1885, Salome takes out-of-doors a head of the Baptist on a platter, and a dove

Fig. 4.11. Gustave Moreau, The Apparition. 1874. Watercolor. Musée Gustave Moreau, Paris. (Photo Credit: Erich Lessing/Art Resource, NY)

descends, hovering over the head. Does Moreau forget that the dove that appeared to John the Baptist signaled the presence of the Christ? The dove appeared, and a voice from heaven said, "This is my beloved son in whom I am well pleased" (Mt. 3:16–17; Mk. 1:10–11; Lk. 3:22; Jn. 1:32–33). The voice was *not* talking about the Baptist. Moreau transfers to the dead Baptist the third person of the Trinity, the Holy Ghost as dove, that identifies the (son of) God.

Yet if the head rises, it also sinks. Anticipating the spirit of Aubrey Beardsley and Jules Laforgue (whose Baptist is Orpheus and whose Salome himself),[71] Moreau painted a *Second Empire Salome* (1885 or 1890), a woman in modern dress, reclining in a chair, a head at her feet. As Pierre-Louis Mathieu observes, the head is a self-portrait or self-caricature.[72] Moreau's features lie on the floor, the head on its side, like Ribera's *Johannischüssel*. He faces away from the woman, the abyss. Of his Salome in the garden, Moreau remarked,

> Quand je veux rendre ces nuances-là je les trouve, non pas dans mon sujet, mais dans la nature même da la femme dans la vie, qui cherche les émotions malsaines et qui, stupide, ne comprend même pas l'horreur des situations les plus affreuses.

> [When I want to render these nuances I find them not in my subject, but in the nature of woman in daily life, who seeks out unhealthy emotions and who, idiotic, does not comprehend the horror of the most frightful situations].[73]

Responsibility for "the most frightful situations"—those Géricault contemplates—is deflected onto the woman who fails to understand, away from the men who act.

According to Françoise Meltzer, Gustave Flaubert was "overwhelmed by Moreau's vision and began research for his *Herodias* in the same month of the same year" that he saw Moreau's *L'Apparition* (1876).[74] When Flaubert's *Herodias* (1877) appeared, Zola suggested Moreau should illustrate the story. Flaubert did not respond. However inspiring he may have found *L'Apparition*, Flaubert put down Moreau's heavy head before Moreau did. In Flaubert, the Baptist's head ends up on the dinner table among the dirty plates and leftovers, "le débris du festin." Not divinized, that head has no spiritual elevation, and it belongs, contradicting the scripture, to the men.

In spite of the title's guilty lure, neither Herodias nor her daughter interests Flaubert. Salome is a sequence of body parts glimpsed by Herod, her dance a scrabbling beetle. There is no scene between Herodias and the head. Salome delivers the head to her invisible mother, where the gospels leave it. In Flaubert, no one in particular brings the head back down to the men at table.

Before he dies, Flaubert's John spouts tirades impersonal, inevitable, and tiresomely predictable: "On avait reconnu Iaokanann" (They recognized Iaokanann) (235).[75] Herod slobbers. Only the Roman Vitellius retains any dignity, and he is hostage to the ephebic Aulus. Contradicting the gospels, where the disciples receive the body, not the head, of John, Flaubert gives John's head to three disciples. They shift it among themselves *alternativement* because it is so heavy. The head provides, in Flaubert, a weightiness, a ballast, a profundity that none of the living possess, including the living Baptist.

When he describes the Baptist's head, Flaubert's language evokes less the open-eyed *Apparition* that inspired him than Solario's serene, Leonardesque Baptist, eyes closed, countenance illumined, eye sockets like pilgrim shells. Of artists ostensibly focusing on Salome, Flaubert is the only one known to have wished to have on his table, as he wrote (or sketched), the head of a guillotined man. The speculative, skeptical Roman audience scrutinize the head, as curious about the signs of decapitation as the writer, equally indifferent to this "frightful situation":

> Ils l'examinèrent.
> La lame aigue de l'instrument, glissant du haut en bas, avait entamé la mâchoire. Une convulsion tirait les coins de la bouche. Du sang, caillé déjà, parsemait la barbe. Les paupières closes étaient blêmes comme des coquilles; et les candélabres à l'entour envoyaient des rayons.

> [They examined it.
> [The sharp blade of the instrument, gliding from above, had cut into the jaw. A convulsion twisted the corners of the mouth. Blood, already clotted, sprinkled the beard. The closed eyelids were pale as shells, and the candles around shed their rays.][76]

The executioner's "sharp-bladed instrument, gliding from high to low," evokes a guillotine as well as the oddly unnamed sword. Playing the tortured or sexual against the serene, Flaubert marks convulsion and blood, but then closes the dead eyes of the *Johannisschüssel*. The "coquille" is the shell of the pilgrim, emblem of St. James. The last words are light, from candles that rest on tables as on altars.

In 1868, E. Lecomte had given to the Louvre Solario's *Head of the Baptist,* where it joined Luini's copy of Solario's *Salome with the Head of the Baptist.* Put on display, it gathered considerable attention, both parodic and reverential.[77] Flaubert never mentions Solario, but on 21 April 1868 he told his niece Caroline not to wait for him to go the Louvre on Thursday, and the *Education Sentimentale* (1869) speaks of going to the Louvre to see old pictures.[78] In the absence of a guillotined head for the writing table, Flaubert is likely to have revisited those old pictures, deliberately countering Moreau's uplifting influence by sinking the head and closing the eyes of the dead. Flaubert does not identify with the Baptist, but he is intent on interrogating the brute and heavy reality of death. Having worked so self-consciously against Moreau, Flaubert, it is not surprising, was silent when Zola missed the point.

Touched by the Baptist's predicament, Odilon Redon copied Solario and adapted Moreau, but he moved beyond the Baptist to the predicament of the modern self, afloat, meaningless, terrified, un-nurtured, intermittently beautiful. Redon began by sketching Solario's head of the Baptist, probably in 1868 or 1869. Explicitly theological, Redon's copy tangles a descent from the cross in the curls of the hair, parallel to the plane of the profile.[79] Making next a "portrait of Salome," Redon reversed Solario's seductive dynamic. A self-portrait as the Baptist, the head on its platter faces Salome's breasts, but the breasts are hard, pointed, metal-capped, spiky. Salome's soft face contradicts the repulsive breasts, but looms above the head, which cannot see it. The gaze flees the breasts for the severed head or Salome's face, but suffers the contradiction between face and breasts. Relationship disappears between the Baptist and Salome, whether amorous or confrontational. Redon's pair never face each other, even when he copies Moreau's *L'Apparition*. From his Baptists, Redon launches an exploration "sincerely and genuinely new [that] —like beauty, after all—carries its meaning within itself," as if heads could be innocent.[80]

Breaking from the specific symbolic correspondences of traditional iconography, Redon's famous "blacks" included separated, unidentified, floating heads. Lacking referentiality, where referentiality is most demanded, huge heads, flying heads, quizzical heads, heads with their eyes open, heads with their eyes closed, challenge, or defy, interpretation. A mark in a huge forehead suggests Goliath. In *Après le supplice* (after the execution), an open-eyed, sad-faced, portrait head set on a Roman marble recalls Géricault's Roman execution and guillotined heads. A dark, hairy floating head has incongruous little wings, like a Renaissance spirit head. Numerous heads are set "sur une coupe," though they bear no resemblance to Solario's head or his cup. No blood drips. As symbols without referents, these heads obtrude not severing, but separation, mystery without violence, "autogenesis and isolation."[81]

Douglas Druick attributes the *noirs* to the death of Redon's father, a loss stimulating an anguished search for the self. The intensity of paternal loss, erasing maternity, Freud confirms in *Civilization and Its Discontents*, "I cannot think of any need in childhood as strong as the need for a father's protection."[82] Beyond biographical, psychoanalytic, or personal loss, Redon's images remember the power of the head, its authority and value, but insist there is no ulterior meaning there.

Many viewers found that discovery unsettling. Redon revealed a mysterious, alternative universe, containing "every imaginable human perversity and animal baseness, and all sorts of terrifying inert and baneful things . . . the grandiose, the delicate, the subtle, the perverse, the seraphic."[83] Huysmans placed the *noirs* a few pages beyond Moreau's *L'Apparition* as "apparitions inconcevables" (inconceivable apparitions). Humanity fled backward in evolutionary decline from primitive culture to animal speechlessness, from "une tête d'un style mérovingien, posée sur une coupe" to "l'homme encore frugivore et dénué de parole" (a head in Merovingian style, poised on a cup [to] man still fruit-eating and speechless).[84]

Eluding his interpreters, Redon changed his topos—heads for flowers. His last *Salome*, two women with a head at their feet, mirrors his *Fleurs lumineuses*, two women with flowers at their feet (1890s).[85] Does Redon remember that flowers are the sex organs of plants? In a 1912 watercolor, *Nude, Begonias, and Heads*, he laid a pink female nude among flowers, a black male head forming one of the flower heads, while several white male heads rise, above flowers and woman. Reading the heads, Druick takes the image as profoundly anti-female, representing woman as primitive, allied to nature and the dark head, above which the white male spirit heads rise.[86] Leaving his *noirs* and floating heads, Redon turned to a simpler, less conflicted, more purely sensual beauty. Thereafter, he painted flowers. At last, no one asked him what his paintings meant.

Heads and flowers are a homology as ancient as heads and penises. With Salome's passion aggrandizing the head as object of physical desire from Heinrich Heine's *Atta Troll* (1843) to Oscar Wilde's *Salome* (1893), it remained for Richard Strauss to identify the Baptist's passion for Christ with Salome's passion for the Baptist in his opera *Salome* (1905). Strauss's libretto is a straightforward German translation of Wilde's text, originally written in French, from which Strauss deleted many of "the overtly sexual lines," among them Salome's knowledge of the meaning of Herod's gaze.[87] His librettist also added a Christological image absent in Wilde: "It is like a crown of thorns placed on thy forehead" ("Es ist wie eine Dornenkrone auf deinen Kopf gesetzt"). Salome, fleeing the banquet and the lecherous Herod, demands to see the Baptist; she desires his body, hair, lips; he scorns her; she dances for Herod, demands the head (to her mother's surprised delight), and kisses it. Horrified, Herod orders her crushed by the soldiers.

To the Baptist, Strauss gives music that aspires to resolution, serenity, in fourths, at ever higher levels. Whether judged "commonplace" or "impressive," his music proposes another world, an alternate reality, a visionary harmony that escapes the impediments of flesh.[88] "He will come," the Baptist sings. Isaiah's language of rejoicing follows. The deserts blossom, the child puts his hand in the adder's lair and leads the lion. When Salome appears on the scene, she disturbs his music, and his language darkens, horrified by lust, until he curses her not in his own key, E-flat, but in her key, C-sharp minor. As Tethys Carpenter puts it, John "loses control of the situation and is sucked progressively further towards her tonal orbit," until he enters it.[89] As Derrick Puffett observes, the tam-tam that punctuates the Baptist's religious utterances is gradually overwhelmed by his quarrel with Salome and turns into an ordinary percussive instrument, its religious associations lost.[90] As she approaches, he rejects, yet his music is also identified with hers. His notes on "he will come" are her notes when she sings, "I will kiss your mouth."[91] In her last aria, as she moves into C-sharp, she also echoes his motives in E-flat, and the orchestra plays two keys against each other. To the memory of his music her last aria aspires and almost, agonizingly, reaches.

Almost to a man, Strauss's critics have been dissatisfied with the Baptist's living music. "Flatulent, over-blown, stilted, shallow as an operetta," it represents religious fervor as less compelling than sexual perversity.[92] Critics have also puzzled over the fact that Strauss's music of religious fervor *is* his music of sexual consummation and desire. The Baptist's melody at the climax of his religious longing reappears in *Der Rosenkavalier* to represent physical consummation between the

Marschallin and her lover.[93] The "vocal climax" Strauss gives his prophet is in a cadence "one more usually associates with the composer's heroines at their moments of greatest triumph or satisfaction," murmurs Osborne.[94] In Wilde's play, Salome and the Baptist imitate each other; each attacks sexuality and condemns the body. In Strauss's opera, the Baptist's music identifies his desire for Christ with Salome's for him. More scandalous than the libretto, the music identifies what the words oppose.

Strauss stages the contest between sexuality and spirituality as simultaneously oppositional and identical. Did he know what he was doing? Cynthia Annmarie McGregor argues that John's music appears in Salome's final aria because, for her, the last aria is a love duet.[95] Salome's longing appropriates the Baptist's, turning his religious harmonies into her frustrated dissonances, incapable of satisfaction. Richard Specht hoped that Salome's sins were to be remitted, since her music was linked through the Baptist with the theme of Christ's coming.[96]

For Strauss, John's asceticism was comical, and his music determined by the need for a contrast with Salome's erotic anguish that did not undermine Salome. For the Baptist's sanctity, he had few kind words: "You know, Jochanaan is an imbecile. I have no sympathy at all for that type of man. In the first place I would have liked him to be a bit grotesque." That was 1907. Thirty years later he claimed,

> I tried to compose the good Jochanaan more or less as a clown; a preacher in the desert, especially one who feeds on locusts, seems infinitely comical to me . . . [but] I had to follow the law of contrast and write a pedantic-Philistine motif for four horns to characterise Jochanaan.[97]

Like Flaubert's, Strauss's Jochanaan lacks his creator's respect. Alive, his visionary denial of the body has value only as it produces Salome's need for his head.

Strauss's friend Romain Rolland insisted that his music for *Salome* deserved a better subject, say, *Lear*, and Strauss, as he usually did with criticism, agreed. But, he complained, he was not Wagner; he could not write his own librettos. Salome's agonized, aspiring, unfulfillable desire articulates modernity's crises, the opposition between body and spirit, female and male, longing and fulfillment. Yet, as representative of modernity's unattainable and infinite desire, Strauss and Rolland agree she ought to have been male.

In its multiplication of Salomes, the nineteenth century engages several of its greatest struggles, redefining gender roles, faith, sexuality, art. The female subject is re-affirmed as bodied, desiring, and predatory relative to a traditionally repressive but now (ostensibly) helpless masculinity. As religion crosses over to sexuality in Strauss, the saintly Baptist, beleaguered, molested, decapitated, remains what every woman wants. It fell to Freud, more sympathetic than Strauss to the Baptist, to explain what that meant.

In the 1920s, Freud theorized decapitation, re-identifying penis and head, in his familiar formula, "decapitation = castration."[98] Making "the sexual theory" foundational for society and the individual, Freud turned Locke's "inclination" and Shaftesbury's "sympathy" into libido, "an internal erotic impulse which causes human beings to unite in a closely-knit group."[99] At work in Vienna, he had been curing thirteen-year-old boys of sexual neurosis at least since 1901 by telling them stories about decapitation.[100] With Medusa's head in mind, Freud insisted that dreams, fantasies, and representations of decapitation symbolized the primordial masculine terror of castration, loss of the penis that defined the boy's (masculine) identity and differentiated him from castrated females, especially his mother. Castration anxiety, grounded in the body, was the terror men had to traverse to become men, while accepting the reality of her castration made a woman.

Freud restored the ancient homology between the penis and the head, castration having become unspeakable about the mid-eighteenth century, as *Tristram Shandy* records. Although Tristram is undone by a falling window, it is "morally impossible [for] the reader to understand" the proposition that "when your possibility has taken place at the hip,—you may as well take off the head too."[101] For a century, our culture's reigning interpretation of decapitation has been Freud's "decapitation = castration."

Historically, as actual practices, castration and decapitation occupy related but distinct positions, carefully calibrated relative to each other. As penalty, castration degrades (feminizes, unmans, mars), while decapitation often honors. Emily Vermeule observes that there are no damages to genitals on the *Iliad*'s battlefields, though Priam fantasies himself castrated.[102] Jean-Pierre Vernant observes that the only mutilations Homer constructs as horrific are genital mutilations.[103] The *Odyssey* systematizes the opposition: the treacherous goatherd is castrated, the last noble suitor decapitated.

As an act of self-abnegation, the Chinese author Ssu-ma Ch'ien (ca. 145–85 B.C.E.) chose castration over decapitation in order to finish his history. Sentenced by his offended emperor to castration, code for a disgrace he was expected to evade by suicide, Ssu-ma Ch'ien reluctantly chose castration. Beheading honored, castration degraded, but a beheaded author cannot write.[104] In the aggravated form of the traditional English sentence for treason, the living head watched its castration before the head was severed. Traditionally, then, men seem to have regarded castration as worse than decapitation, more shameful though less mortal.

When Freud identifies decapitation and castration, he dishonors decapitation, bringing it down to the shameful, hidden private parts. At the same time, he honors castration, made fundamental to the formation of the self, binding identity to the body more intimately than ever. In the fantasy fundamental to the formation of gender identity through the Oedipus complex, the boy, desiring his mother, harbors murderous instincts toward his father and dreads castration at the revenging father's hands. His mother's and little girls' castrated genitals assure him that castration occurs and always threatens. He could lose the pleasure-providing, envied body part on which his identity is founded, so coveted by women and girls who lack his penis and can never have one. The castration complex is fundamental to the healthy male character. The boy affirms his male identity as he accepts the justice of the father's threat and turns his desire from his mother to another woman. The threat of castration, accepted and internalized, always reassures him that (unlike women) he is not castrated.

The little girl adjusts to her painfully deprived difference and accepts her castration as the price of becoming a woman. When she fails to adjust, as frequently happens, she longs to be a man and suffers penis envy.[105] As Charles Bernheimer suggests, "the fantasy of castration forms the core of psychoanalytic theory: without castration, psychoanalysis would lack its oedipal key to differential structures in the psyche, the family, and society."[106] "Reduced" to castration, decapitation becomes the cornerstone of identity, the polite sign of the self in the body, the public representation of anxious privates, private anxieties.

Post-Lacanian theorists de-biologize Freud, reading castration metaphorically as "loss," "narcissistic injury," even death.[107] Castration signifies what decapitation does. In Lacan the phallus as transcendental signifier governs access to the symbolic and to language, generating, as Susan Rubin Suleiman puts it, "the logic of 'phallic' discourse, characterized by linearity, self-possession, the affirmation of mastery, authority, and above all unity."[108] As transcendental signifier, the wanting wand, the phallus "can play its role only when veiled":[109] St. John's head as lingam.

Although he lived surrounded by the erotic topos of Salome, Freud never mentions Salome, Herodias, Herod, or Richard Strauss, yet his single reference to the Baptist in a letter in 1898 inadvertently prophesies both Strauss's opera and the decline of the Baptist topos. In a now familiar pattern, Freud likens the Baptist to Christ and defends him against a decapitating woman, quoted by his correspondent. Ida's remarks are "clever and correct," but she is wrong to reject John as psychoneurotic. Although "the sexual theory" defines an ascetic as defective, Freud defends manly asceticism in terms of its potential for ejaculation. John has, like Christ, the virtues of his defects: visionary, abstinent, virginal. "[I]t is only abstinence that attracts people, as though they were waiting for [the distribution of] what has been stored up. Music of the future!"[110] Salome, waiting for John's love, demanding what he denies, taking his head, blood and all, sings that music.

But John, Freud goes on to observe, has no future. "John the Baptist has all his deeds (as a sinner) behind him; he is incapable of any new deed (except for measures of protection and repentance)." The statement is odd: John as repentant sinner is unknown to the Christian tradition. That is the repentant prostitute's role, to which woman as disciple is confined and reduced. Turning John into Mary Magdalene, Freud castrates and feminizes him before his decapitation. Deeds are only sexual, not symbolic. Like Flaubert and Strauss, Freud sees John as having nowhere to go. Without sexuality, his story is over.

The contrast with Holofernes is instructive. As Margarita Stocker observes, when Freud addresses a decapitating woman, Judith, he selects a modern work (Hebbel) in which Holofernes impregnates Judith (and so does not die forever, but lives on) and an adaptation (Nestroy) in which showing a false head scatters the Assyrian army.[111] Freud sexualizes the decapitated and removes the real head from the woman's hands, where tradition put it. The non-sexual John, his head in women's hands, Freud does not take up, even though it would seem to be the God-given answer to his question, "What do women want?"

Unmasked as lingam, John's head becomes a dead end. Freud's fertile single story replaces John's multiple meanings. When Freudian readings take over, becoming inevitable, conventional, and entirely respectable, the greatest head of all finally subsides, abandoned on its platter.

5

African Heads and Imperial Décolletage
Beheadings in the Colonies

If you can keep your head when all about you
Are losing theirs and blaming it on you.   —Rudyard Kipling, "If"

On a boat crewed by "starving cannibals" whose only intelligible remark is "Eat 'im," Joseph Conrad's Marlow journeys into *The Heart of Darkness*. He hopes he looks more appetizing than the other Europeans on board his ship. Free from ancient fears of ingestion and incorporation, Marlow finds African cannibalism more amusing than frightening. Among the Bangula, following Conrad, Norman Sherry also reports jocular, anecdotal, food cannibalism. The pilot of a steamer, asked if he really ate human flesh, replied, "Ah! I wish I could eat everybody on earth," and a missionary once talked to a man who had reportedly killed and eaten seven of his wives.[1] Europeans are in no danger of being killed by anything except the climate. Yet heads still stun.

Arrived at Kurtz's house, taking in the ornamental "round knobs" on a decaying fence, Marlow startles: "I had suddenly a nearer view, and its first result was to make me throw my head back as if before a blow." The "knobs of wood" are human heads. Most face Kurtz's house, but one faces out, toward Marlow. "I returned deliberately to the first I had seen—and there it was, black, dried, sunken, with closed eyelids,—a head that seemed to sleep at the top of that pole, and, with the shrunken dry lips showing a narrow white line of the teeth, was smiling, too, smiling continuously at some endless and jocose dream of that eternal slumber."[2] Subdued, oddly smiling, this black head does not challenge with open eyes. It does not look back. It neither demands an empathic response nor issues Melville's terrible warning to slaveholders in "Benito Cereno," where the black head on the pole keeps its eyes open and smiles.

Conrad's readers know what such heads mean: African heads = African barbarians. Repellent, fascinating, the dried, museum-quality heads in an African setting are horrifying, thrilling, and predictable. Marlow "was not so shocked as you may think." Africans did that sort of thing. When Europeans in Africa did similar things—as the non-fictional Captain Rom bordered his flowerbed with twenty-one native skulls shortly before Conrad began *Heart of Darkness*—it was reported with horror, but the action characterized Africa, not Europe.[3] That Europeans once spiked heads, and do so no longer, is an article of faith and a mark of the progress of civilization that Kurtz represents, and betrays by his "reversion."

In the code of nineteenth-century European imperial decollations, only barbarians cut off heads, and only barbarians have their heads cut off. The classic formulation is Kipling's "The Head of the District" (1891).[4] Often the native loses his head to superior European technologies, bypassing the intimacy of decapitation and producing the trope of headless native bodies, discovered by Martin Green, associated with "explosions, producing human debris, usually native" in Jules Verne, W. H. G. Kingston, Conrad, and Defoe.[5]

In a preemptive codicil, the civilized lay claim to a superior barbarity, cutting off the heads of barbarians, who are still the only ones to have their heads cut off. Not only does the act of decapitating separate the barbarians from the civilized: they do it, we don't; but submission to decapitation also separates the barbarians from the civilized: they suffer it, we don't.

Civilized people neither cut off heads, nor lose their own. They keep everyone's head in place and improve the heads they find. Thus the civilizing mission defines and justifies its progress abroad. Controlling violence is to the secular civilizing mission what spreading the word of God is to the evangelical. Since there can be no civilizing mission without barbarians to civilize, it is helpful if those-to-be-civilized do something that marks them as conspicuously barbarous.

Cut off, the native head demonstrates its inability to protect itself, to control others' violence, or to create circumstances where heads are secure. Cutting off a head, the native demonstrates both his command of force and his inability to exert power without violence. His may be the excessive manliness of the warrior or the hysterical (feminine) savagery of the crowd. Natives' cutting off one another's heads represent the violent disorder that the European presence enables the native to move beyond to peaceable civility, yet native violence also recalls a vigor endangered by (feminized) peaceable civility. High imperialism reclaims that vigor when white men decapitate, monopolizing violence.

Marking the climax of European imperial ideology, Cecil B. Rhodes claimed, "I am a barbarian. I believe with Ruskin that all healthy men love to fight." Ruskin makes an instructive model of manliness: "Better fight than fuck." Martin Green shows Rhodes's sentiments echoing through Winston Churchill, T. E. Lawrence, Richard Burton, Richard Meinertzhagen, Rider Haggard, and Rudyard Kipling.[6] Writing in 1898–99, Conrad has such attitudes in view in Kurtz, the white man who takes heads, but continues to define himself as civilized against "the brutes."

Already amused by cannibals, Marlow laughs when the Harlequin identifies the heads as "rebels" to Kurtz's sovereignty. The Harlequin's defense reminds Conrad's readers that London too once saw heads on poles, Thames-side. Marlow's laughter rejects the justification and registers embarrassed recognition. Marlow has toyed playfully with the symbolic incorporation of cannibalism, but the heads bring him into western history. Incongruously, he finds restored at this outpost the sign civilization defines itself by abandoning. "[N]ot ornamental but symbolic," most facing the house, the black heads mirror the white Kurtz. They affirm Kurtz's power, the power of whiteness over blackness. But one head faces out, toward Marlow and his auditors, showing what imperialism, idealistic or degraded, comes to in the end.

Although they always mention them, Conrad's critics do little with Kurtz's heads. Like Sherry on cannibalism, they unselfconsciously reenact the trope. For F. R. Leavis, "such things as the heads on posts" (though there are no other "such things") evoke Kurtz's "strange and horrible perversions," a view seemingly shared but not further developed by Albert Guérard, Benita Parry, and others.[7] The heads repel, producing horror at a surging primitive violence that ought to be extirpated, but they also excite. Representing Europe, associated with cultivated women, aligned with progress and civility, in Africa Kurtz makes himself a king (the rebels' heads), a god (the unspeakable rites), and a man (the African woman). The sexually active man ranks highest, climaxing the sequence. For Kurtz's magnificent degradation and reversion to Africa, the heads are the only physical evidence Conrad supplies. They are all he needs.

Yet the only characters in the text (including Marlow) who do not fall under Kurtz's spell are those whose heads surmount the stakes around his house. As "rebels," they resisted Kurtz's charm, Kurtz's divinity, Kurtz's European siren song (Kurtz's greed). Evidently less "rudimentary souls" than the Africans "charm[ed] or frighten[ed]" by Kurtz (51), more courageous than the Europeans at the station who detest Kurtz and his connections, their reward as rational, un-mystified beings is death and dehumanization. Only they knew and rejected his hollowness. Only they saw through him. So they smile.

No one, of course, notices, since the reader also falls under the Kurtzian spell. Unmistakable signs of an alternate subject position, hiding in plain view, the heads enact the colonial silence imposed even when imperialism is attacked or scrutinized as moral quandary. Marlow gazes, disinterested, rational. He overcomes his revulsion through scrutiny, empowered by analysis, and he disallows the Harlequin's justification, but his interest is Kurtz, not the heads. When he laughs at the designation "rebels," he turns Kurtz's opponents into Kurtz's victims, subjects into objects, fear into pity. Conrad both silences African heads and reveals the brutality silencing requires. Yet he also marks the place where speech would be, where speech was.

In modern African fiction, descendants of the heads Kurtz put on poles revise an ancient topos that acquired its racist component relatively recently. As cultural marker, decapitation separates civilization from barbarism to justify domination abroad and to control behavior at home; in modern times it separates white from black. Usually assumed to be eternal, decapitation as cultural marker dates from the Roman period, assumes its modern interracial form in the eighteenth century, and achieves full racist expression with the development of scientific racism in the nineteenth.[8] Conrad and his critics breathe that air, as does American popular culture. The heads obtrusively severed in such recent films as *Resident Evil: The Movie* (2002) or *A.I.* (2001) belong to black people, a corollary to the Hollywood axiom (cited in *Canadian Bacon* [1994]) that the black character dies first.[9] Before we look at what Africans make of severed/severing African heads, we should be clear on how historically specific Conrad's—and our—correlation of decapitation with the darkly barbarous is.

Decollation as Cultural Marker: Civility vs. Barbarity

Girard: Well, why not consider headhunting a bad habit? I really consider headhunting a bad habit, personally.

Rosaldo: Let me tell you what I have to say about that. I am not here as an advocate of headhunting. I feel that it's a bad habit.

Girard: You feel it's a bad habit?

Rosaldo: It's a very bad habit.

—Robert G. Hamerton-Kelly, ed., *Violent Origins: Walter Burkert, René Girard, and Jonathan Z. Smith on Ritual Killing and Cultural Formation.* Commentary Renato Rosaldo. Intro. Burton Mack (Stanford, Calif.: Stanford University Press, 1987), 253.

Cannibalism or decapitation: imperial terror of the colonial subject comes in two fantasied forms. The civilized, who know that eating people is wrong and cutting off their heads is barbaric, discover in the lands they want to settle or to conquer barbarians who think that eating people is right and cutting off their heads heroic. Each practice differentiates civility from barbarity, but they have not always run in tandem as they do in modern cartoons. Cannibalism precedes decapitation as a source of imperial terror in ages of exploration, among Greeks and sixteenth-century Europeans, for Homer as for Montaigne. Among Romans and post-eighteenth-century Europeans, decapitation displaces cannibalism as empire becomes rationalized, its hierarchies clearly defined and empowered, its violence disciplined and othered.

Decapitation has not always served as a cultural marker separating the civilized from the barbarian, even in cultures confident of their situation at the apex of civilization. The Chinese, Japanese, and ancient Israelites found nothing "barbaric" or alien in their own common practice of striking off heads. Nor does it begin with the Greeks. "Barbarous," designating non-Greek-speaking foreigners and their meaningless babble, requires a practice construable as foreign, differentiable from one's own, and supposes a desire to eliminate or restrict the practice.

For the Chinese of the era of the Roman republic, decapitation was an ordinary part of aggressive jurisprudence: "The law officers pursued and beheaded him [Lao Ai] at Hao chih, then his clan was destroyed."[10] Heads were occasionally preserved and used as drinking cups, signifying not reverence, but satisfied anger: "Because of the deep grudge he bore Lord Zhi, Lord Xiang lacquered his skull and used it as a wine vessel."[11]

Decapitation with a saw, as torture, was differentiated from decapitation with a sword, an honorable death, but both torture and execution were legitimate aspects of the legal system.

Few cultures have been more intent on the distinction between empathic courtly elegance and barbarism than Japan engaged in the civil wars recorded in the thirteenth-century epic *Tale of the Heike.*[12] Nor does any other great work take off so many heads so many different ways. What defines the barbarian, however, is not taking off a head but rusticity. So the vulgar, crude Yoshinaka slurps from big rice bowls, puns rudely on visitors' names, and descends the wrong way from an oxcart. Rudeness, inelegance, and failures of etiquette make the barbarian. Cutting off heads belongs to the warrior. Courtly, playing the flute, writing poems, weeping at the beauty of a Chinese chant, he takes no particular notice of the heads coming toward him, carried by allies returning from battle.

Before battle, warriors challenge one another to "take off my head and show it," and they do, lofting the head on a lance and announcing the names of the dead warrior and the warrior who killed him. "Holding [the head] high on the point of a sword Ishida shouted loudly, 'Kiso Yoshinaka, known through the length and breadth of Nippon as the "Demon Warrior," has been killed by Miura-no-Ishida Jiro Tamehisa.'"[13] Fighting Buddhist monks hang heads around the pond on their monastery walls; a loyal retainer severs his master's head to hide it from the enemy. A nurse drowns herself with the severed head of her seven-year-old charge, and a lowly middle-class warrior weeps over a head he takes. Nor are onlookers indifferent to the terrible pathos of heads paraded through the city, a cruelty forced on an unwilling emperor.

The principal bearers of pathos are women, hiding their faces in their sleeves as they identify a husband or son by his severed head, and the people, pitying the lofty aristocrats whose heads are carried through the city. Properly confined to the camp, severed heads figure a difference between warrior and court or city. Death pollutes, and it is inappropriate, all agree, to send heads to the palace.[14] Thematizing the simultaneity of heroic force and empathetic rupture, the tale aestheticizes, ritualizes, and sympathizes with the severed head. No text better reveals what is at stake in a world of war, any world where violence is value and glory is currency.

The ancient Israelites might have been expected to designate taking heads as terrifying, alien, and Assyrian, but they do not. The young lions, their sharp bows, their rapid chariots horrify, but their practice of piling up heads (chap. 1, fig. 1.1) escapes notice, though not imitation. Lacking any aversion to head-taking (or massacre or genocide) when it serves the Lord, the biblical record supplies an Assyrian imitator in Jehu, who demands the individual heads of Ahab's seventy sons and sets them in baskets before the gates of Jerusalem (2 Kings 10:6–11). Named among tributary princes and portrayed bowing on the Black Obelisk of Shalmaneser III (ruler of Assyria 858–824 B.C.E.), "Jehu, son of Omri" is the only king of Israel for whom such an extra-biblical record exists, preceding by several centuries the tallied heads at Nineveh on Ashurbanipal's palace wall.[15] Unlike that careful, bureaucratic documenting of heads and quivers, Jehu's seems to have been a one-time display to secure the succession. By the time 2 Chronicles retells Israel's history, there seems less enthusiasm for an action that remains un-condemned. Manners changing, the heads simply disappear (2 Chronicles 19:2–3, 22:8–10).

Later Talmudic commentary remarks on the number of Ahab's sons, but not on what was done with their heads. Silence is not praise and perhaps suggests reservations about decapitating children. Less reservedly, the Protestant editors of the Oxford Study Bible deprive Ahab of his fertility, making his sons "not literally sons of Ahab [but] leading members of the royal family" and assure their readers that Jehu had to do it: "The whole dynasty of Israel and its Judean allies had to be removed or else the religious issue would not be settled." [16] In their eagerness to justify Jehu's baskets of heads, the Christian editors forget that Josiah's reforms (ca. 620 B.C.E.) and the Exile settled the religious issue, not Jehu's massacre.

Elsewhere, the Bible celebrates decapitation. The two greatest heroes, male and female, of the Jewish tradition flaunt trophy heads taken from the infidel. David and Judith bring home, dripping blood, the heads of Goliath and Holofernes. The significant oppositions are between the faithful and the infidel, the circumcised and the uncircumcised, the chosen and the outcast, and not the civilized and the barbarian as takers of heads.

The Greeks seem at first to be a harder case. They give us the term "barbarian," and they emblematize horror in the gorgoneion, the severed head of Medusa taken up and affixed to Zeus's shield or Athena's aegis. Herodotus notes, with displeasure, the head-taking habits of many peoples: the Issedonians who make cups of their fathers' heads, "but otherwise practice justice"; the Scythians who gain shares of battle loot for bringing heads to the king and who turn enemy kinsmen's heads into cups; the Tauri who protect their houses with heads on poles and seem especially warlike, an implicit antithesis to the settled people of the *polis*.

Cyrus the Persian, decapitated, his head dunked in a skin of human blood by Tomyris, queen of the Massagetae, served Rubens (1577–1640) to figure the civilized male undone by the barbaric female. Andrea del Castagno was less censorious: his fresco of *Uomini famosi* (ca. 1450, Villa Carducci at Legnaia) figured Tomyris with Judith and Esther as a female worthy who saved her nation.[17]

In Herodotus, the head-dunking episode is justified by the death of Tomyris's son and trumped by Massagetaen cannibalism and glorious horse sacrifice. Herodotus recognizes a symbolic, participatory component in Massagetaen cannibalism: they eat the old, who are considered fortunate to die by sacrifice rather than by disease.

The lowest of peoples remain the Androphagi, the man-eaters: savage, without justice, without laws, without symbolism. Unlike other peoples who consume human flesh as an aspect of sacrifice, the Androphagi are mere cannibals, man eaters.[18] As Greek scholars have long recognized, without observing the implications for decapitation, the Greeks defined as the ultimate barbarian not the head-taker, but the cannibal.[19]

Head-taking occurred naturally in battle and was privileged, as in Japan, as heroic. In "Masking Medusa" we saw Odysseus striking off a climactic head in the *Odyssey* while heroes in the *Iliad* resisted the display of their friends' heads and attempted to display their enemies'. Although neither performs it, Achilles and Hector equally desire heads.[20] The Gorgon head, ornamenting houses and fabrics, adorns and protects civility, rather than opposing it.

In Hesiod's *Works and Days*, "Man is the creature that does not eat its fellows."[21] The complete Other encountered by Odysseus, the definitive barbarian, is the cannibal Cyclops. He eats raw food, does not till, and practices no justice. Like the Laestrygonians, Polyphemus, child of a god, inverts the laws of hospitality. Instead of feeding his guests, he feeds on them. Moreover, his lands are suitable for colonies. Homer doubles cannibal encounters, Polyphemus and the Laestrygonians, multiplied by man-eating monsters such as Scylla and man-transforming witches such as Circe. Like early modern explorers in America, the Greeks feared being swallowed up more than losing their heads.

To be ingested by and to disappear within the other, dissolving the boundaries of self and the body: that terrified. Bruno Snell observed that Homer has no word for "mind" or "soul," as a site localizing thought and feeling.[22] In Homer, thinking and feeling are not centered in the head, but dispersed through other parts, including heart and lungs. So too the body is the limbs, *soma* only the corpse. Terror of cannibalism recognizes that dispersal, proposing a monstrous Other, *rakshi,* cyclops, or American, who gobbles up the self with no leftovers in the ultimate *carnivale*: farewell, meat.[23] (In *A Modest Proposal* [1729] promoting enlightened cannibalism, Swift alleges an American source for his project.) To horrified Greek eyes, cannibalism lacks symbolic significance, annihilates heroic identity, and assimilates an individuated but un-localized self-throughout-the-body to another, monstrous body. Cannibals, like the wilderness, swallow up identity without a trace.

To find a clear link between barbarism and decapitation, one must go to Rome, where Conrad found modeled his contempt for cannibalism and antagonism to the displayed head. Seeing themselves as Conrad represents them, Romans developed an imperial ideology that privileged Ciceronian *humanitas* and propagated peace, not war (albeit by war). When Romans represented heads on poles as barbaric, however, they represented themselves as suffering display. Condemning a practice as barbaric not only justifies dominating or extirpating the perpetrator, but also argues against using the practice oneself. The school poet and poet of empire, Vergil, encoded those attitudes for the rest of western civilization, for as long as boys learning Latin would read him.

Dismissing cannibalism as no threat, the *Aeneid* links decapitation with indigenes, monsters, and losers. While severing heads is a recognized tactic in raids, those who collect and spike known heads deserve displacement. Celtic head-display, identified as monstrous, is linked to Aeneas's indigenous Rutulian foes. Hercules is celebrated as the hero who destroyed the head-displaying monster while Trojan-Roman heroes suffer their heads displayed to their fellows. Vergil points to both the Celts and the most recent civil wars, between Caesar and Pompey and between Octavian and Antony.

Despatching cannibalism, Aeneas revisits the blinded Polyphemus. Saving an Ithacan abandoned by Ulysses (Aeneas always takes better care of his people), he loses no men to the bone-crunching, blood-swilling, gut-spilling monster (*Aeneid,* III, 613–83). No longer a serious danger, giant cannibals make an intriguing spectacle, grand and pathetic. What threatens Aeneas is not disappearance into the other, but defeat in which the head identifies the loser.

Like Marlow in Africa, Aeneas in Italy goes upriver to find an ally and discovers a monster. For Aeneas, monster and ally are not the same, and Hercules, prefiguring Aeneas, has already liberated the land and its people. King Evander and his countrymen once suffered the monster Cacus, not Kurtz, who fixed to his doorposts the "pale faces of men": "Fixed to his proud doors / the pale faces of men hung suspended in bitter gore" ("foribusque adfixa superbis / ora virum tristi pendebant pallida tabo" [VIII, 196–97]). Dryden adds the quarters, visible in seventeenth-century England:

> The monster Cacus, more than half a beast,
> This hold, impervious to the sun, possess'd.
> The pavement ever foul with human gore;
> Heads, and their mangled members, hung the door.
> (VIII, 258–61)

As Aeneas learns this story upriver, back in the Trojan camp ("simul"), the loving friends Nisus and Euryalus undertake a nocturnal expedition against the Rutulians. Slashing the heads off sleeping Rutulians, blood soaking his garments and the ground, Euryalus slips into the familiar, self-alienated, frenzied Roman killing lust, *caede atque cupidine*. Nisus and Euryalus abandon the severed heads, Roman style, for other plunder (IX, 314–66), but they are killed making their escape. Turnus's irritated people put their heads on poles, facing Aeneas's camp, and parade them.

Turning themselves into indigenous monsters, Cacus *redivivus*, the Rutulians reenact Cacus's display of heads, now the well-known, beloved heads of Nisus and Euryalus: "On uplifted spears, oh wretched sight, / they transfix the heads, the very heads, and loudly shouting follow / Euryalus and Nisus" ("quin ipsa arrectis [visu miserabile] in hastis / praefigunt capita et multo clamore sequuntur / Euryali et Nisi" [IX, 465–67]). One of Vergil's rare uncompleted lines, the line ends at "Nisi." No words follow the naming.

If the Rutulians perhaps resemble a triumphing legion, Vergil's words closing the scene echo precisely his description of Cacus's doors. "Gore" (*tabo*) ends the line; the "faces of men" (*ora virum*) echo their fixity (*adfixa* and *praefixa*). Pale under Cacus, *pallida*, they go black, *atroque* (*ater*) under the Rutulians. "Black" perhaps approximates the momentary blindness shock produces as the Trojans see their friends:

> The hardy sons of Aeneas set their opposing line on the ramparts'
> left side

(for the right the river girds), hold the broad trenches, and on the
   high towers
stand grieving; moved at once by the faces of men transfixed,
too well-known, too wretched, and dripping black gore.

Aeneadae duri murorum in parte sinistra
opposuere aciem (nam dextera cingitur amni)
ingentisque tenent fossas et turribus altis
stant maesti; simul ora virum praefixa movebant,
nota nimis miseris atroque fluentia tabo.
(IX, 468–72)

In Dryden, Turnus makes himself responsible:

This done—to give new terror to his foes,
The heads of Nisus and his friend he shows,
Rais'd high on pointed spears—a ghastly sight:
Loud peals of shouts ensue, and barbarous delight.
Meantime the Trojans run, where danger calls;
They line their trenches, and they man their walls.
In front extended to the left they stood;
Safe was the right, surrounded by the flood.
But, casting from their tow'rs a frightful view,
They saw the faces, which too well they knew,
Tho' then disguis'd in death, and smear'd all o'er
With filth obscene, and dropping putrid gore.
(IX, 618–29)

Inside their camp, momentarily secure, the Trojans look in grief and horror at known heads both fixed and moving. Word by word, the passage recalls Cacus. Repeated at the end of the line, "tabo" means the rotting matter of the still moist heads, but "tabum" is also a pestilence, physical or moral.

To conquer the Rutulians, as Aeneas must, is to liberate the land from atrocity, specifically the atrocity that displays the severed head as a mark of its power, a sign of its *gloria*.[24] Aeneas, like Hercules, will free the land from such signs by conquest. Whatever their claims from possession or prescription, however indigenous they may be, those who make such monstrous, uncanny signs merit displacement and defeat.

The imperial and pro-Augustan political implications of the trope were clear in first-century Rome. In their imperial expansion into Gaul and Britain, the Romans had encountered the Celtic head cult, now known principally from archeological remains, associated with wells and water spirits. Cacus, with his heads fixed to the doorposts, reproduces the lintels carved with heads or containing niches for embalmed heads found at various Salian settlements throughout Provence, the Roman province.[25] Without mentioning heads, Livy calls Cacus's cave "uncanny," a "loco infesto." Cacus's three heads, mentioned by Ovid though not by Vergil, reproduce Celtic images of three-faced gods.[26] The Celtic practice, whatever its meanings to Celts, figured as opposition to Rome, and on occasion Romans suffered directly from it. Nor did the Romans succeed in extirpating practices associated with the Celtic cult in areas they dominated.[27] In Vergil, Cacus is an archaic figure, long subdued, like the area where the Salian head cult had flourished; but he remains a powerful memory, an indigenous practice to be rejected and repressed, evidence of cultural incommensurability.

If Cacus was no longer a threat, the Rutulians' actions evoked more recent political events among their Roman descendants. The display of well-known heads to an enclosed, fortified camp duplicates Caesar's circling the Pompeian camp at Munda with the heads of his dead son-in-law's supporters. "Son-in-law" is the relation Aeneas aspires to among the Rutulians, and Anchises's anguished cry to Caesar and Pompey, yet unborn, is directed to Caesar, his own blood: "Nor, my boys, nor make such warfare familiar to your souls . . . throw the sword from your hand, my own blood" (ne, pueri, ne tanta animis adsuescite bella . . . proice tela manu, sanguis meus [VI, 832, 835]). Anchises and his readers know that Pompey's head will be handed over to Caesar, after Caesar visits his ancestral haunts at Troy.[28] Recognizing the passage's political immediacy, Dryden applied Anchises' cry to the contest between James II and William of Orange, "his daughter's husband," in 1688–89, and introduced the non-Vergilian notion of a "lawless claim":

> His daughter's husband in the plain attends:
> His daughter's husband arms his eastern friends. . . .
> And thou, the first, lay down thy lawless claim.
> (VI, 1141–45)

Allegorically, the episode also justifies Marc Antony's displacement by Octavian. An Aeneas who chose to stay with Dido, Antony had been destroyed with Cleopatra only a decade earlier at Actium (31 B.C.E.) If the Rutulian display of Trojan heads to Trojans justifies Turnus's displacement by *pius* Aeneas, what did Marc Antony deserve, who had displayed Cicero's well-known Roman head to Romans? In Egypt, Cleopatra's brother had presented Pompey's head to Caesar. Caesar wept: he knew the correct rhetorical demeanor. Like Turnus's *gloria,* Antony's associated him with exerting power over severed heads, a practice Vergil's narrative links to losers.

Cannibalism is the fear of the explorer, decapitation of the empire builder. The explorer disappears into the wilderness, swallowed up, his home, identity, self, being, lost. Loss of self also threatens the empire builder, but the identity threatened is not his being, but his place at the top of a hierarchy, ruling over the strange others he has encountered. Power, control, position: none disappears, but all shift to another head. Successful imperial expansion on the Roman model dominates, subordinates, and stays rather than grabs and goes (the Homeric model) or settles an autonomous colony (the Greek way). It removes indigenous authority and replaces it with its own, in person or through native nominees. Such imperialists preserve the social, legal, religious structures that precede them: the social "body" of the people remains intact, only the head—the lordship—changes.

Between the Vergilian and the nineteenth-century imperial tropes of the head, however, both the decapitated and the decapitator have turned into another, usually darker race, more primitive and more dangerous. Vergil's heroes remain decapitators, on the Homeric model. Both Aeneas and Turnus can take off heads with a single blow. Turnus does so first, with more élan, the helmeted head spinning away (IX, 769–71). Aeneas's exploit figures as retaliation and focuses on the body. The head still pleading, Aeneas spurns the trunk: Aeneas "Stands o'er the prostrate wretch, and, as he lay, / Vain tales inventing, and prepar'd to pray, / Mows off his head: the trunk a moment stood, / Then sunk, and roll'd along the sand in blood" (Dryden, X, 773–76; X, 554–55: tum caput orantis nequiquam et multa parantis / dicere deturbat terrae truncumque tepentem).

Vergil's severed heads belong to ancestral heroes who loved each other and decapitated some (also ancestral) Rutulians before they were in turn decapitated and displayed. Mourned by grieving men, they are immortalized as a named pair, linked in death as in life. Vergil's heads have names; Conrad's do not. Vergil's heads are the same color he is; Conrad's are not. Vergil's heads are same, self; Conrad's are other. Vergil's decapitators engage in an equal contest, which one must win. Conrad's white decapitator discloses a contradiction in the imperial project that is usually concealed by the darkness of the nineteenth-century decapitator.

The differences have two obvious sources: the interracial, intercultural context of European imperialism from the fifteenth century on, and the sentimental othering of violence from the late seventeenth century, displaced onto history and the colonies by the late eighteenth century. Unlike the Romans, eighteenth-century Europeans succeeded in diminishing visible violence within their societies.[29] Although the trope will undergo considerable development, the displacement of decapitator and decapitated onto natives appears already fully formed in Daniel Defoe's *Robinson Crusoe* (1719), the classic text of individualist imperialism. Defoe's Protestant, bourgeois hero reenacts the displacement of cannibalism as terror, and he assumes sovereignty through a decapitation that he himself does not perform. Instead, one savage decapitates another.[30]

Unlike Aeneas and Marlow, the solitary Crusoe genuinely fears cannibals. Shipwrecked on a deserted island in the Caribbean, Crusoe one day sees a single footprint in the sand on the beach. Terrified by the human sign he has longed for, he finds the shore littered with skulls, hands, feet, remains of grisly feasting. Obsessed with ghastly cookery, fascinated by human self-consumption, Crusoe lurks until one sacrificial savage escapes. Crusoe saves the cannibal-victim with a shot from his piece. The saved savage then takes off another savage's head with Crusoe's sword. The technique used is German. Germany was the home of England's new king George I, whose accession had recently been celebrated with numerous decollations:

> I presented my other Piece at the Man, as if I would shoot him, upon this my Savage, *for so I call him now*, made a Motion to me to lend him my sword, which hung naked in a Belt by my side; so I did: he no sooner had it, but he runs to his Enemy, and at one blow cut off his Head as cleaverly, no Executioner in *Germany*, could have done it sooner or better; which I thought very strange, for one who I had reason to believe never saw a Sword in his life before, except their own Wooden Swords; however it seems, as I learn'd afterwards, they make their Wooden Swords so sharp, so heavy, and the Wood is so hard, that they will cut

off Heads even with them, ay and Arms, and that at one blow too; when he had done this, he comes laughing to me in Sign of Triumph, and brought me the Sword again, and with abundance of Gestures which I did not understand, laid it down with the Head of the Savage, that he had kill'd just before me.[31]

Friday, soon to be named, presents Crusoe with a trophy head in sign of fealty and so becomes "my Savage."

Crusoe does not understand all of Friday's gestures, but he understands the principal one. He understands the head being laid at his feet. The next day, Friday proposes they eat the body, but Crusoe declines. The terror aroused by the single footprint, the horror of cannibalism, is past. Crusoe now safely declines assimilation with savages, whether by eating or being eaten. Crusoe emerges from the terror of cannibal incorporation through distanced modern technologies of lethality, the gun, and the dominance signaled by decollation. The "sovereign" is independent of violence while, in the crucial innovation, both the perpetrator and the victim are savages of another color.

For nineteenth-century imperial writers, the common savagery of perpetrator and victim—like racism itself—was crucial to coping with the ideological contradictions of an imperial project in a democratizing age. At home in Europe, popular participation had become fundamental to legitimate rule, yet abroad indigenous populations were excluded from participation in their own governance. Domestic ideology affirmed the rights of man and broached those of woman, grounded sovereignty in consent, and decried violence as savagery. How then could dominion over unwilling others be justified? The reason must be in them, their deficiency and need, their color and racial physiology.[32] Imperial ideology sustained itself by deploying precisely the violence it decried, in the form it most feared—it cut off heads metaphorically, symbolically (and often literally) —while shifting responsibility for that violence onto the feared Other, who is also its victim, his head cut off. The native-native beheading occludes the imperial power that has already beheaded the native.

If imperial writers sometimes used decollated black heads as mirrors, reflecting the darker element in the self, questioning the justice of the imperial project, they were, unlike Vergil, careful not to cut off their own white heads. Had Conrad put white heads on Kurtz's fence, those heads would have turned into atrocity propaganda, inviting reprisals, undoing Conrad's imperialist critique and demonstrating yet again the necessity of the civilizing mission. No matter whose heads they are, beheadings in the colonies argue for imperialism as a sign of cultural difference. This tradition post-colonial writers inherit, and rewrite. Deftly, Africans reweave a topos that originates as terror of them.

Post-Colonial Heads

> If it were you or I how in deep grief you or I would be?
> —Amos Tutuola, *Simbi and the Satyr of the Dark Jungle*, 82.

For the African writer, the imperial conflict between cultures becomes an internal conflict within a culture over the direction of its future and the evaluation of its past. When he condemned *Heart of Darkness* for repudiating human kinship with Africa and representing Africans as subhuman, infantile (speechless) primitives, Chinua Achebe did not rebuke Conrad for his house ringed with African heads or his jesting with cannibalism.[33] Traditional Africans took heads as trophies in war, as sacrifice (life, a head to preserve a head), and as police.[34] Colonialism de-legitimated cannibalism and the trophy head as practice, and colonial subjects learned to write through imperial writers who barbarized both those who took heads and those whose heads were taken.

The civilizing mission had an impact but created a quandary. To repudiate the heads taken by the ancestors was to adopt the empire's view of one's ancestors' barbarity. To ignore the heads was to obliterate the past and an aspect of cultural identity. To revive the practice, as Mishima dreamed, or to affirm the tradition as positive was to renounce modern individuality and to identify with the warrior/decapitator against the decapitated/colonized. To retort the practice onto Europeans, as Zakes Mda does, is just, but evades the question of what one makes of one's own heads, taken and takers.[35] Given decapitation as a cultural marker, dividing the civilized from the barbarians, is it possible for an African writer, enlisted by literacy on the side of the civilized, to address ancestral decapitations without mimicry, without turning himself into a parody of Europe or a parody of Europe's imaginary Africa?

Theoretically difficult, the problem dissolved at the touch of three Nigerian writers of different ethnicities and varied Christian backgrounds: Amos Tutuola (1920–97), Chinua Achebe (1930–), and Ben Okri (1959–). Before Nigeria achieved political independence in 1960,

Tutuola's and Achebe's early novels, published in the 1950s, had established a literary independence that included addressing precisely the problem of human sacrifice and the head as the warrior's trophy. Recycling and reinventing Yoruba tale-telling in English, setting the "Methodist Church of the Bush of Ghosts" in a spirit-landscape unfamiliar to European Christianity, Tutuola took up the desirability of commuting human sacrifice not as an argument between cultures (Europe and Africa) but as a difference of custom within a culture, between villages. In the astonishing and unappreciated parable *Simbi and the Satyr of the Dark Jungle* (1955), Tutuola's female protagonist encounters decapitation, human sacrifice, and cannibalism not as terrifyingly sublime, achingly pathetic, or titillatingly remote, but as intensely disagreeable experiences that she would rather do without. Although no novel appears less to do so, *Simbi* performs as folklore the regulatory function of the civility/barbarity binary. Ignoring "civility's" claims to superior knowledge, power, architecture, humanity, and military discipline, the fiction adopts an insider's perspective, not the dominant warrior, but the pretty girl from another village where they do things differently (and much better). She does not represent a more powerful culture intent on improving and changing the primitive practices she encounters, but an alternative within a culture, so that customs may be criticized and vigorously opposed without participation in the civility/barbarity binary.

The binary Tutuola declines, Chinua Achebe shows imposed. His father a Christian missionary, his ethnicity Igbo (Ibo), Achebe wrote the classic trilogy of a culture destroyed and transformed, beginning with *Things Fall Apart* (1959; *No Longer at Ease*, 1960; *Arrow of God*, 1964, revised 1974). An account of traditional Igbo culture interrupted by English missionaries and bureaucrats, *Things Fall Apart* uses heads not only to figure the difference between traditional culture and the modern reader, but also to reenact the moment when the different way of seeing that separates the reader (and the writer) from traditional culture comes into being. The civility/barbarity binary descends along the swing of a machete, focusing rupture. The warrior's trophy turns into modern criminality. With its fundamental shift in point of view, Achebe's is perhaps the single most important severed head in literature.

Ben Okri, a generation younger, freed by Achebe and Tutuola from the requirement that he address the binary's imperialist connotations, reimagines ancestral head-taking as present nightmare in *Stars of the New Curfew* (1988). Remotely Urhobo, unmistakably postmodern, his parents' house book-filled and literary, Okri adapts Yoruba myths he has learned from books, including Tutuola's. Writing "a kind of realism, but a realism with many more dimensions," he engages a post-independence Nigeria that has lived a history many of its participants would rather not believe in.[36] In his work, the boundaries of the civility/barbarity binary etched by Achebe dissolve, and terror seeps back. The perspective is no longer that of the warrior or the folkloric heroine, but a threatened, modern civilian, less powerful than the one who lost his head when things fell apart.

Perhaps no author in English appears less didactic than Amos Tutuola or argues more subtly against the range of traditional ritual practices that European imperialism conflates as "barbaric." Rather than promoting a superior civility to control and extirpate ritual practices, Tutuola shifts the subject position from the powerful to the powerless. Where the ideology of civility seeks to replace with its own power the warrior or king whose ideology sustains and supports sacrificial violence, Tutuola represents those who suffer the sacrifices: the kidnapped, the enslaved, the traded, the beheaded, and the mothers whose children are sacrificed. That Tutuola appears altogether innocent of such designs is a triumph of genre, of folklore over the realistic novel, of folk speech over standard English, of far too many severed heads.[37]

In *Simbi and the Satyr of the Dark Jungle,* Tutuola blithely lets heads fly. By European standards, everything he does with heads is wrong. He puts them in the wrong place in the narrative, where they lack the meanings they should have. He makes his decapitator the wrong gender, and she cuts off heads for reasons inappropriate to her sex, that is, for her own sake, not for his love or God's. There are too many heads about, and not one is used to a proper dramatic effect. Unlike Achebe's parsimonious and careful disposition of heads, Tutuola wastes precious heads. So too his syntax and his episodes sprout too many heads, head off in too many different directions. With its energetic "'WRONG ENGLISH' etc.," the text seems disorderly, random, abundant but defective in structure. Excessive, it lacks the rational, Aristotelian form that Achebe or Okri provides and the controlling head emblematizes. The structure puzzles, because Tutuola has in his sights more than decapitation's imperial transfer of power. Through the marginal hero characteristic of folklore, more marginal still as heroine, he challenges ritual practices extending from elaborate sacrifices that preserve the king's life, through erratic police, to infant sacrifice, the last surrounded by an unimaginable darkness figured as "cannibalism."

Raised by a rich mother, lacking for nothing, the village's best singer and most beautiful girl, Simbi one day loses her two best friends to a kidnapper. Miserable, tiring of her mother's wealth, she decides to learn "about the poverties and the punishments," Siddhartha's story. Although her mother and others assure her the desire is ill-advised, she persists, consulting the soothsayer, who advises a complex sequence of sacrifices, a cock to her head "to safe [*sic*] your life throughout your journey and to help you to return to your mother," as well as a dog, a pigeon, kola nuts, a broken pot, and palm oil.[38] Placing the sacrifice at a junction two miles from the village where three roads meet, Simbi is seized by Dogo the kidnapper, sold into slavery, and plunged into circumstances that could not be worse. Beaten, starved, pressed down by a "myrmidon" sitting on her head in "the town where nobody sings," she sings, certain she is about to die. When her master dies instead, the townspeople nail her in a coffin to carry his provisions along heaven road and throw the coffin into the river. From miserable life, she passes to certain death in the first three chapters, with nine more to go. What could be worse than slavery followed by burial alive? Perhaps to be saved from the water (like Moses), to find her friends again, and then to be condemned to beheading by a king who sacrifices slaves to his head.

In the aptly named Sinner's Town, the king sacrifices two thousand slaves a year to his head, to preserve his life. Waiting in line for beheading with her friends, Simbi listens to the song of the girl to be beheaded next. Her body will become a jug, pouring blood onto the gods and the king's head: "And when she was singing the song nearly to its end the king beheaded her and the chiefs and the prominent people took her body from the ground, they poured the blood of her neck onto the heads of the gods and onto the king's head as well" (37).[39] Simbi seizes the king's sword, cuts off his head and several others, and flees with her friends and the sword. By all western rules, including folkloric ones, such an adventure should be the climax of Simbi's story. Having beheaded the beheading king, she should return in triumph, with the sword, the order of the world transformed for the better.

Not here. This dramatic adventure occurs at the beginning, not the end. Nor is it the only beheading episode; beheading serves not only ritual, sacrificial purposes, but also a police that tends to be disturbingly erratic. In the town of Multicolored People, the bell ringer dreads the king's summons: "Neither to behead him or to send him to somewhere, he never knew which was which" (59). Betrayed by a hunter whose life she saved, Simbi saves her own life by demanding his head and mixing its blood with a juju powder to bring the king's daughter back to life (63).[40] Elsewhere, she boasts of beheading the king and some chiefs of the Sinner's town, and her act remains an achievement of renown, but along the way she somehow loses the sword (77, 132). Occurring in villages and as part of a well-defined social or ritual structure, beheadings have multiple purposes: they preserve the chief's life, punish injustice, save and restore life as sacrifice, terrify ordinary folk at the chief's prerogative, and thrill ordinary folk when one of them appropriates the chief's power.

On the continuum of beheadings, only Simbi's beheading of the king of Sinner's Town is unambiguously positive. Simbi knows that sacrifice must be displaced. Only pagans and sinners sacrifice slaves instead of fowls and animals (31). When Simbi procures a beheading, her agency is removed and ironic justice emphasized: "The hunter wanted the king to kill Simbi, but he died instead" (65). Among Simbi's punishments, she becomes more complicit in human sacrifice, in the village within the dark jungle.

Beyond the villages where beheadings occur, along the path of Death, is the dark jungle, abode of the satyr, the cannibal. On his apron: "More than one thousand heads of birds were stuck to all over it [*sic*]." His huge, unfed mouth is covered with spiders' webs. His beard is so long he uses it as a broom. He has been there for two thousand years, and "[T]his Satyr was a pessimist, he was impatient and ill-tempered, impenitent and noxious creature" (74). He also intends to eat Simbi and her friends, and it is he, not the beheading king, who is the antagonist of the title. Between bouts with this persistent satyr, Simbi becomes the wife of a woodcutter and loses her child to infant sacrifice, forced to pound her baby with soap to expel death from the town.

The woodcutter's village is contiguous with the land of poverty, where fruits turn to stones and clothes to dust. The juxtaposition suggests that infant sacrifice occurs where desperation is closest. "Having seen this bad habit, she was feeling to go away from this town," and does so when her second baby is sacrificed with others to keep away the locusts (96). The sacrifices implicating Simbi cannot be resisted because they are motivated not by the chiefs' narcissism, that is, individualistically, but by the need to defend the life of the community as a whole. Although Simbi's interests as a mother oppose the sacrifice of her children, her interests are bound up in the life of the town. What is most precious, but also least individuated, is sacrificed in a despair beyond the terrors of cannibalism.

With the help of an old woman and her gift of three gods, Simbi returns triumphantly home, with the girlfriend who gave the advice that enabled her to kill the satyr of the dark jungle. Sneaked back through Sinner's Town in body bags, Simbi and Rali encounter Dogo the kidnapper with three other girls on the outskirts of their village. Beaten by Simbi, he promises no longer to kidnap from her village. She then returns to her mother with a moral not heard since Milton's Adam, who said when it was much too late, "To obey is best" (*Paradise Lost,* XII, 561). In a lesson profoundly repugnant to modern western (and feminist) ideology, Simbi affirms that her mother was right all along and she should have obeyed her and stayed home.[41] "Having rested for some days, she was going from house, [*sic*] to house she was warning all the children that it was a great mistake to a girl who did not obey her parents." Not only does she advise the other children that obedience is best, but she also *tells her mother so*: "Hah, my mother, I shall not disobey you again!" Her mother believes her, and has the novel's last word, "Happy night rest, my daughter" (136).[42]

In Simbi's world, the most powerful adversarial figures are male—the kidnapper, the hunter who is a liar, the satyr of the dark jungle, kings and chiefs—and the female protagonist returns happily to her wealthy mother, free of a marriage plot, assisted by an old woman, her gods, and her girlfriends. Such a pattern supposes a sex-segregated society in which women have considerable autonomy in spheres separate from men's, without horizontal integration. Power remains firmly in men's hands, and a male soothsayer directs her departure and safe return. Trade, however, in women's hands is an alternative source of wealth and status, and presumably the source of Simbi's mother's wealth. Alain Severac characterizes "the social function of woman" in Africa as "glamour girl and/or merchant princess."[43]

Although women's status varies from group to group, Nigeria's Yoruba and Igbo peoples are especially conspicuous for their trading women's groups and women's economic power, such that rich Igbo women may have "wives," and men boast of their mother's wealth.[44] The married woman has her own farm, from which she feeds herself, her children, her husband, in "economic, social, and personal independence."[45] Simbi's attachment to her baby, like her mother's to her, requires little masculine participation. Enabling autonomy, activity, independence, and safety for women, this sexually segregated society finds its happy ending in a return to mother, not in a romance. Yet the heroine's distance from power also prevents the decapitations she performs from fulfilling their modern role: they do not change everything.

The problems with Tutuola's beheadings should be clear: a beautiful, singing woman decapitates several men (not just one), without sexual implications. The decapitation occurs at the beginning, not the ending of the narrative, so it begins things, rather than ends them. The decapitation is not singular and definitive, but multiple and dramatic. It is not worked (bled) for emotional effect. No climactic pattern emerges from the sequencing of the decapitations, which have both police and sacrificial functions. Instead, decapitation is linked with other forms of human sacrifice that continue in spite of the heroine's success. The woodcutter's village in the center of the dark jungle continues to sacrifice infants; Simbi must be sneaked back through Sinner's Town; Dogo will continue to kidnap girls from other villages. In sum, lives are sacrificed, heads are lost, but without providing any culminating meaning, without symbolizing as they ought, without changing everything forever. The western reader stammers that such people place no value on human life, that is, the human head. That reader wants fixity, not mobility, unity, not multiplicity.

To imperial, western, progressive ideologies, Tutuola's narrative structure signals backwardness. Returning to the mother is in and of itself regressive (so Freudians would object). The character's failure to be significantly transformed marks a failure of ego formation and world mastery. In their turn, Marxists and Americans (materialist twins) would complain that such plotting aptly represents a folk society that goes nowhere, suffers much, and fails to progress. Neither controlling nor mastering nature, characters are not transformed and fail to dominate their worlds. They merely accommodate themselves or escape from particularly dangerous places to begin over again, no further along, in the episodic structure loathed by Aristotle. Such narratives reproduce cyclical societies rather than generating the transforming energy of progressive western societies. Such a critique supposes that "the transforming energy of progressive western societies" solves problems eternally (reality as a work of art with a single Aristotelian action), rather than solving some problems and generating others in cyclical and dialectical fashion. Structurally, linguistically, and stylistically, Tutuola's work proposes an alternative vision of reality.

Led by D. O. Fagunwa, who wrote in Yoruba and claimed Edmund Spenser as his literary ancestor, Tutuola invented new folklore from the stories, myths, warnings, and jokes of the ancestors, especially the grandmothers.[46] Although it is tempting to regard his work as "authentic" oral folktale, Tutuola synthesizes an eclectic mix of folkloric, classical, and biblical elements, deployed like trade goods in a bilingual Yoruba context. "Myrmidons," satyrs, gnomes, two-thousand-year-old jungles, and "woes" abut Ife divination and an old woman's gift of three gods, thunder, famine, and iron. "These three gods are the prizes of your faith," she says, as if they were the Sunday School Trinity. Yet Tutuola's world is so bizarre that such elements from ours may well be overlooked.

His strangeness extends to his English, which ran afoul of the civility/barbarity binary. Tutuola's first Nigerian critics charged that his style fed western views of Africa as primitive, energetic, childlike. They disliked the effects admired by such readers as T. S. Eliot and Dylan Thomas, who found their old language renewed, freshened.[47]

Fluid, unpredictable, like his events, Tutuola's sentences take unexpected turns. They bifurcate, add another consideration, rethink a problem, and turn again, slowing—or tripping—the reader: "Alas! Simbi did not believe that a young girl like herself must not attempt to force herself to know of what her parents had warned her for, not to attempt to know." Simple, positive willfulness ("Simbi wanted to know what she wanted to know, regardless of what her parents said") is folded inside negations, making a triple "not." The seemingly artless, repetitive structure of the underlying English sentence ("Simbi did not believe that a young girl must not attempt . . . to know . . . what her parents had warned her . . . not to . . .") goes astray at two points. First, Simbi's desire to know becomes an "attempt *to force herself* to know" as if a power additional to her own desire or will were acting upon her from outside herself. Knowing is something she makes herself, unwillingly, do. Yet if "force" implies something acting on Simbi from outside, the trait is also internal, since, in the second deviation from standard syntax, her parents have "warned her *for*" it, that is, against something she is in the habit of doing. The erratic syntax insists that what is acting on/in Simbi is both inside and outside, regarded as inside Simbi by her parents, and outside her by Simbi. Finally, the artless sentence turns into a rhythmic warning: "not to attempt to know." Waylaid by extraneous phrases characteristic of Yoruba street-speech, for example, the intrusive "for," the syntax sends the sentence in several directions at once, suggesting a reality conceived as multiple or plural.

Simbi's world is dangerous. Heads are the life, but they are not secure. Babies are life, and they are sacrificed. Life itself passes into other forms and shapes, fluidly and unpredictably. As Wole Soyinka observes, "Life, present life, contains within it manifestations of the ancestral, the living and the unborn. All are vitally within the intimations and affectiveness of life, beyond mere abstract conceptualisation."[48] Adopting the subject position of a character threatened with decapitation and child sacrifice, the narrative engages an intracultural dialogue over this "bad habit," situating beheadings in Sinner's Town and infant sacrifice in the heart of darkness, where both are performed by the heroine. Cannibalism, entirely inhuman, belongs to monsters to be killed. Such actions do not occur in the security of Simbi's village. Although Tutuola co-opts the imperial civilizing claim, he sidesteps the warrior's point of view.

In *Things Fall Apart*, Chinua Achebe took up the problem Tutuola left open in the modern literary English Tutuola did not initially claim. Tackling the civility/barbarity binary directly, Achebe makes his hero the warrior who takes heads, and readers grieve for the beheader, not the beheaded, when the warrior takes his last head. Presenting traditional Igbo culture as normative, articulate, and eloquent, Achebe reweaves the heroic of Homer and Sophocles to welcome an Igbo warrior (Akhilleus, Oedipus, Okonkwo). He also impels modern literary critics, who may or may not notice what they are doing, to practice tribal forms of interpretation and divination. Recovering a subject position for the "primitive" tribal world destroyed by colonial "civility," Achebe mingles threads alien and familiar, from simple thematic elements to hermeneutic tactics.[49] In Conrad, dark, primitive, natural energies lie just out of reach: "forgotten and brutal instincts . . . gratified and monstrous passions . . . gleam of fires . . . throb of drums . . . drone of weird incantations" (67), "wild glances and savage movements" (60), "the thrilling thought of their humanity—like yours—the thought of your remote kinship with that wild and passionate uproar" (36–37). This thrilling Otherness Achebe shakes out, into new patterns.

Achebe gives the last words of his novel to a Kurtz who published, rather than perished. In a paragraph notable for its balance, fairness, and length, he introduces a not unsympathetic District Commissioner doing his best, struck by an incident that has just presented itself to him: "The story of this man who had killed a messenger and hanged himself would make interesting reading." It might be worth "a reasonable paragraph" in his projected book, named to close Achebe's novel: *The Pacification of the Primitive Tribes of the Lower Niger.* A world shrivels up at the touch of the civilizing European. No exploitative Belgian, but a hard-working Briton of the kind Conrad admired, far more interested in native cultures than Marlow, he chooses, lovingly and proudly, a title that discloses the poverty of his perspective, all that it misses, all that it takes away. Yet that loss is a condition of the existence of the text: the European is also Achebe's ancestor. Trading places, the District Commissioner has his "reasonable paragraph" in "[t]he story of this man" as the District Commissioner will never know it.

Unlike Tutuola's deliberate strangeness, Achebe naturalizes the strange, so that the geographically challenged American college student may reach the end of the novel with an insistent question, "Are these people black?" Within a marvelous African reality, lucid, recognizable, and strange, the fate of Achebe's protagonist, remote and heroic as Homer, describes a Sophoclean trajectory. A great man risen through his own efforts and personal initiative, Okonkwo is destroyed partly by aspects of his character that created his success, partly by an irrational order beyond his control. Owing both rise and fall to his determination, physical strength, and inflexibility, he has a speech defect that makes his fists more expressive than his words. In a society that prizes eloquence, he is deprived of the "safety of humans [which depends] on their integrity in the use of words."[50] Given the importance of oratory, skill in speech, to preliterate communities, his speech defect is a terrible and fateful wound. As his body brings ruin to him, so ruin is brought on him by historical forces stronger than he, British imperial power, bearing other gods, from outside his world. Outsiders intervene, not as gods from a machine, but as missionaries on bicycles.

The first and longest part of the novel traces Okonkwo's rise within the world of the nine villages until an accident—an exploding gun that kills a clansman—sends him into exile. The last two parts plot Okonkwo's exile and his return to a village invaded by missionaries, colonial administrators, and their opportunistic native hangers-on. Unplanned and natural, his and his community's destruction proceeds from an historic inevitability more iron-hearted and implacable than fate.

Within this resonant narrative structure, Achebe weaves the familiar and the strange, which shift with the reader, who may be African or European, Nigerian or other African, Igbo or other Nigerian. No uncontaminated traditional consciousness exists to read this English work, and it incorporates its most innocent—or ignorant—readers, Euro-Americans, in the European point of view that closes the book. The novel's opening juxtaposes elements as carefully as a cat steps:

> Okwonko was well known throughout the nine villages and even beyond. His fame rested on solid personal achievements. As a young man of eighteen he had brought honor to his village by throwing Amalinze the Cat. Amalinze was the great wrestler who for seven years was unbeaten, from Umuofia to Mbaino. He was called the Cat because his back would never touch the earth. It was this man that Okonkwo threw in a fight which the old men agreed was one of the fiercest since the founder of their town engaged a spirit of the wild for seven days and seven nights.

So Oedipus, who bears the famous name, might be introduced. Only the names disturb the American reader's sense of neighborhood until the ancestor appears, engaging "a spirit of the wild for seven days and seven nights." Wrestling is familiar, "spirit of the wild" alien, "seven days and seven nights" impossible for a wrestling match. Off balance, this becomes not the world we know, our real world. Yet "seven," repeated as the Bible repeats its numbers, yokes this alien story to familiar biblical myths that include Jacob's wrestling with an angel in the wild.

Rather than alluding to the Bible, however, Achebe juxtaposes two systems that catch at a single point. "Seven" signifies in Judeo-Christian and Igbo culture for the same cosmic reason. The moon's cycle is twenty-eight days; the Igbo week has four days, so seven weeks complete the lunar month. Seven days is almost two weeks. Some elements, requiring no translation, establish correspondences between cultures. Untranslatable elements insist on the incommensurability of cultures. Other elements resemble the Möbius strip—incommensurable, they turn over into correspondences, and back again. So the "seven" linking mythic African to mythic western traditions discloses how alien the biblical stories now are. Revealed in passing is an unmarked self-alienation within western culture.

Achebe also establishes a sly correspondence between tribal divination and literary criticism. Interpretive practices performed by critics on texts reproduce the insights afforded by shamans, sensitive to parallels and fragments of meaning. When Ekwefi's baby dies, the last in a long series of her infants' deaths, Okagbue, the medicine man, by questioning, elicits the insight "that the child had died on the same market-day as it had been born. . . . The neighbors and relations also saw the coincidence and said among themselves that it was very significant."[51] Few readers will not feel superior to the village's unscientific account of infant mortality, its ignorance of causes and their effects. Yet the village reads "natural" events as critics read literary events, intent on making meaning where there is suffering. Readers who find significance in repetitions, duplications, and parallels, the writer who puts them there, and the villagers consulting the medicine man, are using similar interpretive procedures for similar purposes—to make a heartbreaking sequence meaningful.

On the larger scale of the narrative's structure, critics attribute Okonkwo's doom to the sacrificial murder of Ikemefuna, a boy from another village given to the clan to compensate for a slain clanswoman. Ikemefuna lives for three years with Okonkwo, calls him father, and befriends his eldest son. Although the narrative proposes no causal link, most critics take the killing of Ikemefuna as the unpunished crime that dooms Okonkwo, rather than the punished accident (his gun explodes at a fête, killing another boy) for which he is exiled.[52] Adopting the tribal perspective as if they were reading Sophocles and urging "fate" as cause, critics point to Obierika's prediction of disaster in the name of the Earth. Okonkwo's friend Obierika tells him he should have stayed away: "What you have done will not please the Earth. It is the kind of action for which the goddess wipes out whole families." When Okonkwo challenges him with the Oracle's order, Obierika replies, "[I]f the Oracle said that my son should be killed I would neither dispute it nor be the one to do it." Yet when Okonkwo hangs himself, committing another "offense against the Earth," Obierika blames not the goddess or the Earth but the English District Commissioner (190–91). Making Ikemefuna's death the cause, the critic attests his faith in the powers of Earth and the goddess.

Achebe's next novel *No Longer at Ease* offers an alternate hermeneutic: Okonkwo's Christian son, like the literary critic, attributes Okonkwo's fate to the death of Ikemefuna, but his interpretation is biblical. When his father died, he thought of Ikemefuna, not the court messenger Okonkwo had just killed, and said to himself, "He who lives by the sword will perish by the sword." At the time, the narrator observes, others in the village thought it unwise to lift one's hand against a boy who called one "father."[53] Tribal, Christian, and literary: multiple systems of interpretation contend for the same mysterious conclusion. Although there is no narrative connection, Ikemefuna's death determines Okonkwo's.

Yet the fiction contains as well the secular, historical perspective that finds no "necessity" in Okonkwo's doom except that it happened. As Wole Soyinka observes, placing Achebe on the fault line between "true" African spirituality and secular social vision:

> [A]lthough the spiritual and the mysterious are never absent or invalidated—certainly the affective or responsive in the lives of the community is constantly used to reinforce this dimension of reality—yet the strongest arguments in favour of a divine factor . . . are subverted by . . . the preponderant claims of a secular wisdom.[54]

Authorizing "secular wisdom," Achebe plays systems of interpretation against and through each other, engaging his characters in frequent debate among themselves over custom and cultural difference. Tribal, Christian, and literary readings are incommensurable and simultaneous.

A corollary of such debates is that when imperialism enters to shatter this world, its effects are not entirely negative.[55] More eloquent than western characters, Achebe's characters share such values as hard work, ambition, social mobility. They value merit over ancestry, wish a talented daughter had been a boy, and accept a woman's leaving one husband for another she prefers. Yet Achebe also exposes intolerable cultural differences. Such practices as wife beating and intertribal warfare as social practice challenge recently minted western norms. Others challenge more ancient norms: the abandonment of twins, human sacrifice, head-taking in war.

Change brings advantages to some, disaster to others, as the balance of power within the community shifts seismically with the disruptive advent of Christian ideology, administrative order, and market forces. A mother who has repeatedly given birth to twins converts to Christianity: she will no longer have to abandon her babies to the bush. An entire class of inhabitants, the outcasts or *osu,* become visible for the first time. They have not existed for a successful son of the nine villages, or his reader.

From a statistical point of view, counting by surviving heads in the modern way, the villagers probably experience more gains than losses: twins live, *osu* are recognized, wars are prohibited, money circulates, men who could not prosper in traditional ways find new opportunities with the colonial master and administration. Such change is the stuff of imperial self-congratulation on the humanitarian progress of the civilizing mission. Yet while Achebe, the son of a Christian minister, product of a broken, remade world, specifies benefits, he makes his readers feel the losses, even over the single image that shows most decisively exile from the village: the severed head. In this irrevocable transformation, the severed African head moves from ritual to rupture, from African to modern meanings.

Achebe defers Okonkwo's heads until the second chapter when their taking is introduced as both natural and special: "Unlike his father [Okonkwo] could stand the look of blood. In Umuofia's latest war he was the first to bring home a human head. That was his fifth head; and he was not an old man yet. On great occasions such as the funeral of a village celebrity he drank his palm-wine from his first human head" (14). Drinking from a skull and calling that skull one's "first human head" are alienating images. The heads trip Firchow, who indexes "skull" but not "head," and triumphs over Achebe by observing that "his protagonist Okonkwo returned from battle with five human heads, from one of which he continued to drink on ceremonial occasions."[56] Achebe proposes several battles and five heads, not one battle with five heads taken. Although Christian Franks used skulls for similar purposes, we no longer recognize in their act our ancestors, though James Boswell did.[57]

Achebe recognizes the difficulty because he shares it. He gives squeamishness to Okonkwo's father, who could not "stand the look of blood," locating oppositional attitudes in Okonkwo's context. He sets the activity in wartime and emphasizes its role as a sign of vigor and prowess— "he was not an old man yet." Finally, the head is sanctified by its use— "great occasions," "funeral of a village celebrity." The respect due the occasion, the respect due the taker of the head, and the respect due the head reciprocally reinforce each other. The head is not made common by use or display. Nor is it a dismal *memento mori,* mocking men's hopes. Instead, as a head, not a skull, it sustains a continuing symbolic relationship between the living and the dead. The treasured head is present at the feast.

Yet instead of representing the ritual taking of a head in warfare, Achebe proposes the more painful sacrifice of the child hostage Ikemefuna. Having lived with Okonkwo's family for three years, not knowing he is to be killed for a murder committed by his clansmen, Ikemefuna is told he is going home. An elder warns Okonkwo to avoid the sacrifice, demanded at last by the Oracle. Yet Okonkwo goes along, walking behind the puzzled Ikemefuna, who begins to think of his almost forgotten mother and sisters and his favorite songs. He carries a pot of palm wine on his head. Okonkwo drops behind the men. A man raises his machete, "Okonkwo looked away. He heard the blow. The pot fell and broke in the sand." The metonymy is not the end; the sacrificer will not be an anonymous Other.

Ikemefuna runs toward Okonkwo crying out, "My father, they have killed me!" And Okonkwo acts: "Dazed with fear, Okonkwo drew his machete and cut him down. He was afraid of being thought weak" (59). Neither Okonkwo nor the reader sees what happens to Ikemefuna's head. It is concealed as the focus shifts to the executioner, who has killed his foster son, his own son's best friend. As Emeka Nwabueze observes, Okonkwo must kill Ikemefuna precisely because he has tried to avoid participating in the act. He has withdrawn to the back; there is no one behind him. If he does not strike him down, the boy demanded by the oracle will escape into the bush to be hunted.[58] Okonkwo is caught by an unlucky fate, a hostile *chi,* and the broken pot augurs a broken world.

At the end of the novel, Achebe finally shows Okonkwo taking a head with two blows of a machete. As Okonkwo severs the head, his world comes to an end, separating as cleanly and permanently from its past as the head from the body. In the same moment that the decollator's world ends, that of the decollated begins. Henceforward, the privileged point of view will belong to the threatened head, not to the warrior. In Achebe's syntax, as the head comes off, the new world materializes, comes into being, in what the sentence sees. Two adjectives do it: "man's" and "uniformed."

Okonkwo kills the head court messenger the same way he must have killed Ikemefuna. As the village meets and Okonkwo hopes for war against the white men, the head messenger announces that the white man has ordered the meeting to stop. Once again Okonkwo acts without speaking, without registering self-conscious thought. "In a flash Okonkwo drew his machete. The messenger crouched to avoid the blow. It was useless. Okonkwo's machete descended twice and the man's head lay beside his uniformed body" (188). Okonkwo does not take this head. He leaves it on the sand. The tribe will not go to war; they have let the other messengers escape. He wipes his machete and goes away. Soon he will hang himself.

The weapon drawn, the cowardly crouch of the messenger, the inevitability and strength of Okonkwo's arm: the warrior's heroic force is admired in battle, contests, and executions. The sentence should end in victory, the head rolling away as in Homer, or Okonkwo's holding the head by the hair in a sign of triumph. Instead, Achebe focuses on the victim, whose body bears the sign of our disciplined world, "uniform," and who is designated by the enlightenment abstraction, "man." The phrase "the man's head," redundant in common Nigerian usage, makes the head something that belongs to the man, rather than the part that stands for the whole. The possessive turns the person and his life into property. In turn the body, ordinarily merely an adjunct of the head/person, assumes the dominant position, ending the sentence. "Uniformed," eliminating the universality of the body, makes the body a modern civil servant's, one of those uniform, unheroic men in uniform. One of us has lost his head, for the first time in a long time. More swiftly than Okonkwo's twice-descending machete, Achebe's sentence transforms one world into another, Okonkwo's into ours.

Paradoxically, the reader horrified by the sacrifice of Ikemefuna pities Okonkwo rather than the murdered messenger. Cultic murder and ritual skulls produce a frisson of uncanny horror. Self-sacrificing revolutionary action against overwhelming imperial power and its slimy representatives elicits admiration and pity. One may even share Okonkwo's frustrated rage at snippy, domineering bureaucrats. No matter: Achebe signals the change of worlds by the way we see the head. The carefully constructed continuities of the trophy head and skull cup within the ritualized rhythms of tribal life vanish. The severed head becomes a climactic sign of rupture, an ending. Its meaning changes as new systems of interpretation and power arrive.

Only after *Things Fall Apart* had secured its classic perch did Achebe attack Conrad for the wound *Heart of Darkness* inflicts on the African reader. *Things Fall Apart* was published in 1959, the attack on Conrad's racism in 1977. Neither Amos Tutuola nor Ben Okri suffers that wound as Achebe seems to have done, and neither of them aimed a novel to pierce Conrad's darkness, to illuminate that heart. Achebe's resentment surfaced in *No Longer at Ease* (1960) when his protagonist characterizes Mr. Green, his supervisor, as feeling himself called to bring "light to the heart of darkness . . . [to] tribal headhunters performing weird and unspeakable rites." Achebe names the offending novel, but only after a discussion of "the modern novel . . . from Graham Greene to Tutuola," alternatives invoked against the spirit of Kurtz. By *Arrow of God* (1964) he restrained himself to muttering briefly about Capt. T. K. Winterbottom's terror of drums in the night and "unspeakable rites." Meanwhile, a colleague of Winterbottom's quotes George Allen's "call" to the civilizing mission in his *Pacification of the Primitive Tribes of the Lower Niger.*[59]

The essay on Conrad's racism exorcised the demon, saying at last what white literary critics did not care to notice about Conrad's mythography: that our most powerful anti-imperial critique celebrates white men's dionysiac energies at the expense of Africans' enlightenment (and Christian) claim to equal humanity. Ignoring African minds, Conrad needs African bodies to symbolize a lost, recoverable difference. Whether oppressed and exploited, defended and pitied, or admired as thrilling romantic primitives, the natives can neither save themselves nor speak for themselves. Exclusion is the usual native fate in triangular quarrels among whites over their responsibility for native objects, whether imperial or post-colonial. White guilt, taking on responsibility for pitiable natives against all-powerful whites, silences the natives even more thoroughly than charges of black barbarism, which recognize a site of resistance.

Once the problem has been recognized, there is little point in complaining about ethnocentrism—why expect the dog to tell the lamb's story? But when the ram butts and the ewe kicks for herself, the dogs yip painfully. Achebe's exorcism raised other spirits.

So Peter Firchow's valuable *Envisioning Africa* accepts as a purely aesthetic preference a description of African faces as "grotesque masks" and soothes European "brutality" with African comparisons: "But brutal as Leopold and his representatives were, they did not introduce cannibalism, human sacrifice, shamanism, or tribal dances into the Congo."[60] Firchow's Kurtz does not put heads on poles; he mounts "skulls," the human identity Conrad insists upon stripped away by his defender. Against such predictable responses Achebe raises Okonkwo's skull cup. In *No Longer at Ease,* the village elders tell the grandson of the hero of *Things Fall Apart,* "Umuofia would have required of you to fight in her wars and bring home human heads" (12). Now Umuofia's son does something else with heads—he studies abroad.

Achebe's heads are both African and modern. He wants to keep them on, but recognizes the enduring urge to "chop off" the head of an opponent, political or amorous, the casual modern version of the tribal level of enmity called *"kill and take the head."*[61] In *A Man of the People,* Edna, a modern girl, asks Odili, "Where is he going to find all the money the man has paid on my head?" She means her education, but also herself and bride price. Odili, the modern protagonist, declares himself willing to "chop off Chief Nanga's head so as to get" the girl, while the modern Chief Nanga hypocritically affirms continued friendship even when Odili runs against him for Parliament: "Those who don't know us may think we are about to cut off one another's heads."[62] Against such threats asserted by denial, a man lays claim to his head and the heads of his family.

"Civil Peace," a story from the war of the Biafran secession (1967–70), begins with Jonathan Igwebu counting himself "extra-ordinarily lucky. . . . He had come out of the war with five inestimable blessings— his head, his wife Maria's head and the heads of three out of their four children. As a bonus he also had his old bicycle—a miracle too but naturally not to be compared to the safety of five human heads."[63] This unsettling synecdoche celebrates the firmly fixed head that asserts itself as liminal and vulnerable to appropriation by others who value such signs of person, life, individuality, identity, and power. Precarious, heads are always in danger, but Igwebu's family survive, "carrying five heads on their shoulders."[64] Although Africans still threaten African heads, the heads belong to subjects who desire to keep them.

African heads continue to come off even though the practice is no longer authorized. The violence disciplined, canalized, marginalized, and statistically diminished by Enlightenment institutions in Euro-America (and their indigenous equivalents in Asia) re-emerges not as thrilling Sado-Nietzschean sweet delight, but as a real threat that needs to be dodged. As Nathan Nkala puts it, "They really turned bad. . . . They started cutting off heads all over the North. And they wanted *mine* too!"[65]

For Ben Okri, heads are both less problematic and more troubled than they were for his elders. A generation younger than Achebe and Tutuola, Okri is admired by Achebe and often linked stylistically with Tutuola.[66] In *Stars of the New Curfew* (1988), severed heads belong to the nightmare of the past, yet the future holds no clear promise. The troubled present of Nigeria is far more pressing than western perceptions of one's ancestral practices, yet the terror of those ancestral practices still threatens the present. Suspicious of affirmations of cultural synthesis, Okri represents the powerful as appropriating traditional practices to terrorize the people. Doing so reclaims the violence appropriated by white imperialism, by Kurtz, yet also enables those threatened to speak.

Like Achebe in "Civil Peace," Okri uses "head" as equivalent to "person"—opaque, solid, alive. In Okri, people in a crowd do not turn to look at a man raving in the street; instead, "four terracotta heads" turn. A friend does not search for a restless, jumpy little man; he looks for his friend's "restless head."[67]

Like Tutuola, Okri leads with the head. In "Stars of the New Curfew," decapitation enters the text early, in dreams, only to be obscured at the climactic moments in the text where a western writer or Achebe uses it, to mark an irreparable difference between worlds. Animal heads and "a special part of my anatomy," the penis, replace references to decollation. At the same time, references to machetes, bodies, and blood suggest decollation metonymically, but shyly.

The ancestral practice of head-taking has moved to the region of nightmare, and there is no nostalgia for that heroic past. Both horrible and terrifying, it terrifies most those on whom the hopes of the future rest, the children at school. For perpetrators and hunters, heads promise protection. For victims and the hunted, no power cures or protects. The imperial promise of protection and civilization has long blown up, its wreckage strewn in fragments:

> We passed several victims of accidents on the way: cars that had run into iroko trees; cars that had sped over bridges, with blood on the rocks below; lorries that had crashed into one another, entangled, their engines still purring; vehicles that had overturned. My escape from the city was like a journey through nightmares. (109–10)

In this condition of modernity, the escape into the country reveals only different nightmares, darker forests. The pretty promise of life as a fleeting dream is replaced by the grim suspicion that life is an unending, suppurating nightmare.

In "Stars of the New Curfew," the protagonist is a patent-medicine salesman. As the "head" designates the person, his life, and his powers, so "medicine" is a traditional African designation for power, healing, influence, and cures.[68] In Achebe's *Things Fall Apart* "medicine" is spiritual, political, moral, and healing power. It explains why things happen, and it makes things happen. In Okri's "Stars," "medicine" has at first only its modern, secondary meaning of patent medicine, aimed at curing the ills of the body. The salesman's medicine makes people sicker. New, more powerful medicines, "power-drugs," kill more children and cripple more mothers. As the salesman's "medicine" fails to cure the people and sickens the society, "medicine" resumes its older, traditional meanings even as the power of any medicine to cure this society's ills is questioned. The powerful create the drugs, make others sell them, and own the world. In the salesman's nightmares, the stars themselves are auctioned off to the rich, who pay with money, penises, or children's heads:

> When the stars were being auctioned I would realize with a shock that the people who bought them paid either with huge sums of money, a special part of the human anatomy, or the decapitated heads of newly-dead children. When the day's proceedings were over, when the lights had dimmed in the firmament, the auctioneer would look at the moon through a huge spy-glass, would laugh, and mutter: "One day! One day!"

After the stars and before the moon, every night, the salesman dreams that he himself is put on the block for auction, "me, the nameless and underfed salesman who would sell anything." The situation defines the protagonist as colonial subject and as victim in the traditional African context of the slave auction. The man for sale, however, is also a man who sells. Imagining himself as victim, the perpetrator fears for his head.

No longer confined to white Europeans, the culturally and racially diverse powerful include one's own:

> representatives of all races, all nations, all colours. They had bloated faces, indifferent eyes. Their expressions were acutely wise and callous about the resources and the costs of power. . . . I saw the face of an army general, an English aristocrat, an Asian millionaire, an American tycoon. (The rich belong to one country.) I saw the pinched face of a Yoruba chief, his agbada made from the skin of antelopes. I saw a senator . . . coming to canvass votes in the ghetto of Ajegunle.

What these powers want is his head, and for it they are prepared to offer other valuable things: "Someone, whom I never saw, offered a thousand naira for my head. Another offered ten cows. A third offered the heads of three children who had come first in their respective classes" (93–94). In the healing magic that uses body parts, heads are especially valuable, and the heads of children carry special power.[69] In his dreams, the salesman has value, and his value makes him vulnerable.

When the salesman eventually awakens from these nightmares, the heads recede, but the terror increases. Exploiting the past's signs and rituals, present power terrorizes to maintain control. Okonkwo's machetes still clash, but they now serve the rich families of the town, who buy elections from a famished people and who control perception. The new version of Achebe's masked dancers of the ancestors is no longer communal. Nor does art or literature re-create reality. Instead the rich and the powerful "create our realities, and . . . encircle themselves with dread . . . the great magicians of money, masters of our age" (127, 136). In that degraded reality, Africans continue to decapitate Africans, especially the youngest, the most hopeful, the children who come first in their classes.

There is no nostalgia for the terrors of the past. In the protagonist's childhood, the drums told "of dread, of death, of sacrifice." The mysterious head of the cult, it was said, "needed blood for his elixir." The young "lived in fear of returning late to school. We lived in terror of all the stories about the bright students who had vanished, of those that had been killed, their bodies found by the wayside, miles from town." Now, in the present, the machetes sound, and the nightmares move into an hallucinatory present:

All around I could hear the noises of the rival cults clashing, could hear them engaged in an eternal battle for power and ascendancy. It has never been revealed how many heads have been lost in the encounters. It is the town's secret. . . . I saw the secrets of the town dancing in the street . . . I passed the town's graveyard and saw the dead rising and screaming for children. It seemed as if the unleashing of ritual forces had released trapped spirits. Nightmares, riding on two-headed dogs, their faces worm-eaten, rampaged through the town. (128–29)

These powers surge from the ground, erasing boundaries, trampling divisions, undoing discipline, subverting rational control. It is not a pretty sight.

In Okri's world, there is no boundary to separate the civilized from the barbarians, restricting to barbarians violence suffered and inflicted. Instead, violence erupts at the core of culture, not affirmed, not approved, but not eradicable. Amid wealth that looks like civility, warrior figures, stuffed lions' heads, blue glass coffee tables, and Chippendale furniture, the protagonist is invited to "pour his blood into the basin." The machetes clash, the victims fall, the victors bring back "the bodies and the spoils of the defeated" (131). By the civilized rule that occludes victims' heads, "bodies" are brought back, not "heads." Okri does not romanticize the "wild and relentless" victors, the warriors, the men with machetes, the Kurtzes. In the civility/barbarity binary, the eruption of violence is a return of "the archaic" that modernity has disciplined and controlled.[70] Okri enables us to see what the binary obscures, that the cult, though archaic, is present and adaptive, serving the most modern and up-to-date purposes, controlling resources and elections. While the old binary provides both a sense of security and the thrill of transgression, here both the security and the thrill vanish. What remains is the unending clash of competitive realities, always dangerous, never resolved. Such clashes may seem resolved, as in the modern west, but resolution means violence has been dominated, displaced, or disciplined, not dissolved.

Like Achebe and Tutuola, Okri has reclaimed both the decapitator and his victim. "Where will it end? Like most of our leaders, he creates a problem, then creates another problem to deal with the first one—on and on, endlessly fertile, always creatively spiraling to greater chaos." Rationalist heads promise to control reality and bring order, but the salesman encounters the proliferating heads of folklore in the postmodern. New problems created by solving old ones rampage everywhere, like nightmares on two-headed dogs.

Epilogue
Craniate Origins and Headless Futures

The earliest vertebrates did not have bony vertebrae; in the vertebrate pantheon, distinct heads with a braincase and external bone
evolved first. Since heads, not backbones, are the basic defining feature of all that follows, John Maisey [the curator] wanted to replace
the word *vertebrate* with *craniate*. However, a Hall of Craniate Origins did not have the recognition factor of Hall of Vertebrate Origins, and hence the misnomer remains.
— Henry S. F. Cooper, Jr., "Origins: The Backbone of Evolution,"
Natural History 105:6 (June 1996): 31–44

Now nobody really controls Congress.
— R. W. Apple, Jr., "Gone Are Political Wise Men and the Culture
That Bred Them," *New York Times,* 12 October 1998, A16

And that's what is scary about this year's Davos: . . . [T]he world
economy today is just like that Internet: everybody is connected but
nobody is in charge.
— Thomas L. Friedman, 2 February 1999, *New York Times,* A19

The instant, see how it's just fallen, between Saint John: the body is
still living, but already the head is dead.
— Hélène Cixous, "Without End," *New Literary History,*
24 (1993): 101

The Leader has no head!   — Eugene Ionesco, *The Leader,* 1958

No head, no body, I'm empty now, empty all over . . . Eurydice!
— Jean Cocteau, *Orphée,* 1927

Discontinuity is the jump-off point of any new risk or problem.
— Michel de Certeau, *Heterologies,* 183

Fig. Epi.1. Vladimir Velickovic, Descente FIG. XXI, 1989. (© 2004 Artists
Rights Society [ARS], NY/ADAGP, Paris)

Heads, the body's metaphor for hierarchy and metonymy for wholeness, are in trouble. This is not news, save that the observation has moved from the avant garde to popular platitude. In the 1930s, Georges Bataille celebrated the *Acéphale,* the headless man, and his new world. *Acéphale,* a journal published by dissident surrealists between 1936 and 1939, with an acephalic man for emblem, lived only four issues. Freed from his head as a prisoner from prison, headless man plunges into a world without foundation and without head, committed to destruction and the death of God, merging with the superman, reviving the energies of the body in mythic community.[1] In the 1990s, *Le Monde* chose as the cover for its Science issue, a painting of a headless man on a staircase (Fig. Epi.1).

The metaphor motivating the choice seems transparent. Now headless and anonymous, Science advances. Moving endlessly upward, human knowledge no longer requires traditional forms of dominance and control. Progress continues, even though something we have always expected to find has come up missing, viz., the sign of perfection in the complete human form. The imperfect body can be trusted. Yet in *Le Monde*'s ascent of man, the figure is actually descending. Vladimir Velickovic titled his painting *Descente Fig. XXI,* and closer inspection reveals that the left leg is not rising, but is extended backwards, reaching down to the step behind.[2] Beginning just below the painting's vertical midpoint, the five steps start at the horizontal midpoint, ascend a quarter of the diagonal, and end nowhere. If the man had a head, he might be able to see beyond the diagonal incline he ascends to something else, outside the picture plane. But he has no head.

The moral is clear. From a distance, in public, we affirm progress and headlessness, the seductions of virtual realities and the joy of market stampedes, the fluidity and autonomy of self-sustaining, open-ended networks, democratic and anti-hierarchical. We like being connected, hooked up, plugged in, *au courant electrique, cablé.* From closer up, in private, reading the title rather than responding only to the image, we are compelled to rethink our enthusiasms as potential dangers, our currency flows as loss of control, our interconnectedness as emptying of self, our endless movement as without direction. In sum, real losses are inextricably linked to real gains, as we balance beheaded on the stair, one foot in the air.

What we do not question at all is the absence of a head. Art, science, and politics have been divesting themselves of heads for the last three hundred years, and it would now be embarrassing to be forced into the position of preferring heads to bodies. Precisely that embarrassment confronted New York's Museum of Natural History when it redesigned its exhibits for the millennium. Forced to choose between origins in the body or in the head, the museum dodged, obscuring the issue as best it could.

The discovery that the earliest vertebrates lacked backbones but had heads produces modernity's usual condition, a quandary. In "vertebrate origins," one bone leads to another, branching from the body. So Emerson admired Goethe for seeing the head as "only the uppermost vertebra transformed. 'The plant goes from knot to knot, closing, at last with the flower and the seed. So the tapeworm, the caterpillar, goes from knot to knot, and closes with the head. Men and the higher animals are built up through the vertebrae, the powers being concentrated in the head.'"[3] Darwin and Wallace improved Lamarck by locating evolution in mindless activities of the body (the accidental survival of offspring as motor of natural selection), rather than mindful adaptations transmitted by inheritance. Yet if vertebrates actually originate in "crania," that is, in heads without bodies, the head replaces the body as fundamental, as origin. The truer this may be as fact, the more conceptually incorrect it becomes. Not only does "a Hall of Craniate Origins [lack] the recognition factor of Hall of Vertebrate Origins," but it also makes the head, not the body, "the basic defining feature of all that follows."[4]

For a popular, public institution such as the Museum of Natural History to assert the evolutionary primacy of a head would be indecorous. The struggle against the head in science as in politics has too recently been won to be symbolically given away, even for the sake of accuracy in nomenclature. "Head," it seems, cannot be a neutral descriptive category. So the museum fudges, and science revives a forgotten word: braincase.[5] Outside the Hall of Vertebrate Origins, the "Vertebral Column and Braincase" are linked together, vertebra first, the braincase's origins and relations to the vertebral column unstated. Inside, the first station is "Jaws," a popular-culture allusion that acknowledges the primacy of the head it masks. Jaws, like brains, are in the head, but not of it, and mark the head's voracious origins. Heads appear to have originated some 700 million years ago as a cluster of nerve cells around the mouth of wormlike, soft-bodied creatures. Concentrating nerve cells at the animal's mouth made the head itself "a driving force in evolution," since the ability to locate prey more efficiently prompted evasive responses by prey and further improvements in the head's sensory equipment.[6] Such origins never promised non-violence.

When Darwinism replaced Design as explanation for the origin and characteristics of species, the body replaced the head. Not, however, without a struggle: the resourcefulness of human heads should never be underestimated. Disdaining their neo-Aristotelian demotion, resentful heads flipped Darwinism over, turning creation on its head, but preserving its anthropocentric ends. The Designer's creation had proceeded from a Head, speaking its Word; Darwin's evolution was made to move *to* a head, capable of language and laughter, cookery and culture.

For most of its history, Darwin's theory has been felt as progressive, an evolutionary movement up a chain of being, impelled by a teleological urge. For the Reverend James Freeman Clarke in 1874, Darwinism promised "perpetual improvement . . . perpetual progress."[7] Now Edward O. Wilson dubs man's journey an "evolutionary epic" in which man sets out on a new "journey . . . farther and better than the one just completed." This heroic Odyssey culminates in a neo-Enlightenment desire for "a more detached view [that envisions] the history and future of our genes against the background of the entire species. A word already in use intuitively defines this view: nobility."[8]

Opposing man's tendency to situate himself above, overlooking all below in an "equal, wide survey," museum time charts are linear. Meant to show man's humble brevity in time, Carl Sagan's popular "year" diagram places man at the last second before midnight. Nothing follows him, for "the last shall be first." Viruses, bacteria, termites, and ants appear somewhere in the middle muddle, disappearing from view as the plotting moves on to its denouement in man. Life moves from single-celled organisms to self-reflective consciousness, from chaos to us.

In Darwin's own time, the theory of evolution by natural selection met opposition from Richard Henry Dana's theory of "cephalization." As Plato's round head argued static perfection, Dana held that life's progress meant progress in dominance by the head. As creatures ascended the scale of life, the head became ever larger, more in control of the forelimbs and body. Unlike other body parts, the head has "uses" peculiar to it of a more elevated, if unspecified, kind:

> While all other Mammals have both the anterior and posterior limbs as organs of locomotion, in Man the anterior are transferred from the locomotive to the cephalic series. They serve the purposes of the head, and are not for locomotion. The cephalization of the body—that is, the subordination of its members and structure to head uses—so variously ex-

emplified in the animal kingdom, here reaches its extreme limit. Man, in this, stands alone among Mammals.[9]

Dominance of the head, the cephalos, and bipedalism, standing alone, alone standing, transmute man as physical object into symbolic object of value.

Although Dana represents the dominance of the head in physical terms as control over the arms, "head uses" are evidently distinct from other subordinate, bodily activities carried out by the head, such as sniffing, spewing, spitting, sneezing, and blinking. Paradoxically, Dana's cephalic theory would be ill-served by vertebrates' beginning with heads and descending into backbones. There would be no "rising" to the head, only hungry development from it, biting, tearing, swallowing.

"Caputocentric" fantasies, whether popular or learned, have been displaced in every modern discipline, starting with evolution itself. Darwin's preferred metaphor was the "tree of life," an image that combines extensive branching with a vigorous phallic thrust from the root. Although trees branch non-hierarchically, they have identifiable tops, called "crowns." Darwin's acolyte, the late Stephen Jay Gould, reduces life's form to the more egalitarian "bush," branching in unpredictable directions. As metaphor, "bush" is feminine and bodily (and slang for the mons veneris). Crown-free, bushes have no heads.

Such contests between "heads" and "bodies" have occurred in every discipline, and the heads have lost every time. Current theory glorifies the body—the mass, the collective, the common, the unconscious, the genetic, the genetic junk—and either cuts off the head or assimilates it to the body. A general epistemological phenomenon extending from the sixteenth century to the present, the process began in religion as Reformation mutilated the unified body of the church and removed its head, the pope.

Coinciding with the invention of man, in Foucault's terms, mutilation moved to politics as Hobbes's sovereignty fell to Locke's contract theory. So Charles I lost his head and James II his throne. In the marketplace of ideas, Mandeville's grumbling hive demonstrated the unintended consequences of bodily vices' producing public benefits, while conscious virtues produced public deprivation. The body worked as long as the head left off tinkering and moralizing. In 1776, as Americans elaborated a new contract, rid themselves of a traditional head, and initiated postcolonial consciousness, Adam Smith replaced rational control of markets with the "invisible hand." Smith's hand replaces both the conscious heart of the butcher—it is not from his benevolence that we get meat—and the head of the regulating ruler, establishing monopolies, controlling trade, attending to the needs of his people.

Other disciplines took the contagion. In history, unconscious forces replaced the intentions of actors, producing "master" narratives now in turn displaced by *bricolage*. In psychology, Reason passed control to the passions early in the eighteenth century and then disappeared altogether into mathematics and arbitrary social constructions.[10] No one dares doubt that mathematics is the realm of reason, but in no other area of human endeavor is "reason" now held to operate purely. For Emmanuel Lévinas, language precedes and "constitutes reason." For Donald Calne, "reason" is a construct, proceeding by certain rules, also constructed.[11]

The fluid self, so distressing to classical thinkers from Horace to Alexander Pope, still intermittently exercises reason, but is itself formed initially by others and remains irrevocably relative ("Head Matters"):

> Our depths who fathoms, or our shallows finds,
> Swift whirls, and shifting eddies, of our minds? . . .
> On human actions reason though you can,
> It may be Reason, but it is not Man.[12]

With the unconscious determining the self without its knowledge, "Freudianism dismantles individualism."[13] The self is constituted by significant others in George Herbert Mead, and by language and its exchanges between agents in Jürgen Habermas.[14] The subjectivist cultural objective "to find oneself" means, in practice, to cease regarding the self and to hook into an Other for definition: a profession, a love, an activity that erases "self"-awareness. To find the self is to lose it—and to be blithely unaware that one has lost anything at all.

In science, great minds with names are superseded by great minds on research teams, and truth becomes the paradigm that has not yet been displaced. Pursuing truth (singular), science constantly annihilates old truths with new ones, so that there is the least stability in the practice that lays claim to the most and that all accept as foundational. Alan Stone, diagnosing psychoanalysis's loss of scientific standing, laments that "without the claim of science there is no privileged text."[15] Yet science always eats its texts, turning the most privileged into history or literature. In art and literature, romanticism was always the living dead, an eighteenth-century gentleman pressed to death by mass culture, restored to life by the mantra "everyone is unique, but especially me."

In the early twentieth century, Giorgio de Chirico (1888–1978), Carlo Carrà (1881–1966), Giorgio Morandi (1890–1964), Filippo de Pisis (1896–1956), and José Clemente Orozco (1883–1949) decapitated the bourgeoisie. They attacked the well dressed, the elegant, the powerful, and mocked their cultural claims by replacing classic and bourgeois heads with crypto-phallic dummy heads. In 1916, de Chirico turned *Hector and Andromache*, the ideal classical married couple, into dummies, their heads replaced by the thumblike crypto-phallus at the top of a tailor's dummy. The next year, Carlo Carrà's *Madre e Figlio* implicated the twentieth-century bourgeois family; the son in his sailor suit, the portly mother, staunchly erect, dummies from head to foot, posed before mirrors (fig. Epi.2). De Chirico (*Disquieting Muses*) and Carrà (*Musa metafisica*) having dummied the artist's muse, Giorgio Morandi put a similar dummy's head into a *nature mort* where it replaces the shattered antique head whose presence gave dignity to the proceedings. In 1927, de Pisis' *Onions of Socrates* took the head off an antique statue on its plinth, turning Numa's saving gesture into absurdity. Socializing and politicizing the project, the Mexican José Clemente Orozco replaced with spikes the heads of contemporary oligarchs in *Mannikins* (1930). In tuxedo, red dress, and dangerous high heels, a beautifully dressed but headless couple discourse courtship on a bench, a bust on a marble column behind them, a vase toppling.[16]

The Mexican Marxist David Alfaro Siqueiros exhorted the proletarian (male) to get a head on his shoulders. Woman without a head (*Paisaje humano*, 1945) embodies nature, her arms and breasts the human landscape all traverse. She has no need for a head. With a head, helmet, and broken chain added to the same torso, woman allegorizes the struggle for natural freedom, *Nueva democracia* (1944–45). Men without heads need them. Siqueiros crops a man's torso at the neck and pubis in *Adoración* (1951), clasped hands yearning upwards. He replaces the face with a giant head of stone in *Nuestra imagen* (1947, Our Image), hands outstretched for help.[17] Enlightened, skeptical, self-sufficient heads are wanted here. By the 1950s, up north, moving further and faster than other fields of endeavor, art abolished representation, heads and bodies together.

Now the sculptor Magdalena Abakanowicz exhibits fields of headless children, lines of headless men (without genitals) and headless women (with bumps on upper torsos). These lumpish, gray, concrete, mesh, wire,

Fig. Epi.2. Carlo Carrà, Mother and Son, 1917. Pinoteca de la Brera, Milan. (Reproduced under license from Italian Ministry for Cultural Goods and Activities)

rough anthropomorphisms, installed on the roof at the Metropolitan Museum of Art in New York City (fall 1999), appeared in the summer at the Palais Royal in Paris. Regarded by their creator with a certain contempt, a herd without a leader,[18] these headless crowds abreast, obedient, anonymous, drew strolling tourists, who stopped to look, moved meditatively around them, drawing closer, pulling back. The tourists did not slow down for the abstract sculptures in the garden. The headless crowd, awkward, sympathetic, helpless, seems natural, but disturbing.

Today, when a thinker imagines a unified theory of knowledge, he posits a network linking many brains, the bodily insides of heads. "Culture is created by the communal mind, and each mind in turn is the product of the genetically structured human brain. Genes and culture are therefore inseverably linked. . . . The mind grows from birth to death by absorbing parts of the existing culture available to it, with selections guided by the epigenetic rules inherited by the individual brain."[19] These brains, "growing," "absorbing," "guided," "inherited," "existing," sound more like bowels than they do any other part of the body. Their unconscious, externally determined behaviors form the great mat of culture, endlessly extruding more culture as they go.

Current research in many fields pursues the production of orderly, complex, cooperative behavior in aggregations that lack both consciousness and central control.[20] Anywhere one picks up a theorist, one finds a theory in which a pattern emerges from randomness or intended patterns collapse into randomness, and there is no central control at home. Richard Dawkins's memes speed through the culture into J. M. Balkin's *Cultural Software: A Theory of Ideology.*[21] James P. Crutchfield's cellular automota collide and transfer information in mathematically describable patterns. John Horton Conway's "Game of Life" produces complex structures from individual blinking squares; it can be played on the Web. Complexity theory writes programs to mimic the behavior of a flock of birds, "their behavior patterns . . . not determined by centralized authorities but by the collective results of interactions among independent entities."[22] Edward O. Wilson's brains morph contentedly, like slime molds. The sociobiologists and mathematicians are delighted by patterns that precede thought and produce it.

Most self-conscious about the unmaking of the rational subject have been post-modern theorists, credited by themselves and others with displacing the subject and multiplying subjectivities, denying hierarchy and deifying multiplicity, losing origins in endless folds and vanishing traces.[23]

As Alexander Nehamas puts it, the once autonomous, sovereign subject is now "permeated or even fully constructed by lines of impersonal power, domination, and normalization (Foucault), by codes whose ability to communicate fully is undermined by their own structure (Derrida), by unconscious forces and desires (Lacan), or by economic and social factors (Bourdieu, Althusser)."[24] Foucault laments the loss of metaphors of dominion, the eagle and the sun, and awaits the erasing of man, that sixteenth-century European construct, "like a face drawn in sand at the edge of the sea."[25] Bataille, Derrida, Lacan, Kristeva "disarticulate the Enlightenment concept of the rational, stable self."[26] Having once exercised their skills discovering patterns, relationships (genealogies of influence), meaningful wholes, erstwhile humanists, now practitioners of "antihumanist literary criticism," chop wholes into fragments, furiously blending schools of thought—structuralism, poststructuralism, deconstruction.[27]

Studies of *The Body in Parts* or *The Body in Pain* find no place for heads and snipe at "cerebral primacy."[28] With Roland Barthes, reading dissolves the face into "the breath, the gutturals, the fleshiness of the lips, a whole presence of the human muzzle . . . the anonymous body."[29] Charmingly insouciant, the leading disseminator of grafts without bodies and skews without straight lines, Jacques Derrida, assures us that "[t]o lose one's head, no longer to know where one's head is, such is perhaps the effect of dissemination."[30]

So there we are. Losing one's head has a pleasant aura of liberation. Post-colonial or post-modern, the liberated subject casts down heavy heads, burdensome empires, weighty authorities. Shattered bits and pieces may be picked up as the passerby pleases, or left for the next comer. Fragments may be shored against ruin, dumped on the dustbin of history, or consigned to the resale shop of reenactments and reinvented wheels. A certain playfulness, a distinct lightheadedness attach to making do without a head. The art of having no head is zen, and the diligent student may consult such works as *On Having No Head,* to be read with the eye of the headless mind, charcoaled by Redon.[31]

Headlessness is freedom, equality, democracy, release from the weight of reason, obedience, domination, conscious control. The processes of the body take over, linking one body with other bodies to generate new, unforeseen forms of culture. The de-centered Web or Net, the displacement of national planning by global market forces, the preference of process over product, the creation, in effect, of *The Horizontal Society* and the spread of "Viral Culture" promote the currency of an ideology of

Fig. Epi.3. Ptiluc, En fin libre, 1996. Autograph. (Reproduced by permission of the artist)

headlessness (heedlessness).[32] To celebrate the absence of heads is to recognize unconscious process in culture, in language, in society at large, and in individuals. Headlessness affirms the vitality moving the hierarchical structures of institutions and endorses the indefinite potential of the body, its power, energy, life, longing for release, demanding release, breaking through, breaking away.

Yet having broken through, where does one go? Freed, what does one do next? Embracing acephalic man, how do we kiss?

Ptiluc puts it well. A French hardcover comic-book artist, master of the *bande dessinée*, Ptiluc sees the world through verminous eyes: the rat. In his *Faces de rat* (1987), three gleeful rats reread Camus's *La peste*, giggling helplessly, slapping their little thighs, squatting on the dump among rotted apple cores and toxic barrels. Ptiluc understands shifting the subject position and letting the marginalized—who more marginalized than a rat?—speak. In another image, "Enfin libre!" (Free at last!) shouts the ugly signature rat, as his head is blown off (fig. Epi.3). A little blood spatters the page. The cartoon, however, does not appear in the book proper. It is the author's autograph, created on the spot for his fans. They line up under the plane trees, clutching their new copies, hoping at most for a scrawled signature, a trace of the artist's presence, an enduring sign of a momentary link between the work, the author, and the reader/buyer. For his faithful readers, daring to desire only his name, the artist mutilates his book, ripping a hole in the page or rending the cover.

As in Velickovic's ambivalent image, the decapitator is the artist himself, in a gesture of creative destruction jabbing at the self, art, commerce, the book. A sneaking sense intrudes that, however jolly headlessness may be, getting there requires being beheaded, a prospect much less genial. With the body the last locus of the sacred, those who would subvert must strike at the head. The networks of power that Foucault analyzes and decries are, as he observes, us. Since what beheads also constitutes and empowers, the subject encounters a paradox sidestepped by choosing headlessness over beheadings. Chosen, headlessness produces a surfeit of detached heads.

We know the heads must be gone because the place is crawling with heads. Loose severed heads turn up relentlessly, in horror films and comedies, in cartoons, high art, and front-page images of the dictator's fallen head. Absent a cultural symbolism that promotes veneration for severed heads, the head displayed encodes hostility, proposing a more or less visible violence. "Talk your head off," chirps the cell-phone ad featuring a decapitated parrot. Yet veneration remains possible, and pressing. We still build pyramids of severed heads, heaping the whitened skulls of the victims of genocide in Cambodia and Rwanda. The sign of victory turns shrine, commemorating victims, an important public purpose. Day of the Dead altars juxtapose skulls and photographs, memories more private, but inviting participation.

To figure destruction is not to destroy but to make a new figure. Whether "self," "art," "commerce," or "the book" is the principal object of Ptiluc's destructive gesture, the violence directed against all these categories as he mutilates (what was) his own text generates another work of art and, of course, commentary. The rat is blown up; the book is ripped apart; the pristine sanctity of property, bought and paid for, is violated; annihilation and freedom are one. Ptiluc's destructive act is also aggressively creative: a new work is added to the book, destruction creates value, and both work and process provoke criticism. Although the freed, destroyed rat remains trapped in the memory of a commercial transaction as well as a book, the damage to the book is also a gift, free, unasked, supererogatory.

Heads, severed and not, continue to do major cultural work. We need heads for ethics: to make ethical judgments and to perform unethical acts. Only someone with a head can with certainty of success shove Velickovic's headless *Le Monde* man off his staircase. In Will Self (British novelist), Joel-Peter Witkin (American photographer), and Emmanuel Lévinas (Lithuanian-born French philosopher, Jewish theologian), three roads meet that define the ethical contradictions of our moment in what they do with heads. These names do not, on the face of it, belong in the same sentence. Controversial in the contemporary mode, that is, offensive and acclaimed for it, the two artists play with heads. Self dabbles in Nietzschean explorations of evil. Witkin decorates and photographs mutilated corpses in the name of sacred beauty. Lévinas, whose commentators include Derrida, Irigaray, and Lyotard, devises a postmodern version of Judeo-Christian ethics, finding a way "to keep ethics afloat without external support."[33]

In Lévinas, the head, unsevered, stages a comeback. Hierarchy re-insinuates itself, as preference for the other over the self-same. At the same time, wholeness is given up: the head comes back not as "head," but as "face." In his luminous "phenomenology of sociality based on the face," Lévinas restores not the head as dominant or whole, but the face as a part that enters into discourse.[34] He begins not from the subject position of the autonomous self (as, for example, John Rawls and Martha Nussbaum do), but from the other: the face is "not me," "what I myself am not," since the face is always for others.[35] Nor is the face before me my equal, in a relation of reciprocity. It is above me, not in power, but in obligation: "The face is not in front of me (*en face de moi*), but above me; it is the other before death, looking through and exposing death. Secondly the face is the other who asks me not to let him die alone, as if to do so were to become an accomplice in his death."[36] The other, separate, irreducible, unique, a "being identical to itself," assumes the value self often monopolizes.[37]

In just such terms, Nietzsche trumpets self against the loathly religion of sympathy or fellow-feeling. "We, however, *want to become those we are*—human beings who are new, unique, incomparable, who give themselves laws, who create themselves."[38] Splitting Nietzsche's "we" and taking "me" out, leaving "him" in, Lévinas equally rejects sympathy that proceeds from recognizing the self, an "alter ego," in the Other, that reduces the Other to the same. Yet in this refusal to reduce the other, responsibility devolves on the self, the I.[39] As David Steiner puts it, "Levinas' account supplies, as it were, the missing history of the pre-socialized self: the political animal is itself a consequence of the ethical call of the other's visage that summons me to an autonomy already cast as responsibility."[40]

Like "jaws," the face supposes a head, but removes its traditional associations: reason, dominance, wholeness. The face replaces reason with relationship, dominance with discourse, and wholeness with parts invoking one another. Possession and violence equally threaten the Other. "The partial negation which is violence denies the independence of beings: they are mine. Possession is the mode by which a being, while existing, is partially denied."[41] Violence always tempts: one need not awaken toward the other, one may commit evil, one may reduce the "not me" to "mine." "Evil is the order of being pure and simple."[42] Yet to be in relation with the other "face to face" precludes violence. To look "straight at him. [To look] him in the face. . . . To be in relation with the other face to face— is to be unable to kill. This is also the situation of discourse." And "The essence of discourse is prayer."[43]

Theologian as well as philosopher, Lévinas keeps his practices separate, but the beauty of his ethics is the beauty of holiness. "Religion" he defines, without naming God, as the bond with the Other, who is not represented but invoked, called. "To go toward the other is the penetration of the human into being, an 'otherwise than being.' . . . [T]he ideal of holiness is what humanity has introduced into being. An ideal of holiness contrary to the laws of being."[44] Radically revising Genesis, where a good world is spoiled by human evil, Lévinas supposes the world before man to be evil. He postulates the incursion of good into evil, the insinuation of humanity within nature's hungry jaws, the emergence of faces where there were only heads.

As if embracing Lévinas, certainly sharing his terms of value, Will Self deploys the precise antithesis of Lévinasian ethics to represent evil, "the Holocaust writ small" in a single action. Locating absolute negation in the violation of the face of the Other, his protagonist imagines himself beheading a fellow subway passenger, fucking the corpse's neck, looking at the head, and watching the face die: "[H]is personality, his soul, his identity? What you will, I watched it retreating, going away."[45] This Lawrentian affirmation of the self-through-sex takes a turn through degradation, fucking a wrong opening in the body to figure self-conscious despair. The self is asserted; the Other, possessed, negated. Yet to exert such power over the Other is simultaneously to lose it: the Other disappears.

Condemning himself, the narrator appropriates the reader's judgment. Seduced into identification with the narrator, the reader cannot escape the "ghastly, anti-human horror . . . the moral equivalent of a cosmological singularity." Mired in bodily fluids, the reader takes up the narrator's point of view as semen and blood mingle. That leaves everyone, protagonist, reader, author, feeling sticky. Since the imagined beheading opens the book, rather than closing it, no significant rupture transforms the persistent probing of the repulsive intimacies of the body. The innards are plumbed, the surfaces picked scabby, to serve the high-minded, moral purpose of exposing and experiencing the human potential for evil, inside and outside at the same time.

The revelation Self proposes at the moral level, the American photographer Joel-Peter Witkin proposes at the aesthetic. Lévinas's and Self's explicit ethical norms Witkin violates in the name of art, "beauty," "prayers," and the artist's "spiritual quest." Setting two contemporary ideologies, the Other-identified self and art, against each other, Witkin violates the ethical for the sake of the transcendental, a thrilling and disturbing human habit as ancient as severed heads. Photographing such voluntary subjects as naked dwarfs, legless men, and pre-op transsexuals, Witkin also photographs involuntary, anonymous corpses and body parts, secured from a Mexico City morgue—severed torsos, hands, arms, legs, feet, men's and babies' severed heads.[46] *Nuestra imagen,* indeed, but not "our" image: for an American audience, a Jewish-Russian American artist manipulates Mexican heads, in a way Siqueiros might have found disagreeable but not surprising. Descending from Géricault, this *abattoir* has a peculiarly American abundance. Witkin has been awarded a retrospective at the Guggenheim, featured in *Photo,* hailed in exhibitions, and mocked by Cintra Wilson at salon.com.[47] Unlike Géricault and Champmartin, however, Witkin poses body parts in elaborate tableaux, alluding densely to earlier artworks and religious symbolism. The ethical problem these images pose is that human heads have been appropriated for a private, self-expressive artistic discourse in which their faces do not participate.

Above the closed eyes and grimacing mouth of a man's plump, bald, severed head, lilies, roses, and baby's breath emerge from a hole cut out of half the forehead (*Still Life, Marseilles* [1992]). Vegetables placed in the head's emptied cranium and below the chin make a Mayan warrior's elaborate headdress and profile (*Harvest, Philadelphia* [1984]). De Chirico-izing, *Story from a Book* (1999) sets a blindfolded head with classical profile on an antique book. Because the skull has been cut away, a platter with apples rests where a laurel wreath would. (These and other images may be found on the Web.)[48] Like any model, these silent, severed heads have been appropriated for purposes not their own: the artist has possessed them, made them "his," to serve his artistic, spiritual projects. Yet unlike the empathic, public purposes of a St. John's head, the formal arrangements of these heads preclude discourse.

They have been decorated as if they were trophy heads or seventeenth-century anatomical specimens, fussed over, gussied up, and tricked out, and they make no argument against their treatment.[49] Many of the heads are in profile or blindfolded. Most, like Conrad's, have their eyes closed. Unlike Géricault's, these heads do not look back at the viewer, challenging anything.[50] Unlike Champmartin's, their adornments attract attention to themselves and away from the head, conflicting with the attention Champmartin's drape or Géricault's open eyes argue that a severed human head demands.

Interpreting the image requires turning away from the head toward the paraphernalia—the roses and lilies of the *Song of Songs* or the sinful knowledge of a platter of apples on a book. The classical profile contrasts with greasy hair, apples with wens on the neck. Subordinated to an interpretive project, the head leads to contemplation of the artist-god. Not objectionable when the head belongs to a willing participant, when the head belongs to a corpse incapable of consultation, sociocultural norms defining the body as property, as private, and as sacred are violated in favor of artistic self-expression and the spectator's self-knowledge. Although the artist has turned headhunter, the heads are not venerated. Veneration is reserved for the artist and his vision, violating the face of the Other. That remains an ethical quandary.

Witkin's admirers address that quandary by appropriating the moral ground. Calling his work his "prayers" and "sacred," Witkin serves the cultural ideal of Art and the Artist's Autonomy. His photographs violating the face hallow it: the ethical dimension is seen as continuous with the transcendental. So Germano Celant, curator of contemporary art at the Guggenheim during Witkin's 1995 retrospective, affirms the higher didacticism: "The formless and the deformed, the base and the terrifying must be brought into the light. . . . [T]he notion of 'cruelty' is no longer hostile but is transformed into a cognitive nucleus purged of its dark and negative side."[51] Once a system of meaning takes over, brute cruelty dissolves into meaning ("cognitive nucleus") and vanishes, liberated into light. Charles Mann makes the dialectical argument more banally, blending religion and art, identifying the dead and the deformed: "Using cadavers, hermaphrodites, and hunchbacks, Witkin creates visual paradoxes that challenge our perception. Often criticized for sensationalism and the exploitation of his subjects, he actually redeems them—makes them central to his spiritual quest. Once photographed, they enter the eternal stream of art."[52]

Others focus on the self-discovery Witkin affords his viewers. As Maria Villaseñor admiringly puts it, "He plunges into the deepest and darkest recesses to develop an image that will help us to fathom our own depths."[53] Serving his audience's self-discovery, the artist enables audience and maker to transcend the ordinary limits of experience and to discover radiance through darkness. Manipulating and decorating the head, playing imaginatively over dead parts that once were human, Witkin's viewer discovers pleasures of mystery and mastery once denied to all but medical students, now also available through Von Hagen's "Bodyworlds." Two hundred years ago, in Delacroix and Ingres, the terms of this debate were fresh.

By contrast, Witkin's detractors mount an aesthetic attack. They seem, like Okonkwo, afraid to be thought "weak," that is, moralistic or aligned with retrograde forces, like medieval clerics opposed to dissection. Charles Hagen at the *New York Times* calls Witkin's work atrocity photojournalism masked by "artiness."[54] Cintra Wilson mocks the work as sentimental and pretentious kitsch, likening Witkin's banal "freak show" to Anne Rice. Indeed, Celant's light emanates from severed heads in Rice's *Vittorio the Vampire*. Yet in the absence of formal criteria of evaluation, when "provocative," "disturbing," "challenging" are prized aesthetic qualities, calling the provoking and disturbing work "sentimental kitsch" seems to reveal only that the critic, provoked and disturbed, has lost the challenge.

When a subject appears in kitsch, cartoons, and children's stories, we know we have reached the heart of ideology, the core of culture, the rag-and-bone shop of identity, the moving toyshop of self. If French cartoonists encounter existential despair and Lévinasian critique, American children's stories promote self-help. Among the Victorians, the Red Queen cried, "Off with her head!" The Red Queen, it will be remembered, was an enemy to be flouted, resisted, and overturned with the full force of a little girl's contempt. Beheadings imposed by powerful, punitive, visible others are no longer the mode. The revolutions are over. We encounter losses sustained by no known or resistible agency, but think we must cope with on our own. Yet even though sovereign artists may claim the right to finger, photograph, and catalogue severed human heads, other heads reserve the right to object. Many of us do not want anyone making off with our heads.

Consider the fable of Irv Irving from Pinsk. A children's story, *It Happened In Pinsk* is the story of Irv Irving, a prosperous shoe salesman who wishes, constantly, he were someone else.[55] Why am I not strong like the wrestler? Why am I not rich like the banker? Why do I not own a great mansion like the widow? Why do I have to be me, Irv Irving; why can't I be someone else? One morning, he wakes up, and while eating his sugared doughnut, he realizes he has no head. His wife makes him a new one, and he goes searching for the old one. It is a terrible day. He is constantly mistaken for someone else, for someone he does not want to be—a criminal, someone's beloved old uncle, a hated debtor. He is always on the run, poor headless Irv Irving. Finally, he finds his own head posing as a dummy in a hat shop; he tries to buy it, fails, and steals it at a run. Thereafter, once he has gotten it back on, he is rarely ever again heard to complain.

This is a sweet modern fable with a debt to Gogol's Nose. The head disappears by non-violent means, and it causes no break in sense of self or rupture of consciousness. And the moral is a happy one—be content with who you are, because you wouldn't want not to be you, would you? If others define you, you might not like it. The story strikes a nice, wholesome balance between contentment with one's lot and individuality. Although it happened in Pinsk, it is wonderfully American in its insistence that everybody is unique, everyone is an individual, even though everyone is so much like everyone else. By no accident, Irv Irving's initials are I. I.: self (I), affirmation (aye aye), and a cry of pain (ai ai).

Decollation has become an obsessive, often comic trope for the vulnerability of the modern self, ideologically the ultimate source of value, but undermined by technological networks that erase the individuals they depend upon. When the single head was sovereign, the hydra, sprouting two heads for every one cut off, figured the people as irrationally prolific Other. Curled up in a corner, lost to fame, no longer terrifying, hydra now raises one head every fifteen minutes for a photo-shoot. If too many heads seem sometimes like none at all, Irv Irving reminds us that there is a difference. If Self and Witkin were playing with Irving's head down some darker alley, he would snatch it from them as readily as from the hat shop: "Not with my head, you don't." We are as attached to our heads as if our lives depended on them. For the foreseeable future, we are likely to remain so, eyeball to eyeball, eye to eye, face to face, head to head.

Notes

1. John Noble Wilford, "In Ancient Skulls from Ethiopia, Familiar Faces," *New York Times,* 12 June 2003, A1, 8.

2. Bernard Weinraub, "At the Movies: Mutual Admiration," *New York Times,* 19 November 1999, E20.

3. *Prairie Home Companion,* National Public Radio, 7 January 2001.

4. Judith Butler, *Bodies That Matter* (New York: Routledge, 1993), ix–x.

5. Norbert Elias, *The Civilizing Process,* 2 vols., trans. Edmund Jephcott (New York: Urizen Books, 1978); Michel Foucault, *Discipline and Punish,* trans. Alan Sheridan (New York: Vintage Books, 1979); Pieter Spierenburg, *The Spectacle of Suffering* (Cambridge: Cambridge University Press, 1984). Daniel Gerould and Daniel Arasse on the guillotine: *The Guillotine: Its Legend and Lore* (New York: Blast Books, 1992); *La Guillotine et l'imaginaire de la Terreur* (Paris: Flammarion, 1987); Jean-Louis Voisin on the Romans: "Les Romains, chasseurs de têtes," in *Du Châtiment dans la cité* (Rome: Ecole française de Rome, 1984); Mary Flavia Godfrey on Old English poetry: "*Beowulf* and *Judith*: Thematizing Decapitation in Old English Poetry," *Texas Studies in Language and Literature* 35:1 (Spring 1993): 1–43; Renato Rosaldo on the Ilongot of the Philippines: *Ilongot Headhunting 1883–1974* (Stanford, Calif.: Stanford University Press, 1980); Robert F. Murphy on the Brazilian Mundurucú: *Headhunter's Heritage: Social and Economic Change among the Mundurucú Indians* (Berkeley: University of California Press, 1960); Geoffrey Bryan for a general history and Paul-Henri Stahl for the near Orient in the nineteenth and twentieth centuries: *Off with His Head* (London: Hutchinson, 1934), *Histoire de la Décapitation* (Paris: Presses Universitaires de France, 1986); Howard Engel on executioners: *Lord High Executioner* (London: Robson, 1997); Stephen R. Wilk on *Medusa: Solving the Mystery of the Gorgon* (New York: Oxford University Press, 2000); Mireille Dottin-Orsini on *Salome* (Paris: Editions Autrement, 1996); and Margarita Stocker on *Judith: Sexual Warrior* (New Haven: Yale University Press, 1998).

6. A surprising exception is Jack Morgan's *The Biology of Horror* (Carbon-

dale: Southern Illinois University Press, 2002). Although Morgan says that Melville's "Benito Cereno" inspired his study, he does not mention the severed head that ends the story.

7. Claudia Dreifus, "Following the Wolves, Number by Number: A Conversation with Douglas Smith," *New York Times*, 29 July 2003, F3.

8. Terrence W. Deacon, *The Symbolic Species: The Co-evolution of Language and the Brain* (New York: Norton, 1997).

9. Jonathan Israel, *Radical Enlightenment: Philosophy and the Making of Modernity 1650–1750* (Oxford: Oxford University Press, 2001), 20.

NOTES TO THE PROLOGUE

1. Edward O. Wilson, *On Human Nature* (Cambridge, Mass.: Harvard University Press, 1978), 111–15; Lionel Tiger and Robin Fox, *The Imperial Animal* (New York: Holt, Rinehart, and Winston, 1971), 205–7; Robin Fox, "The Human Nature of Violence," in *The Challenge of Anthropology: Old Encounters and New Excursions* (New Brunswick, N.J.: Transaction Publishers, 1994), 87–94. Steven Pinker, *The Blank Slate: The Modern Denial of Human Nature* (New York: Viking, 2002), 294, 44, 306–36; Nicholas Wade, "In Nature vs. Nurture, a Voice for Nature," *New York Times*, 17 September 2002, F1, 4.

2. Avshalom Caspi, Joseph McClay, Terrie E. Moffitt, Jonathan Mill, Judy Martin, Ian W. Craig, Alan Taylor, and Richie Poulton, "Role of Genotype in the Cycle of Violence in Maltreated Children," *Science* 297:5582 (2 August 2002): 851–54; Charlotte Schubert, "Gene Tripped by Violence," *Nature Medicine* 8:9 (September 2002): 941.

3. Stephen R. Wilk, *Medusa* (New York: Oxford University Press, 2000), 189.

4. Muriel Beadle, *The Cat: History, Biology, and Behavior* (New York: Simon and Schuster, 1977), 34–37; Dennis C. Turner and Patrick Bateson, *The Domestic Cat: The Biology of Its Behaviour* (Cambridge: Cambridge University Press, 1988), 116, 119, 120.

5. Jane Van Lawick Goodall, *In the Shadow of Man* (1971), 205, 212, quoted in Emily Vermeule, *Aspects of Death in Early Greek Art and Poetry* (Berkeley: University of California Press, 1979), 115. The chimp slams the juvenile baboon's head against the ground, a gesture echoed in Psalm 137, "Happy shall he be, that taketh and dasheth thy little ones against the stones."

6. Ernst Robert Curtius, *European Literature and the Latin Middle Ages*, trans. Willard R. Trask (Princeton, N.J.: Princeton University Press, 1973), 293. *Works of the Right Reverend Thomas Newton*, 3 vols. (London, 1782), III, 33. Nicephorus's tale is reprinted in Mireille Dottin-Orsini, *Salome* (Paris: Editions Autrement, 1996), 74–75.

7. For the difficulties, see L. Dérobert, *Médicine légale* (Paris, 1974), cited in

Jean-Louis Voisin, "Les Romains, chasseurs de têtes," in *Du Châtiment dans la cité* (Rome: Ecole française de Rome, 1984), 257–58.

8. *Rethinking Symbolism* (Cambridge: Cambridge University Press, 1975), 48.

9. Elisabeth Bronfen, *Over Her Dead Body: Death, Femininity and the Aesthetic* (New York: Routledge, 1992), 195.

10. *Natural Symbols: Explorations in Cosmology* (New York: Pantheon Books, 1970), vii.

11. Smell identifies the wasp as from the nest, while facial markings determine place or rank within the nest. "Wasps Can See the Difference," *Discover* 23:1 (January 2003): 64.

12. Larry Spear, "The Halloween Mask Episode," *Natural History* 97:5 (June 1988): 4–8. "Maa-maa's Boys," *Discover* 19:12 (December 1998): 20. Fostered female sheep and goats return to their own kind. See also Stephen Budiansky, *If a Lion Could Talk* (New York: Free Press, 1998), 6, 51.

13. C. Gross, C. Rocha-Miranda, and D. Bender, "Visual Properties of Neurons in Inferotemporal Cortex of the Macaque," *Journal of Neurophysiology* 35 (1972): 96–111; Stephen J. Gould, "Bacon, Brought Home," *Natural History* 108:5 (June 1999): 30; Hillary R. Rodman, "Face Recognition," in *MIT Encyclopedia of the Cognitive Sciences*, ed. Robert A. Wilson and Frank C. Keil (Cambridge, Mass.: MIT Press, 1999); Leslie Brothers, *Friday's Footprint: How Society Shapes the Human Mind* (New York: Oxford University Press, 1997), 38.

14. R. L. Fantz, "Pattern Vision in Newborn Infants," *Science* 140 (1963): 296–97.

15. J. Bowlby, "The Nature of the Child's Tie to His Mother," *International Journal of Psychoanalysis* 41 (1958): 350–73. H. R. Schaffer, ed., *Studies in Mother-Infant Interaction* (New York: Academic Press, 1977), 119–20, 239, 248–49.

16. Wilson, *On Human Nature*, 61–63. The manipulative power of the smile accounts for the irrational dislike provoked by ingratiating "smiley-faces" used as periods or for dotting i's. A less significant squiggle, say a Daffy Duck logo, would not produce the same hostility.

17. "Exploring Antisocial Aspects of Autism," *New York Times*, 25 April 2000, F8; Douglas S. Fox, "The Inner Savant," *Discover* 23:2 (February 2002): 44–49; Brothers, *Friday's Footprint*, 15–16.

18. Charles Darwin, *The Expression of the Emotions in Man and Animals*, intro. Konrad Lorenz (Chicago: University of Chicago Press, 1965), 15–16, 131. Human facial expressions are often coded differently, as expressing different feelings, so sociobiologists and culturalists differ on the mutual intelligibility of facial signs. Paul Ekman, "Biological and Cultural Contributions to Body and Facial Movement in the Expression of Emotions," in *Explaining Emotions*, ed.

Amélie Oksenberg Rorty (Berkeley: University of California Press, 1980), 78–80; Carroll E. Izard, *The Face of Emotion* (New York: Appleton-Century-Crofts, 1971); Linda A. Camras, Elizabeth A. Holland, and Mary Jill Patterson, "Facial Expression," in *Handbook of Emotions*, ed. Michael Lewis and Jeannette M. Haviland (New York: Guilford Press, 1993), 199–200.

19. Merlin Donald, *Origins of the Modern Mind* (Cambridge, Mass.: Harvard University Press, 1991), 180.

20. Stephen R. Wilk, *Medusa*, 156–59. "Eye-Tracking Movements," in *MIT Encyclopedia of the Cognitive Sciences*.

21. Margaret Power, *The Egalitarians, Human and Chimpanzee: An Anthropological View of Social Organization* (Cambridge: Cambridge University Press, 1991), i, xvii, 3, 240. Influenced by feminist analysis and James Woodburn's accounts of egalitarian foraging systems among surviving hunter-gatherer groups, Power proposes "a fluid role relationship of mutual dependence between many charismatic chimpanzees of both sexes and other more dependent members," so as to modify the current view of chimpanzee society as "aggressive, dominance seeking, and fiercely territorial." She attributes the latter character to stress-induced adaptation to artificial feeding at Gombe. Since chimpanzee social organization is adaptive, artificial feeding at Gombe produced competition within the group and altered "the loosely structured mutual dependence system which is the normal adaptation and optimal strategy for foraging their natural habitat, to a rigidly structured, hierarchical form of social organization." Although opposed to hierarchy, Power is unable to rid chimp society of differentiation between "charismatic" and "other more dependent members." See also Frans de Waal, *Chimpanzee Politics: Power and Sex among Apes* (New York: Harper and Row, 1982), for the view that hierarchy is "a cohesive factor, which puts limits on competition and conflict" (213).

22. Marco Costa and Pio Enrico Ricci Bitti, "Face-ism Effect and Head Canting in One's Own and Others' Photographs," *European Psychologist* 5:4 (December 2000): 293–301.

23. Edward O. Wilson, *Sociobiology: The New Synthesis* (Cambridge, Mass.: Harvard University Press, 1975), 548; William R. Leonard, "Food for Thought," *Scientific American*, 287:6 (December 2002): 109–12.

24. Chimpanzees using mirrors for self-exploration have included a female studying her genitals. Karen Wright, "The Tarzan Syndrome," *Discover* 17:11 (November 1996): 88–99.

25. Steve Jones, Robert Martin, and David Pilbeam, eds. *Cambridge Encyclopedia of Human Evolution* (Cambridge: Cambridge University Press, 1992), 241–51; Eric Delson, Ian Tattersall, John A. Van Couvering, and Alison S. Brooks, eds. *Encyclopedia of Human Evolution and Prehistory* (New York: Garland, 2000), 652–53; Wilson, *Sociobiology*, 548. "Globular" distinguishes people from giraffes, whose heads are also conspicuously above their bodies.

26. 1 April 1717. *Letters from the Levant during the Embassy to Constantinople 1716–18* (New York: Arno Press, 1997), 107.

27. Colwyn Trevarthen, "Communication and Cooperation in Early Infancy: A Description of Primary Intersubjectivity," in Margaret Bullowa, ed., *Before Speech: The Beginning of Interpersonal Communication* (New York: Cambridge University Press, 1979), 321–23; "The Foundations of Intersubjectivity: Development of Interpersonal and Cooperative Understanding in Infants," in David R. Olson, ed., *The Social Foundations of Language and Thought: Essays in Honor of Jerome S. Bruner* (New York: Norton, 1980), 317–18, 322–23; "Descriptive Analyses of Infant Communicative Behavior," in H. R. Schaffer, ed., *Studies in Mother-Infant Interaction* (New York: Academic Press, 1977), 232–24; "Predispositions to Cultural Learning in Young Infants," *Behavioral and Brain Sciences* 16 (1993): 534–35; "Growth and Education in the Hemispheres," in *Brain Circuits and Functions of the Mind*, ed. Colwyn Trevarthen (Cambridge: Cambridge University Press, 1990), 341–42; Daniel N. Stern, *The Interpersonal World of the Infant* (New York: Basic Books, 2000), xii, xxii; Michael Tomasello, *The Cultural Origins of Human Cognition* (Cambridge, Mass.: Harvard University Press, 1999), 66.

28. Tomasello, *Cultural Origins of Human Cognition*, 64–66.

29. Michael Tomasello, "On the Interpersonal Origins of Self-concept," in Ulric Neisser, ed., *The Perceived Self: Ecological and Interpersonal Sources of Self-Knowledge* (Cambridge: Cambridge University Press, 1993), 182. See also Phillippe Rochet, ed., *Early Social Cognition: Understanding Others in the First Months of Life* (Mahwah, N.J.: Lawrence Erlbaum Associates, 1999); Walter Goldschmidt, *The Human Career: The Self in the Symbolic World* (New York: Basil Blackwell, 1990).

30. Jacques Lacan, "The Mirror Stage," in *Ecrits* (New York: Norton, 1977).

31. Michel de Certeau, *Heterologies*, trans. Brian Massumi (Minneapolis: University of Minnesota Press, 1986), 56.

32. Brothers also observes that the ability to read others' intentions puts evolutionary pressure on the ability to deceive; see *Friday's Footprint*, 25.

33. Tomasello, *Cultural Origins of Human Cognition*, 21.

34. For the cosmic analogy, see Richard Broxton Onians, *The Origins of European Thought about the Body, the Mind, the Soul, the World, Time and Fate* (1951) (Cambridge: Cambridge University Press, 1988); Bruce Lincoln, *Myth, Cosmos, and Society* (Cambridge, Mass.: Harvard University Press, 1986); Leonard Barkan, *Nature's Work of Art: The Human Body as Image of the World* (New Haven: Yale University Press, 1975).

35. Francis Macdonald Cornford, ed., *Plato's Cosmology: The "Timaeus" of Plato Translated with a Running Commentary* (London: Routledge and Kegan Paul, 1937), 150, sec. 44d; 353, sec. 90; 282, sec. 69.1.

36. Jacques Le Goff, "Head or Heart? The Political Use of Body Metaphors in the Middle Ages," in *Fragments for a History of the Human Body,* part 3, ed. Michel Feher (New York: Zone Books, 1989), 22.

37. Cornford, *The "Timaeus" of Plato,* 150, sec. 44d; 353, sec. 90; 282, sec. 69.

38. 151, sec. 45.

39. Onians, *The Origins of European Thought,* 98–99.

40. Elisabeth Bronfen, *Over Her Dead Body* (New York: Routledge, 1992), 96.

41. *Totem and Taboo,* trans. James Strachey (New York: Norton, 1950), 141–42; *Violence and the Sacred,* trans. Patrick Gregory (Baltimore: Johns Hopkins University Press, 1977).

NOTES TO CHAPTER 1

1. *Life,* 60th Anniversary Issue, 19:11, 12 (1996): 16.

2. Richard Broxton Onians, *The Origins of European Thought about the Body, the Mind, the Soul, the World, Time and Fate* (1951) (Cambridge: Cambridge University Press, 1988), 96, 100, 108, 154, 236; Leonard Barkan, *Nature's Work of Art: The Human Body as Image of the World* (New Haven: Yale University Press, 1975).

3. For Saussure, the sign is a unit formed of a signifier (an acoustic element) and a signified (a concept); Ferdinand de Saussure, *Course in General Linguistics,* trans. Wade Baskin (New York: McGraw-Hill, 1959), 65–67.

4. "The Uncanny" (1919), in *Standard Edition of the Complete Psychological Works of Sigmund Freud,* vol. 17 (London: Hogarth Press, 1957), 218–56.

5. C. S. Peirce distinguishes index, icon, and symbol: the index "maps" what it represents; the icon points to what it represents, as smoke signals the presence of fire; the symbol is arbitrary (like a word, or a flag representing a nation); Charles S. Peirce, *Selected Writings: Values in a Universe of Chance,* ed. Philip P. Wiener (New York: Dover, 1958), 368, 391, 407. As index, the head is the person; it "maps" the face. As icon, the severed head points to death, the absence of life. As symbol, the severed head is arbitrary: life, peccary spirit mothers, justice, schism in Dante.

6. Julia Kristeva elaborates the distinction as follows: "[T]hese elements (symbols) refer back to one (or several) unrepresentable and unknowable universal transcendence(s); univocal connections link these transcendences to the units evoking them; the symbol does not 'resemble' the object it symbolizes; the two spaces (symbolized-symbolizer) are separate and do not communicate. The symbol assumes the symbolized (universals) as irreducible to the symbolizer (its markings). . . . The sign [retains] the fundamental characteristic of the symbol: irreducibility of terms, that is, in the case of the sign, of the referent to the signi-

fied, of the signified to the signifier, and, in addition, all the 'units' of the signifying structure itself. The ideologeme of the sign is therefore, in a general way, like the ideologeme of the symbol: the sign is dualist, hierarchical, and hierarchizing. A difference between the sign and the symbol can, however, be seen vertically as well as horizontally: within its vertical function, the sign refers back to entities both of lesser scope and more *concretized* than those of the symbol. They are *reified* universals become *objects* in the strongest sense of the word. Put into a relationship within the structure of sign, the entity (phenomenon) under consideration is, at the same time, transcendentalized and elevated to the level of theological unity. The semiotic practice of the sign thus assimilates the metaphysics of the symbol and projects it onto the 'immediately perceptible.' The 'immediately perceptible,' valorized in this way, is then transformed into an *objectivity*—the reigning law of discourse in the civilization of the sign. Within their horizontal function, the units of the sign's semiotic practice are articulated as a *metonymical concatenation of deviations from the norm* signifying a *progressive creation of metaphors.*" *Desire in Language,* ed. Leon S. Roudiez, trans. Thomas Gora, Alice Jardine, and Leon S. Roudiez (New York: Columbia University Press, 1980), 38, 40.

7. Ian Tattersall, *The Last Neanderthal: The Rise, Success, and Mysterious Extinction of Our Closest Human Relatives* (New York: Macmillan, 1995), 165–70. Some skull arrangements have been dated to 400,000 years ago, well before the emergence of language in *Homo sapiens,* 50,000 to 100,000 years ago. Merlin Donald, *Origins of the Modern Mind: Three Stages in the Evolution of Culture and Cognition* (Cambridge, Mass.: Harvard University Press, 1991), 277. Baruch Arensberg and A. M. Tillier, "Speech and the Neanderthals," *Endeavour* 15 (1991): 26–28, argue that Neanderthals could have produced speech. See also Deacon, *The Symbolic Species,* 370–73.

8. John Noble Wilford, "In Ancient Skulls from Ethiopia, Familiar Faces," *New York Times,* 12 June 2003, A1, 8.

9. "Les Romains, chasseurs de têtes," in *Du Chatiment dans la Cité: Supplices corporels et peine de mort dans le monde antique* (Rome: Ecole française de Rome, 1984), 242.

10. Herodotus, *The History,* trans. David Grene (Chicago: University of Chicago Press, 1987), IV, 26; Geoff Marsh and Barbara West, "Skullduggery in Roman London?" *Transactions of the London and Middlesex Archaeological Society* 32 (1981): 95.

11. Michel Ragon, *The Space of Death,* trans. Alan Sheridan (Charlottesville: University of Virginia Press, 1983), 10–11.

12. Barry Goldensohn, "Margaret Roper (after Holbein's drawing)," in *The Marrano* (Orono: University of Maine, 1988), 70.

13. Stahl does not speculate on the origins of the heads, in *Histoire de la Décapitation,* 138–40. Like the gospels' authorship, the heads' identities do not re-

ally matter: all are equally children of God, so any head can represent all. Still, that is not what the churches advertising their relics argued.

14. Robert F. Murphy, "Intergroup Hostility and Social Cohesion," *American Anthropologist* 59 (1957): 1024–25. Successful headhunters presuppose less successful ones.

15. Claude Lévi-Strauss, *The Raw and the Cooked*, trans. John and Doreen Weightman (New York: Harper and Row, 1969), 85–86, 99, 101. Lévi-Strauss does not mention these myths when he discusses Mundurucú headhunting in *The Origin of Table Manners*, trans. John and Doreen Weightman (New York: Harper and Row, 1978), 101–3, 93.

16. *Violence and the Sacred*, trans. Patrick Gregory (Baltimore: Johns Hopkins University Press, 1977), 12.

17. Alison Futrell, *Blood in the Arena: The Spectacle of Roman Power* (Austin: University of Texas Press, 1997), 191, 179, 180, 196, 207. Terence Chong spoke for Sabah's Engineering Institute. Melinda Liu, "Beware of the Headhunters," *Time*, 11 December 1989, 62.

18. Jay A. Levenson, ed., *Circa 1492: Art in the Age of Exploration* (New Haven: Yale University Press, 1991), 573.

19. *Appian's Roman History*, 4 vols., trans. Horace White (Cambridge, Mass.: Harvard University Press, 1933), III, 385, book 2, sec. 86. Plutarch calls Cicero's assassin Herennius the centurion; Appian calls him Laena the centurion. Appian, *Civil Wars*, book 4, sec. 20, in *Appian's Roman History*, IV, 173–75. Roman orators favored Laena, as a former client defended by Cicero on a capital charge. He then took off the head of the eloquence that had saved him. Amy Richlin, "Cicero's Head," in *Constructions of the Classical Body*, ed. James I. Porter (Ann Arbor: University of Michigan Press, 1999), 195.

20. *Discipline and Punish*, trans. Alan Sheridan (New York: Vintage Books, 1979), 50, 53–54.

21. T. G. E. Powell, *The Celts* (1958) (New York: Thames and Hudson, 1980), 180. Pierre Lambrechts, *L'Exaltation de la tête dans la pensée et dans l'art des Celtes* (Brugges, Belgium: de Tempel, 1954), 23. An exception is Anne Ross, *Pagan Celtic Britain* (1967) (Chicago: Academy Chicago Publishers, 1996), 125–27.

22. Onians, *Origins of European Thought*, 109, 122–23, 203, 239, 243, 534, 537–38.

23. Powell, *Celts*, 161.

24. *Roquepertuse et les celto-ligurians*, Musée Archéologique Mediteranée, vol. 14. Lattes, France: A.D.A.M., 1991.

25. Alain Duval and Danielle Heude, *L'art celtique en Gaule* (Paris: Ministère de la Culture Direction des Musées de France, 1983), 134, pl. 155, 160; 134, pl. 154; 139, 141, pl. 163, 164, 166; 140, pl. 165ab.

26. Lambrechts, *L'Exaltation de la tête*, 51.

27. "Warriors from Ancient France," *New York Times*, 3 June 2002, A9.

28. David Rankin, *Celts and the Classical World* (London: Routledge, 1996), 75–76, 51. Lincoln, *Myth, Cosmos, and Society*, 61.

29. Diodorus of Sicily, ca. 90–20 B.C.E. Barry Cunliffe, *The Ancient Celts* (New York: Oxford University Press, 1997), 198–99.

30. Cunliffe, *The Ancient Celts*, 209–10.

31. Powell, *Celts*, 11, 13–15; Lambrechts, *L'Exaltation de la tête*, 39, nn. 1–4.

32. Herodotus, IV, 103; Grene, 318–19.

33. Ralph Merrifield, *The Archaeology of Ritual and Magic* (New York: New Amsterdam, 1987), 27–29, 37, 45–46, 60, 74–75, 82.

34. Ralph Merrifield, *The Archaeology of Ritual and Magic*, 45; Geoff Marsh and Barbara West, "Skullduggery in Roman London?" 90n. 17; M. Harman, T. I. Mollesen, and J. L. Price, "Burials, Bodies and Beheadings in Romano-British and Anglo-Saxon Cemeteries," *Bulletin of the British Museum (Natural History), Geology* 35:3 (1981): 162–64.

35. Lambrechts, *L'Exaltation de la tête*, 40n.

36. Pliny, *Natural History*, 10 vols., book 28, sec. 4, trans. W. H. S. Jones (Cambridge, Mass.: Harvard University Press, 1963), VIII, 13.

37. According to Geoffrey, in the late second century C.E., in response to the Romans' wasting British villages, Demeti, Albani, Deiri, and Venedoti united to exterminate Roman power. Although the British leader was inclined to accept the surrender of Gallus's last legion, the Venedoti preempted him. Advancing "in formation," the Venedoti alone systematically decapitated the surrendered legion. The heads were thrown in the brook or heaped beside it, not appropriated as personal emblems or placed on house fronts. There they were found in the 1860s. Geoffrey of Monmouth, *History of the Kings of Britain*, trans. Lewis Thorpe (New York: Penguin, 1966), 129–30, 19, 44n. 29. Merrifield suggests that the heads recovered from the Walbrook were later votive offerings; *The Archaeology of Ritual and Magic*, 26–29. Marsh and West suggest the heads inspired Geoffrey, "Skullduggery in Roman London?" 86.

38. Isaiah 44:9–20, 41:29, 46:1–7, Jeremiah 10:1–16. As John Dryden puts it, "Gods they had tried of every shape and size,/ That god-smiths could produce or priests devise," *Absalom and Achitophel*, ll. 49–50.

39. Powell, *Celts*, 154–56.

40. Alain Duval and Danielle Heude, *L'Art celtique en Gaule*, 197, pl. 258; André Varagnac and Gabrielle Fabre, *L'Art gaulois*, 2nd ed. (Paris: Zodiaque, 1964), 272, 275, pl. 63.

41. Voisin, "Les Romains, chasseurs de têtes," 283n. 190, and intervention by Dominique Briquel, 292.

42. Jeffrey Jerome Cohen, "Decapitation and Coming of Age: Constructing Masculinity and the Monstrous," in Keith Busby, ed., *The Arthurian Yearbook*,

III (New York: Garland Press, 1993), 173–92. *The Mabinogion,* trans. Gwyn Jones and Thomas Jones (London: J. M. Dent, 1993), 31–33. For other stories, see Anne Ross, *Pagan Celtic Britain,* 155–61.

43. Kate Greenspan, "Hairoic Virtue," Senior Week Symposium, Skidmore College, May 2002.

44. George Lyman Kittredge, "Disenchantment by Decapitation," *Journal of American Folklore* 18:68 (1905): 10.

45. Lucretius, *On the Nature of Things Books I–IV* (Chicago: Henry Regnery, 1949), 91.

46. The Ilongot in the Philippines throw away the head immediately after the decollation, which is often performed from ambush. Renato Rosaldo, *Ilongot Headhunting 1883–1974* (Stanford, Calif.: Stanford University Press, 1980), 63–64, 139–42, 260–61. At almost every point, Ilongot procedures invert those of the Mundurucú.

47. Cornford, *Plato's Cosmology: The "Timaeus" of Plato,* secs. 44e–45, 151.

48. Vermeule, *Aspects of Death,* 107.

49. Hans van Wees, "The Ethics of Anger," in *Status Warriors: War, Violence, and Society in Homer and History* (Amsterdam: J. C. Gieben, 1992), 126. Renato Rosaldo attributes Ilongot headhunting to rage management; they express rage at loss in mourning and find "vitality and energy" in anger. Robert G. Hamerton-Kelly, ed., *Violent Origins: Walter Burkert, René Girard, and Jonathan Z. Smith on Ritual Killing and Cultural Formation.* Commentary by Renato Rosaldo. Intro. by Burton Mack (Stanford, Calif.: Stanford University Press, 1987), 241–43, 247.

50. As Jean-Louis Voisin observes, only heroes are able to strike off heads with a single blow. "Les Romains, chasseurs de têtes," 259. Voisin has Aeneas and Turnus in mind, *Aeneid* IX, 769–71; X, 554–55.

51. Homer's Greek precedes the lines in the translation quoted, identified by the translator, here George Chapman, admired by Keats, the translation dating 1598–1611. Alexander Pope lets blood spurt, but misses the stillness at the end that Chapman finds in the Greek:

Penelaus . . .
from the spouting Shoulders struck his Head;
To Earth at once the Head and Helmet fly;
The Lance, yet sticking thro' the bleeding Eye,
The Victor seiz'd; and as aloft he shook
The goary Visage, thus insulting spoke.
Trojans! your great *Ilioneus* behold!
Haste, to his Father let the Tale be told. . . .
Dreadful he spoke, then toss'd the Head on high;

The *Trojans* hear, they tremble, and they fly:
Aghast they gaze, around the Fleet and Wall,
And dread the Ruin that impends on all.
(XIV, 582–98)

52. Jean-Pierre Vernant, *Mortals and Immortals: Collected Essays,* ed. Froma I. Zeitlin (Princeton, N.J.: Princeton University Press, 1991), 121.

53. Hesiod, *Theogony,* trans. Richmond Lattimore (Ann Arbor: University of Michigan Press, 1959), ll. 276–81. Jean-Pierre Vernant, *Mortals and Immortals,* 144, 136, 146. Zeitlin, *Mortals and Immortals,* 136n, 146n.

54. *The Medusa Reader,* ed. Marjorie Garber and Nancy J. Vicker (New York: Routledge, 2003), does not play the game. This invaluable collection of interpretations does not remark the Gorgon-Medusa distinction and assumes that Homer's Athena and Agamemnon go to battle wearing "Medusa's" head, 9.

55. Wilk, *Medusa: Solving the Mystery of the Gorgon,* 186–87. Photographs from Keith Simpson, *Forensic Medicine,* 5th ed. (London: Edward Arnold, 1964), 187–88. Later editions drop those images.

56. Vernant, *Mortals and Immortals,* 124–25.

57. "The Generation of Monsters in Hesiod," *Classical Philology* 88:2 (April 1993): 109.

58. Vernant, *Mortals and Immortals,* 149, 112. Lambrechts, *L'Exaltation de la tête,* 21.

59. "The Mask of the Underworld Daemon—Some Remarks on the Perseus-Gorgon Story," *Journal of Hellenic Studies* 75 (1955): 11–12, 14.

60. Croon, "The Mask of the Underworld Daemon," 13 and n. 54. Jane E. Harrison, *Prolegomena to the Study of Greek Religion* (Cambridge: Cambridge University Press, 1922), 188.

61. Vernant, *Mortals and Immortals,* 131.

62. Vermeule, *Aspects of Death,* 236n. 3.

63. Ross, *Pagan Celtic Britain,* 125. The masks are British and of uncertain date.

64. Vernant, *Mortals and Immortals,* 138n.

65. A. L. Frothingham, "Medusa II. The Vegetation Gorgoneion," *American Journal of Archeology* 19:1 (January–March 1915): 13–23.

66. Art Institute of Chicago, Volute Krater (funerary vessel), Greek from Apulia, ca. 330/320 B.C.E. Earthenware, red-figure technique, attributed to the Painter of Copenhagen 4223 and a painter of the White Saccos Group. Katherine K. Adler Fund, 1984.7 and 8.

67. Harrison, *Prolegomena to the Study of Greek Religion,* 465–66.

68. Philip Slater, *Glory of Hera: Greek Mythology and the Greek Family* (Boston: Beacon Press, 1968), 18–20, 309. For a positive view of that disorder, see Luce Irigaray, "This Sex That Is Not One," trans. Claudia Reeder; and

Hélène Cixous, "Laugh of the Medusa," trans. Keith Cohen and Paula Cohen, in *New French Feminisms,* ed. Elaine Marks and Isabelle de Courtivron (Amherst: University of Massachusetts Press, 1980), 103–5, 245–64.

69. Eva C. Keuls, *The Reign of the Phallus* (Berkeley: University of California Press, 1985).

70. Vernant, *Mortals and Immortals,* 111.

71. *Timaeus,* 42B, 144; 90E–91, 356–57. Jaroslav Pelikan, *What Has Athens to Do with Jerusalem?* (Ann Arbor: University of Michigan Press, 1997), 83.

72. *The Theban Plays,* trans. E. F. Watling (Baltimore: Penguin, 1947), 136.

73. Bronfen, *Over Her Dead Body,* 70.

74. XX, 249; Vermeule, *Aspects of Death,* 101. Wilk reproduces the first known beautiful Medusa from 475 B.C.E., *Medusa,* 41.

75. *Selected Writings,* ed. Mark Poster (Stanford, Calif.: Stanford University Press, 1988), 169.

76. John Stambaugh, *The Ancient Roman City* (Baltimore: Johns Hopkins University Press, 1988), 222.

77. Futrell, *Blood in the Arena,* 184–85.

78. Ovid, *Fasti,* III, 330ff.

79. Futrell, *Blood in the Arena,* 190, 204, 203, 206.

80. Futrell, *Blood in the Arena,* 203.

81. *Aeneid,* VIII, 262–63; *Annals,* book 1, sec. lxi, in *Works of Cornelius Tacitus,* trans. Arthur Murphy (Philadelphia: Thomas Wardle, 1836), 28.

82. Lambrechts, *L'Exaltation de la tête,* 49.

83. Jean-Louis Voisin, "Les Romains, chasseurs de têtes," 244, 285–92. *Appian's Roman History,* III, 421, book 2, sec. 105.

84. Futrell, *Blood in the Arena,* 191.

85. "Cicero's Head," 199.

86. Richlin, "Cicero's Head," 193–94.

87. Ramsay MacMullen, "Judicial Savagery in the Roman Empire," *Chiron* 16 (1986): 163.

88. Richard A. Bauman, *Crime and Punishment in Ancient Rome* (New York: Routledge, 1996), 1, 151; Peter Garnsey, *Social Status and Legal Privilege in the Roman Empire* (Oxford: Clarendon Press, 1970), 155.

89. MacMullen, "Judicial Savagery," 149. Eusebius affirms that Marcus Aurelius's distinction was obeyed, Roman citizens were beheaded, non-citizens thrown to beasts, in the persecution at Lugdunum, ca. 178 C.E. James Rives, "The Piety of a Persecutor," *Journal of Early Christian Studies,* 4, no. 1 (2000): 22.

90. Voisin, "Les Romains, chasseurs de têtes," 278.

91. Bauman, *Crime and Punishment,* 19. Helen Grace Zagona, *The Legend of Salome and the Principle of Art for Art's Sake* (Geneva: Librairie E. Droz,

1960), 15; Plutarch, *Lives of the Noble Grecians and Romans,* trans. John Dryden, rev. Arthur Hugh Clough (New York: Modern Library, n.d.), 462–63.

92. *De ira,* cited in Voisin, "Les Romains, chasseurs de têtes," 278; Carlin A. Barton, *The Sorrows of the Ancient Romans* (Princeton, N.J.: Princeton University Press, 1993), 57, 61.

93. Suetonius, *The Twelve Caesars,* trans. Robert Graves (Harmondsworth, U.K.: Penguin, 1957), 165–66, book 4, sec. 30, 32, 33.

94. *Appian's Roman History,* IV, 175, book 4, sec. 20.

95. "Galba," in *Twelve Caesars,* 252–53, book 7, sec. 19–20.

96. *History,* 358–60, I, 41–44, 47.

97. *Discipline and Punish,* 82.

98. John Keegan, *A History of Warfare* (New York: Random House, 1993), 266; Dudley, *Urbs Roma* (London: Phaidon, 1967), 144; Keith Hopkins, *Death and Renewal* (Cambridge, 1983), 29, cited in Stambaugh, *The Ancient Roman City,* 369n. 16; Futrell, *Blood in the Arena,* 170.

99. Roland Auguet, *Cruelty and Civilization: The Roman Games* (London: George Allen and Unwin, 1972), 192; Barton, *Sorrows of the Ancient Romans,* 23, 39.

100. Michael Pye, "Headless Body!" *New York Times Book Review,* 20 February 2000, 17. The author of *The Missing Head* is Antonio Tabucchi, "an Italian academic, theoretician and translator, a devotee of Portuguese literature."

101. *The Random House Book of Poetry for Children,* ed. Jack Prelutsky (New York: Random House, 1983), 186.

102. Samuel Y. Edgerton, *Pictures and Punishment: Art and Criminal Prosecution during the Florentine Renaissance* (Ithaca, N.Y.: Cornell University Press, 1985), 14.

103. Ian Fisher, "Congo's War Turns a Land Spat into a Blood Bath," *New York Times,* 29 January 2001, A3.

104. *Murder Most Foul: The Killer and the American Gothic Imagination* (Cambridge, Mass.: Harvard University Press, 1998), 4.

105. Norman S. Fiering, "Irresistible Compassion: An Aspect of Eighteenth-Century Sympathy and Humanitarianism," *Journal of the History of Ideas* 37 (1976): 195–218.

106. Robert D. Keppel and William J. Birnes, *The Psychology of Serial Killer Investigations: The Grisly Business Unit* (Oxford: Academic, 2003); Laurent Montet, *Tueurs en série: Introduction au profilage* (Paris: Presses universitaires, 2000); Elliott Leyton and Linda Chafe, eds. *Serial Murder: Modern Scientific Perspectives* (Burlington, Vt.: Ashgate, Dartmouth, 2000); Stephen J. Giannangelo, *The Psychopathology of Serial Murder: A Theory of Violence* (Westport, Conn.: Praeger, 1996); Lionel Dahmer, *A Father's Story* (New York: W. Morrow, 1994); Brian Masters, *The Shrine of Jeffrey Dahmer* (London: Hodder and Stoughton, 1993); Richard Tithecott, *Of Men and Monsters: Jeffrey Dahmer*

and the Construction of the Serial Killer (Madison: University of Wisconsin Press, 1997); John Gordon Cater, "The Social Construction of the Serial Killer," *RCMP Gazette* 59 (2): 2–21; Kenneth A. Bennett, "Victim Selection in the Jeffrey Dahmer Slayings: An Example of Repetition in the Paraphilias?" *Journal of Forensic Sciences* 38 (5): 1227–32; Stéphane Bourgoin, *Le Cannibale de Milwaukee* (Paris: Editions Méréal, 1998); David T. Lykken, *The Antisocial Personalities* (Hillsdale, N.J.: Lawrence Erlbaum, 1995); Theodore Millon, Erik Simonson, Morton Birket-Smith, and Roger D. Davis, eds. *Psychopathy: Antisocial, Criminal, and Violent Behavior* (New York: Guilford Press, 1998).

107. Richard Tithecott, *Of Men and Monsters: Jeffrey Dahmer and the Construction of the Serial Killer,* 55, 169, 178; Deborah Cameron and Elizabeth Frazer, "Cultural Difference and the Lust to Kill," in *Sex and Violence: Issues in Representation and Experience,* ed. Penelope Harvey and Peter Gow (New York: Routledge, 1994), 165–67; Michael D. Kelleher and C. L. Kelleher, *Murder Most Rare: The Female Serial Killer* (London: Praeger, 1998).

108. *Dissemination,* trans. Barbara Johnson (Chicago: University of Chicago Press, 1981), 301–2.

109. E-mail from Terence Diggory, sent on the anniversary of the beheading of Charles I.

NOTES TO CHAPTER 2

1. Geoffrey Bryan, *Off with His Head* (London: Hutchinson, 1934), 15, 20, 56. For administrative centralization, see Norbert Elias, *The Civilizing Process,* I, xiv, and *Power and Civility* (New York: Pantheon Books, 1982), II, 3–9, 15–30, 91–98; Pieter Spierenburg, *The Broken Spell* (New Brunswick, N.J.: Rutgers University Press, 1991), 2–5, 11–13. For staging, Pieter Spierenburg, *The Spectacle of Suffering* (Cambridge: Cambridge University Press, 1984), 44–57; Lacey Baldwin Smith, "English Treason and Confessions in the Sixteenth Century," *Journal of the History of Ideas* 15:4 (1954): 471–98; Penry Williams, *The Tudor Regime* (Oxford: Oxford University Press, 1981), 360; Peter Burke, *Popular Culture in Early Modern Europe* (1978) (Burlington, Vt.: Ashgate, 1994), 197; J. A. Sharpe, "'Last Dying Speeches': Religion, Ideology and Public Execution in Seventeenth-Century England," *Past and Present* 107 (1985): 157–61, 165; Douglas Hay, "Property, Authority and the Criminal Law," in Douglas Hay et al., *Albion's Fatal Tree: Crime and Society in Eighteenth-Century England* (New York: Pantheon, 1975), 17–64; Richard J. Evans, *Rituals of Retribution: Capital Punishment in Germany, 1600–1987* (New York: Oxford University Press, 1996), 72.

2. Robert Chambers, *The Book of Days: A Miscellany of Popular Antiquities,* 2 vols. (London: W. and R. Chambers, n.d.), II, 233.

3. Norbert Elias, *The Civilizing Process: I. The Development of Manners;*

Clare Gittings, *Death, Burial, and the Individual in Early Modern England* (London-Sydney, 1984), cited in Spierenburg, *The Broken Spell,* 161; Spierenburg, *The Broken Spell,* 213, 220; David Garland, *Punishment and Modern Society: A Study in Social Theory* (Chicago: University of Chicago Press, 1990), 225; Keith Thomas, *Man and the Natural World: Changing Attitudes in England 1500–1800* (New York: Oxford University Press, 1983); Foucault, *Surveiller et punir [Discipline and Punish]*; V. A. C. Gatrell, *The Hanging Tree: Execution and the English People 1770–1868* (Oxford: Oxford University Press, 1994), 15–17, 226, 331–32; Randall McGowen, "The Body and Punishment in Eighteenth-Century England," *Journal of Modern History* 59 (December 1987): 651–79. Thomas finds the new Enlightenment sensibilities attested in the Middle Ages, 152–53, and Renaissance, 173–74.

4. Sir Edward Coke, ca. 1605, on the Guy Fawkes conspirators, Leon Radzinowicz, *A History of English Criminal Law and Its Administration from 1750 to 1833* (New York: Macmillan, 1948), 222.

5. Jörg Fisch, *Cheap Lives and Dear Limbs: The British Transformation of the Bengal Criminal Law 1769–1817* (Wiesbaden, Germany: F. Steiner Verlag, 1983).

6. *Commentaries on the Laws of England,* vol. 4, *Of Public Wrongs,* adapted by Robert Malcolm Kerr (Boston: Beacon Press, 1962), 510.

7. V. A. C. Gatrell, *The Hanging Tree,* 32, 544; E. P. Thompson, *Whigs and Hunters: The Origin of the Black Act* (New York: Random House, 1975), 23, 254–55; Frank McLynn, *Crime and Punishment in Eighteenth-Century England* (New York: Routledge, 1989), xi–xiv; James Turner, *Reckoning with the Beast: Animals, Pain, and Humanity in the Victorian Mind* (Baltimore: Johns Hopkins University Press, 1980), 34.

8. Thomas Rowlandson's *A Gibbet* (1790s?) is reproduced in Gatrell, *Hanging Tree,* 178. 25 Geo. II, c. 37; 2 & 3 Will. IV, c. 75, s. 16; 4 & 5 Will. IV, c. 26, s.1. William Blackstone, *Commentaries on the Laws of England,* vol. 4, *Of Public Wrongs,* 225.

9. Thanks to Professor Susan Kress for my copy.

10. Michel Foucault, *Discipline and Punish,* 8, 82; T. R. Haskell, "Capitalism and the Origins of the Humanitarian Sensibility," *American Historical Review* 90, nos. 2, 3 (April, June 1985): 339–61, 547–96.

11. Hobbes, *Leviathan,* ed. C. B. Macpherson (Baltimore: Penguin, 1968), pt. 1, chap. 13, 185–87, chap. 14, 189–90. John Locke, *Two Treatises of Government,* ed. Peter Laslett (Cambridge: Cambridge University Press, 1966), *Second Treatise of Government,* chap. 3, sec. 21, 323; chap. 8, sec. 95, 375; chap. 9, sec. 127, 397–98; John Colman, *John Locke's Moral Philosophy* (Edinburgh: Edinburgh University Press, 1983), 184–86; C. B. Macpherson, *The Political Theory of Possessive Individualism: Hobbes to Locke* (Oxford: Oxford University Press, 1962).

12. Henry Bienen, *Violence and Social Change: A Review of Current Literature* (Chicago: University of Chicago Press, 1968), 74.

13. *Second Treatise*, chap. 3, sec. 16–17, sec. 19, 321.

14. *Second Treatise*, chap. 5, sec. 27, 328. Kirstie M. McClure, *Judging Rights: Lockean Politics and the Limits of Consent* (Ithaca, N.Y.: Cornell University Press, 1996), 222–24; John W. Yolton, "Locke's Man," *Journal of the History of Ideas* 62:4 (2001): 665–83; E. J. Hundert, *The Enlightenment's Fable: Bernard Mandeville and the Discovery of Society* (Cambridge: Cambridge University Press, 1994).

15. Gillian Brown, "Lockean Pediatrics," *Annals of Scholarship* 14:3 and 15:1 (2001): 11; G. S. Rousseau, "Nerves, Spirits, and Fibres: Towards Defining the Origins of Sensibility," in R. F. Brisenden and J. C. Eade, eds., *Studies in the Eighteenth Century III. Papers Presented to the Third David Nichol Smith Memorial Seminar, Canberra 1973* (Toronto: University of Toronto Press, 1976), 137–57.

16. *An Essay Concerning Human Understanding* (1690), ed. Peter H. Nidditch (Oxford: Clarendon Press, 1975), book 3, chap. 7, sec. 1, 362; chap. 9, sec. 127, 397.

17. *An Essay Concerning Human Understanding* (1690), book 2, chap. 22, sec. 11, 336–37.

18. Sarah Maza, "Only Connect: Family Values in the Age of Sentiment," *Eighteenth-Century Studies* 30:3 (1997): 208–9; Adam Smith, *Theory of Moral Sentiments*, ed. D. D. Raphael and A. L. Macfie (Indianapolis: Liberty Classics, 1982), 9–10; Adam Ferguson, *An Essay on the History of Civil Society*, 1767, ed. Duncan Forbes (Edinburgh: University of Edinburgh Press, 1966), 19.

19. Randall McGowen, "The Body and Punishment in Eighteenth-Century England," *Journal of Modern History* 59 (December 1987): 651–79.

20. Edgerton, *Pictures and Punishment*, 135; Richard J. Evans, *Rituals of Retribution*, 224, 221, 366, 373, 879.

21. Patricia Fumerton, *Cultural Aesthetics* (Chicago: University of Chicago Press, 1991), 3–10; Donald T. Siebert, "The Aesthetic Execution of Charles I: Clarendon to Hume," in William B. Thesing, ed., *Executions and the British Experience from the 17th to the 20th Century: A Collection of Essays* (Jefferson, N.C.: McFarland, 1990), 7–27.

22. Sir Roger Manley, in Fumerton, *Cultural Aesthetics*, 9.

23. Edward [Hyde], Earl of Clarendon, *History of the Rebellion and Civil Wars in England* (Oxford: Oxford University Press, 1843), book 11, 697; Thomas Hobbes, *Behemoth: The History of the Causes of the Civil Wars of England*, ed. William Molesworth (New York: Burt Franklin, n.d.), part 3, 193; Milton, *Complete Poems and Major Prose*, ed. Merritt Y. Hughes (New York: Odyssey, 1957), 786; Marvell, *An Horatian Ode upon Cromwell's Return from Ireland*, ll. 63–70.

24. Anne Gordon, *Death Is for the Living* (Edinburgh, U.K.: Paul Harris, 1984), 112.

25. *ECSTC; Chronicles of Crime, Or The New Newgate Calendar,* 2 vols., ed. Camden Pelham (Paris: Charles Carrington, 1900), I, 301, 308.

26. [Midgley, Dr. Samuel], *Halifax and its Gibbet Law placed in a true light: Together with a description of the Town. . . .* (London: Printed by J. How for William Bently, at Halifax in Yorkshire, 1708), 56–57. Holinshed observes that the gibbet once bounced a head into the hamper of a lady riding by; Bryan, *Off with His Head,* 23–24.

27. *England's Black Tribunal: Containing, I. The Compleat Trial of King Charles the First, II. The Loyal Martyrology. . . .* 5th ed. (London, 1702).

28. Edward [Hyde], Earl of Clarendon, *History of the Rebellion,* book 11, 741, 700–701.

29. *The Tryal of William Stayley, Goldsmith; For Speaking Treasonable Words Against His Most Sacred Majesty: And Upon Full Evidence Found Guilty of High Treason, And received Sentence accordingly, on Thursday November the 21th 1678* (London: Robert Pawlet, 1678).

30. Melinda Zook, "Violence, Martyrdom, and Radical Politics: Rethinking the Glorious Revolution," in *Politics and the Political Imagination in Later Stuart Britain,* ed. Howard Nenner (Rochester, N.Y.: University of Rochester Press, 1997), 87–88.

31. Frank McLynn, *The Jacobites* (London: Routledge and Kegan Paul, 1985), 127. William E. H. Lecky, *A History of England in the Eighteenth Century* (London: Longmans, Green, 1919), I, 269.

32. [Daniel Defoe], *The Annals of King George* (1718, 1721).

33. James Boswell, *Life of Johnson,* ed. R. W. Chapman (London: Oxford University Press, 1961), 106–7.

34. Karen Halttunen, "Humanitarianism and the Pornography of Pain in Anglo-American Culture," *American Historical Review* 100:2 (1995): 303–34. James Turner argues that pain becomes obscene and "instinctively" aversive only in the nineteenth century; see *Reckoning with the Beast,* xii, 11, 79–80.

35. McLynn, *The Jacobites,* 127; Bruce Lenman, *The Jacobite Risings in Britain, 1689–1746* (London: Eyre Methuen, 1980), 201.

36. *Gentleman's Magazine* 16 (1746): 383. R. Chambers's *The Book of Days,* II, 233, reports that the heads of Francis Townley and George Fletcher were fixed on poles over Temple Bar and blew down in 1772.

37. *Gentleman's Magazine* 23 (1753): 293. By 1753, disemboweling had become an action one ought not to watch. Walpole complained that the officiating clergyman, hastening down the scaffold into his landau, had lowered the top better to view the "emboweling." Assuming his reader will be shocked by a clergyman's securing the best view, as if at a sporting match, Walpole deflects disapproval from the event to one spectator. To Sir Horace Mann, 12 June 1753, in

Selected Letters of Horace Walpole, ed. W. S. Lewis (New Haven: Yale University Press, 1973), 46.

38. *Chronicles of Crime*, I, 301.

39. Horace Bleackley, *The Hangmen of England in State Executions Viewed Historically and Sociologically* (Montclair, N.J.: Patterson Smith, 1977), 81.

40. A Gentleman who attended his Lordship in his last Moments, *A Candid and Impartial Account of the Behaviour of Simon Lord Lovat, From The Time his Death-Warrant was deliver'd, to the Day of his Execution. Together with a faithful Narrative of the particular Incidents which happen'd that Day in the Tower, in the Sheriff's Apartment, and on the Scaffold* (London: J. Newbury, 1747), 26.

41. *A Short and True Narrative of the Rebellion in 1745: Beginning with the Young Chevalier's Entry into the West of Scotland, until his Banishment out of France; With an Account of his bad Treatment, for his good Service to the French King. Together with the Trials of the Scotch Lords Who were Beheaded on his Account. The whole being the shortest and most Authentic Account That can be given of that troublesome Time* (Edinburgh: The booksellers, 1779), 68. Touring the Hebrides with Samuel Johnson, Boswell had bad dreams at Lord Errol's, thinking of the lord's father, Kilmarnock.

42. A Gentleman of the Family, *Genuine and Impartial Memoirs of the Life and Character of Charles Ratcliffe, Esq; Who was Beheaded on Tower-Hill, Monday, December 8, 1746. With an Account of his Family, and how far he was concerned in the Rebellion in 1715; the Inducements that occasioned his coming over to England, in 1725; and also the last Time with the Officers of Dillon's Regiment in the Irish Brigade in the French Service. To which is Added, A true Account of his Dying Behaviour and Last Words. Also A full Answer to the Letter inserted in the Daily Advertiser on Saturday, December 6, 1746, relating to these Memoirs* (London: B. Cole, 1746), 29.

43. Gatrell, *Hanging Tree*, 83–84, 88, 98, 104, 158; Robert Kee, *The Green Flag: A History of Irish Nationalism* (London: Weidenfeld and Nicolson, 1972), 167–68; John F. McCaffrey, *Scotland in the Nineteenth Century* (London: Macmillan, 1998), 22.

44. Howard Engel, *Lord High Executioner* (London: Robson, 1997), 119; David D. Cooper, *The Lesson of the Scaffold* (Athens: Ohio University Press, 1974), 4.

45. Ida Macalpine and R. Hunter, *George III and the Mad-Business* (London: Pantheon Books, 1991), 310–16; John Barrell, *Imagining the King's Death: Figurative Treason, Fantasies of Regicide 1793–1796* (New York: Oxford University Press, 2000), 559.

46. Radzinowicz, *A History of English Criminal Law*, 519.

47. Blackstone, *Commentaries on the Laws of England*, vol. 4, *Of Public Wrongs*, 446.

48. L. A. Parry, *The History of Torture in England* (Montclair, N.J.: Patterson Smith, 1975), 108. Bryan, in *Off with His Head*, 157–59, attributes the use of the axe to the Prince Regent.

49. McLynn, *Crime and Punishment in Eighteenth-Century England*, 269.

50. Pelham, ed., *Chronicles of Crime*, I, 394.

51. Pelham, ed., *Chronicles of Crime*, II, 19. Radzinowicz, *A History of English Criminal Law*, 226–27.

52. *Gentleman's Magazine* 90 (1820), 460. J. B. Priestley, *The Prince of Pleasure and His Regency 1811–20* (New York: Harper and Row, 1969), 261. Nina Athanassoglou-Kallmyer, "Géricault's Severed Heads and Limbs: The Politics and Aesthetics of the Scaffold," *Art Bulletin* 74:4 (1992): 603, 605.

53. Cited by William Makepeace Thackeray in 1840, going to see Courvoisier hang. John Lofland, *The Dramaturgy of State Executions in State Executions Viewed Historically and Sociologically* (Montclair, N.J.: Patterson Smith, 1977), 299; Gatrell, *Hanging Tree*, 113, 306.

54. Bibliothèque nationale de France, Paris, BN R150913.

55. Gerhard F. Strasser, "War and Poetry: Personal Experience of Renaissance Warfare and Visual Representation of Its Horrors in the Work of Agrippa D'Aubigné," in *Actes du VIIIe Congrès de l'association internationale de littérature comparée (Proceedings of the 8th Congress of the International Comparative Literature Association)*, 2 vols., ed. Bela Kopeczi and Gyorgy M. Vajda (Stuttgart, Germany: Kunst und Wissen, Erich Bieber, 1980), I, 173–81; David Freedberg, "The Representation of Martyrdoms during the Counter Reformation in Antwerp," *Burlington Magazine* 118 (1976): 128–38.

56. Gertrud Schiller, *Iconography of Christian Art*, 2 vols., trans. Janet Seligman (Greenwich, Conn.: New York Graphic Society, 1972), II, 96–97, 100; John R. Martin, "The Dead Christ on the Cross in Byzantine Art," in *Late Classical and Medieval Studies in Honor of Albert Mathias Friend, Jr.* (Princeton, N.J.: Princeton University Press, 1995), 189–90. For these references, I thank Professor Penny Jolly.

57. Locke's patron Shaftesbury, Achitophel to Monmouth's Absalom in Dryden's poem, had fled to Holland in 1682, dying in 1683. Resident in Shaftesbury's household since 1667, Locke left England for Holland in 1683, remaining there until 1689. Locke published his *Essay* and his *Treatises* in 1690.

58. *A Letter from Dr. William Lloyd, Bp. of St. Asaph, to Bp. Fell, concerning the Execution and last Behaviours of the Duke of Monmouth*, July 1685, in *Walteri Hemingford, Canonici de Gisseburne, Historia de Rebus Gestis Edvard I. Edvard II. & Edvard III*, 2 vols. (Oxford: Sheldonian Theatre, 1731), II, clxxviii–xix.

59. Robert Clifton, *The Last Popular Rebellion: The Western Rising of 1685* (New York: St. Martin's Press, 1984), 228.

60. *An Account Of what Passed at the Execution of the Late Duke of Mon-*

mouth, On Wednesday the 15th of July, 1685. on Tower-Hill (London: Robert Horne, John Baker, and Benjamin Took, 1685).

61. Timed in 1905 by Dr. Beaurieux on the murderer Languille, who opened and focused his eyes when the doctor called his name after decapitation. Alister Kershaw, *A History of the Guillotine,* reprinted in *Harper's Magazine,* August 2003, 29. Life's disappearance as process was noted by Lucretius. In Lafcadio Hearn's "Diplomacy," the Japanese have no doubts about continuing consciousness in the head. A servant about to be executed rages against his master's injustice and threatens to return as a spirit to torment the household. The master scoffs, saying if the servant thinks he can return he should show it by biting the stone a few feet away. When the servant assures him he will, the master cuts off the head. The head bounces to the stone and bites it furiously. The other servants are terrified, the master entirely calm. A few days later he explains that they need never worry about that ghost. When he died, he was thinking only about biting the stone. All thoughts of anger at the master and the household were out of his mind, so he would never return. And he never did. Professor Robert Mahony drew my attention to this tale. Among recent bouncing heads in film, the trio in *Spirited Away* pay homage to a great tradition.

62. Joseph Addison, *Freeholder* 12, 14, 28, in *Works of Joseph Addison,* 6 vols., ed. Richard Hurd (London: George Bell, 1901–9), IV, 445, 486, 493.

63. *Freeholder* 7, 17, 20, in *Works,* IV, 474. Jonathan Swift, *Miscellaneous and Autobiographical Pieces, Fragments and Marginalia,* ed. Herbert Davis (Oxford: Blackwell, 1962), V, 254.

64. *Remarks on the Speech of James Late Earl of Derwentwater, Beheaded on Tower-Hill for High-Treason, February 24, 1715/16* (London: R. Burleigh, 1716), 3; Samuel Rosewell, *A Sermon Preach'd On the Solemn Occasion of the Deaths of the Lords Who Were Beheaded on Tower-Hill for High-Treason, February 24, 1715–16* (London: M. Lawrence, 1716).

65. Randall McGowen, "'He Beareth Not the Sword in Vain': Religion and the Criminal Law in Eighteenth-Century England," *Eighteenth-Century Studies* 21:2 (1987–88): 195.

66. Although many critics have hoped there was a contemporary historical source for this tasteless episode, Gay's source was literary. Regina Janes, "Gay and Ariosto: Bouncing Heads," *ELH* 70:2 (2003): 447–63.

67. *Works of Sir William Temple* (London: J. Rivington, 1814), II, 100.

68. *Gulliver's Travels,* ed. Herbert Davis (Oxford: Blackwell, 1959), 119–20.

69. Robert Mitchell, "The Violence of Sympathy: Adam Smith on Resentment and Executions," in *1650–1850: Ideas, Aesthetics, and Inquiries in the Early Modern Era* 8 (New York: AMS Press, 2003), 321–41.

70. R. Janes, "Jonathan Swift Bounces a Head," in *1650–1850: Ideas, Aesthetics, and Inquiries* 8 (New York: AMS Press, 2003), 315–16; Dennis Todd,

"The Hairy Maid at the Harpsichord: Some Speculations on the Meaning of *Gulliver's Travels,*" *Texas Studies in Language and Literature* 34 (1992): 249.

71. I owe this reference to my student Robert Koeth III. In 1800, J. Salmon veiled the bounces, describing the three fountains that sprang up from St. Paul's bouncing head as "the three spots his head moved to after it was taken off." *An Historical Description of Ancient and Modern Rome; also of the works of art,* 2 vols. (London, 1800), II, 76.

72. *Miscellanies in Prose and Verse* (London, 1740), 56–57. Her visit to Paris was 1720. I owe this anecdote to Liz Bohls.

73. Jeanne Duportal, *Bernard Picart 1673 à 1733* (Paris: G. Van Oest, 1928), 392. In 1732, an elaborate edition of *Ovid's Metamorphoses,* including Gay's translations along with many other hands, featured "Sculptures, by B. Picart, and other able Masters. Amsterdam." *Gay's Poetical Works,* ed. G. C. Faber (Oxford: Oxford University Press, 1926), 95hn.

74. *The Sense of the People: Politics, Culture, and Imperialism in England 1715–1785* (Cambridge: Cambridge University Press, 1995), 214–16.

75. *Catalogue of Prints and Drawings in the British Museum,* I [1320–1689], II [1689–1733], ed. G. Stephens (London: Trustees of the British Museum, 1870); ed. M. D. George, *Catalogue of Political and Personal Satires* (London: British Museum Prints and Drawings, 1935), V, #4950, #4956.

NOTES TO CHAPTER 3

1. Jacques de Flesselles, merchant and acting head of the provisional government of the city of Paris, had denied ammunition to the crowds at the Hotel de Ville. The Marquis de Launay was the governor of the Bastille.

2. *The Correspondence of Edmund Burke,* ed. Thomas W. Copeland et al. (Chicago: University of Chicago Press, 1967), VI, 10; 9 August 1789.

3. Albert O. Hirschman, *The Passions and the Interests* (Princeton, N.J.: Princeton University Press, 1977), 14–31. Henrietta Moore, "The Problem of Explaining Violence in the Social Sciences," in *Sex and Violence: Issues in Representation and Experience,* ed. Penelope Harvey and Peter Gow (London: Routledge, 1994), 138–55. Pierre Saint-Amand, *The Laws of Hostility: Politics, Violence, and the Enlightenment,* trans. Jennifer Curtiss Gage (Minneapolis: University of Minnesota Press, 1996), 2–8.

4. Jean Jacques Rousseau, *Discourse on the Origin of Inequality* in *The Social Contract and Discourses,* trans. G. D. H. Cole (New York: E. P. Dutton, 1950), 249. In this discourse Rousseau contradicts his argument in the *Discourse on the Arts and Sciences.* In the latter, society corrupts and enervates the primitive, martial, Roman virtues. J. G. A. Pocock has shown how important the image of republican virtue was to the Revolution and in eighteenth-century

thought, *Virtue, Commerce, and History* (Cambridge: Cambridge University Press, 1985). Such virtue controlled both its own violence and that of others.

5. *Reflections on the Revolution in France,* ed. Conor Cruise O'Brien (Baltimore: Penguin, 1969), 159. Emphases added.

6. *Reflections,* 164–65. Emphases added.

7. Seneca, *Thebais,* Act I, in *Seneca: His Tenne Tragedies,* trans. Thomas Newton, intro. T. S. Eliot (Bloomington: Indiana University Press, n.d.), 101.

8. *Correspondence of Edmund Burke,* VI, 73, 17 January 1790. More recently, Albert Soboul tells us much about the price of bread, but little about the hazards of baking it.

9. *Correspondence of Edmund Burke,* VI, 153–54, 3 and 4 November 1790; emphasis added.

10. *Correspondence of Edmund Burke,* VI, 113, 12 May 1790. Contradictory explanations proliferate in Cloots's rush of syntax. Responsibility for the few heads cut off rests elsewhere, with those who have deluded and ensnared the poor people. The people have a right to those heads, which are justly culled.

11. George Rudé, *The Crowd in the French Revolution* (Oxford: Oxford University Press, 1959), 56, 76, 78, 227; Alfred Cobban, *Aspects of the French Revolution* (New York: George Braziller, 1965) and *A History of Modern France: I* (Baltimore: Penguin, 1957); Albert Soboul, *A Short History of the French Revolution 1789–1799,* trans. Geoffrey Symcox (Berkeley: University of California, 1977); Georges Lefebvre, *The French Revolution,* 2 vols., trans. Elizabeth Evanson, John H. Stewart, and James Friguglietti (New York: Columbia University Press, 1964); R. B. Rose, *The Making of the Sans-Culottes: Democratic Ideas and Institutions in Paris, 1789–1792* (Manchester, U.K.: Manchester University Press, 1983). Lynn Hunt remarks on the "horror" of the prints that represented the deaths of Foulon and Bertier and moves on to a less grisly topic. "The Political Psychology of Revolutionary Caricatures," in *French Caricature and the French Revolution, 1789–1799,* ed. James Cuno (Los Angeles: University of California, 1988), 35.

12. Rudé, *Crowd,* 56.

13. Regina Janes, "Beheadings," *Representations* 35 (1991): 26.

14. Alan Wintermute, *1789: French Painting During the Revolution* (New York: Colnaghi, 1989), 148.

15. No. 117, Cuno, ed., *French Caricature and the French Revolution,* 78.

16. Assemblée Nationale, *Journal des débats et des décrets,* 1 December 1789. The abolition of differential sentencing had also been proposed by parliamentary courts during the English civil war.

17. Michel Foucault, *Discipline and Punish,* trans. Alan Sheridan (New York: Vintage Books, 1979), 33.

18. Liancourt is quoted in John Wilson Croker, "The Guillotine," in *Essays on the Early Period of the French Revolution* (London: John Murray, 1857),

532. In 1791, Maury's argument was repeated by M. Lachèze, *Ancien Moniteur,* 4 juin 1791.

19. The radical implications of movement have been explored in another context by Maurice Agulhon, *Marianne into Battle: Republican Imagery and Symbolism in France, 1789–1880,* trans. Janet Lloyd (Cambridge: Cambridge University Press, 1981), 88.

20. *Ancien Moniteur,* 18 December 1789.

21. Daniel Arasse observes that the authorities' ambivalence toward their own project was reflected in the official refusal to allow the fabricator of the machine to patent it. Daniel Arasse, *La Guillotine et l'imaginaire de la Terreur* (Paris: Flammarion, 1987), 35–36. They separated death from commerce, from profit.

22. Of the surrender at Lyon in October 1793, the *Annual Register* wrote from a safe distance: "The miserable victims, who were too numerous for the individual operation of the guillotine, were driven in great numbers, with the most savage and blasphemous ceremonies into the Rhone, or hurried in crowds to the squares, to be massacred by the more painful operation of fire arms and artillery" (1793, 279). The following year, word of Carrier's revolutionary weddings and death ships at Nantes caused the same periodical to recoil even further, to phrases of prophetic incredulity: "In a country and nation hitherto respected for its civilization, its hospitality, its manners, and its eminence in arts, in knowledge, and whatever adorns and refines human life, Europe beheld, and posterity will learn with astonishment and horror, that for the space of several months a tribunal existed in the large and populous city of Nantz, legally commissioned by public authority to exercise the most merciless and cruel despotism, and to condemn to the most unfeeling and scandalous modes of destruction, whole tribes and districts of their fellow-citizens" (1794, 95).

23. The identification between the guillotine and radicalism, charted by Ronald Paulson for England in "The Severed Head," was first made in France; see "The Severed Head," in *French Caricature and the French Revolution,* ed. Cuno, 55–66.

24. *Ancien Moniteur,* 7 April 1794; 18 germinal, l'an 2.

25. Dorinda Outram, *The Body and the French Revolution* (New Haven: Yale University Press, 1989), 118–21, 111–14.

26. *Ancien Moniteur,* 22 January 1795, 3 plûviose, l'an 3. Champain-Aubin made the motion; annihilating the guillotine was the second in a series of resolutions abolishing the death penalty offered to the Convention; they met with the same success as Robespierre's proposal to end capital punishment in 1791.

27. *Ancien Moniteur,* 23 messidor, l'an 3; 11 July 1795. Mass deportations replaced mass guillotinings.

28. *Representations of Revolution* (New Haven: Yale University Press, 1983), 270.

29. *The French Revolution* (London: E. P. Dutton, 1906), I, 115; part I, book 4, chap. 4, "The Procession."

30. Croker, *Essays on the Early Period of the French Revolution*, 542. Sir Walter Scott's account, which Croker is using, is slightly less voluptuous: "He mounted the scaffold with great firmness, and embracing the engine by which he was to suffer, declared it the sweetest maiden he had ever kissed"; *Miscellaneous Prose Works* (Edinburgh: Robert Cadell, 1838), XXIV, 281; "Tales of a Grandfather: Scotland." Argyle's father, the Marquis of Argyle, had been beheaded in 1660 by the Maiden, introduced in 1565.

31. Arasse, *La Guillotine et l'imaginaire de la Terreur* 34.

32. Neil Hertz has shown that the presiding genius of such representations was Medusa, "Medusa's Head: Male Hysteria under Political Pressure," *Representations* 4 (Fall 1983): 27–54. When they tired of festoons of snakes, artists worked in the guillotine. Cruikshank's *Republican Belle* and *Beau* parody the popular revolutionary images of pretty sansculottes and clean, well-turned-out National Guardsmen.

33. Madame Defarge, tricoteuse extraordinaire, mechanical in her motions and in her motivations, incarnates the guillotine in the image structure of the novel. Both are silent, implacable, determined, sharp, female, and newly born in the Revolution. Although Madame Defarge is not given to drunkenness, she does run a wine shop, and Dickens's guillotine, the "sharp female, newly born," consumes wine insatiably. Suspended until the end of the novel is the discovery that Madame Defarge is a handsome woman, sister to the beauty raped by aristocrats. Dickens describes her in strikingly sensual terms, and just before he kills her, he shows us her legs: "Walking with . . . the supple freedom of a woman who had habitually walked in her girlhood, bare-foot and bare-legged, on the brown sea-sand, Madame Defarge took her way along the streets." Within a few pages, Madame Defarge will be dead, killed by the homely Miss Pross and one glimpse of those legs, bare and white on the sea-sand of the past.

Dickens also paints the monstrous carnival of the carmagnole and puts the dance under the sign of the guillotine. Like Burke's, Dickens's images recognize the festive character of the dance even as they turn festivity into dangerous, alien frenzy. "The Wood-Sawyer" chapter begins with "La Sainte Guillotine," the saw of the wood sawyer, "stationed" in his window. After the carmagnole, Madame Defarge appears, and the chapter closes with the tumbrils of the guillotine rolling by. *A Tale of Two Cities* (1859) (Baltimore: Penguin, 1970), 307–8.

34. While the image of Marie Antoinette emerges from the radical, antimonarchical left, the pretty, lethal whore, Democracy and 93, emerges from late nineteenth-century Montmartre, the Chat Noir cabaret, and the saucy superiority of the Chat Noir masthead: "What is Montmartre? Nothing! What should it be? Everything!" The Abbé Sieyès would not have approved, nor was he meant to. Mariel Frerebeau, "What is Montmartre? Nothing! What should it be?

Everything!" *Art News*, 72: 3 (March 1977): 60–62. I owe this reference to Heather Ferguson.

35. Remarked with horror by the Earl of Mornington, *Parliamentary History*, XXX, 1188, January 1794.

36. *Reflections*, 120.

37. *Considérations sur les principaux événemens de la Révolution Française* (London: Baldwin, Craddock, and Jay, 1818), II, 141–42. George Rudé, ed., *Robespierre* (Englewood Cliffs, N.J.: Prentice Hall, 1967), 126.

38. "The Severed Head," 58.

39. *The French Revolution*, II, 285; part 3, book 3, chap. 6, "Risen against Tyrants."

40. Swift, *Verses on the Death of Dr. Swift.*

41. *Explosion in a Cathedral*, trans. John Sturrock (New York: Harper and Row, 1963), 7–8.

NOTES TO CHAPTER 4

1. Helen Grace Zagona, *The Legend of Salome and the Principle of Art for Art's Sake* (Geneva: Droz, 1960), 95–96.

2. In serial form, Laforgue's "Salome" appeared in *La Vogue* in 1886; as part of *Moralités légendaires* it appeared posthumously in 1887. Zagona, *Legend* of *Salome*, 103.

3. Pierre-Louis Mathieu reproduces some seventeen Salomes, most with Baptist, *Gustave Moreau* (Paris: ACR Edition, 1998). See also Geneviève Lacambre, *Gustave Moreau: Between Epic and Dream* (Chicago: Art Institute of Chicago, 1999).

4. For a "selection draconienne parmi près d'un millier de titres," see the bibliography in Mireille Dottin-Orsini, *Salome*, 166–70. Other famous names in Dottin-Orsini's select list include Sue, D'Annunzio, Louys, Schwob, Apollinaire, Cocteau, Desnos, Leiris, Arrabal, Delacroix, Regnault, Willette, Munch (1898, and a self-portrait in 1903), Roualt, Corinth, Klimt, Picasso, Dali (staging for a production of Strauss); many films and many ballets, including one by Martha Graham. Salome in twentieth-century choreography has been treated by H. Williams, "Salome: Biblical Mythology and Twentieth-Century Dance," *Journal of the International Council for Health* 35:3 (Spring 1999): 8–11. The most important omissions in Dottin-Orsini are Paul Delaroche's *Hérodiade* (1841), and the American, J. C. Heywood, *Salome* (Cambridge, Mass., 1862), reviewed by Wilde in 1888, "The Poet's Corner," *Pall Mall Gazette* 47 (20 January 1888): 3. Herodias, not Salome, kisses the head of John the Baptist. Richard Ellman, "Overtures to *Salome*," in *Oscar Wilde: A Collection of Critical Essays* (Englewood Cliffs, N.J.: Prentice Hall, 1969), 74.

5. Krafft, cited by Mireille Dottin-Orsini in *Salome dans les collections*

françaises, ed. Catherine Camboulives et al. (Saint Denis: Musée d'Art et d'Histoire de la Ville de Saint-Denis; Tourcoing, Musée des Beaux-Arts; Albi, Musée Toulouse Lautrec; Auxerre, Musées, 1988–89), 14. Bettina L. Knapp, among others, uses the figure without attribution, "Herodias/Salome: Mother/Daughter Identification," *Nineteenth-Century French Studies* 25:1–2 (1996–97): 179.

6. Excluding the composite "Michael Field," the painters Ella Ferris Pell and Juana Romani (1890), and a few twentieth-century authors, the list is conspicuously masculine. Women danced the choreography, acted the parts, and sang the roles, but the only woman of genius to take up the subject was Martha Graham (1944). The Baptist's decollation having become the Salome topos, female scholars dominate the field in criticism.

7. The topos never disappeared, although Zagona puts Salome into "artistic hibernation" (Bentley's phrase) between the seventeenth and nineteenth centuries, *Legend of Salome*, 21, an account followed by Françoise Meltzer, *Salome and the Dance of Writing* (Chicago: University of Chicago Press, 1987), 16; Toni Bentley, *Sisters of Salome* (New Haven: Yale University Press, 2002), 20; Megan Becker-Leckrone, "Salome©: The Fetishization of a Textual Corpus," *New Literary History* 26:2 (Spring 1995): 238. For an alternative view, see Regina Janes, "An Eighteenth-Century Absence? Salome, Daughter of Herodias," Northeast American Society for Eighteenth-Century Studies (NEASECS) (Boston), October 1997.

8. Bram Dijkstra, *Idols of Perversity: Fantasies of Feminine Evil in Fin-de-Siècle Culture* (New York: Oxford University Press, 1986), vii, 3–19, and *Evil Sisters: The Threat of Female Sexuality and the Cult of Manhood* (New York: Alfred A. Knopf, 1996); Debora Silverman, "The 'New Woman,' Feminism and the Decorative Arts in Fin-de-Siècle France," in *Eroticism and the Body Politic*, ed. Lynn Hunt (Baltimore: Johns Hopkins University Press, 1991), 144–63; Michael Mason, *The Making of Victorian Sexuality* (New York: Oxford University Press, 1994), 57–61; Lynn Hunt, "Freedom of Dress in Revolutionary France," *From the Royal to the Republican Body*, ed. Sara E. Melzer and Kathryn Norberg (Berkeley: University of California Press, 1998), 224–49.

9. Dijkstra, *Evil Sisters*, 3–7.

10. *Jewish Antiquities*, trans. Louis H. Feldman (Cambridge, Mass.: Harvard University Press, 1965), XVIII, cxvi–cxviii, 81–85; ccxl–cclvi, 145–51; lxiii–lxiv, 49–51; cxxxviii, 93.

11. Since the name "Salome" occurs with reference to Herodias's daughter only in Josephus, writers dependent on the biblical account always name Herodias's daughter "Herodias," as she is named in several early manuscripts, or "the daughter of Herodias," as she is called in manuscripts of equal authority. As late as 1859, Delacroix called a painting of the Baptist and Salome that he was copying for a friend, a "St Jean et Herodiate [*sic*]." Arlette Sérullaz, Vincent Pomarède, and Joseph J. Rishel, *Delacroix, Les Dernières Années* (Paris: Réunion

des Musées Nationaux, 1998), 310. So too Mallarmé's poem is *Hérodiade,* not Salome. The modern rejection of the name "Herodias" for both daughter and topos insists on daughterly autonomy and denies maternal power. "Salome" emphasizes the individuality of the daughter; "Herodias" or "daughter of Herodias" emphasizes the power, sexuality, and political interests of the mother. Françoise Meltzer makes much of the "confusion" of names, in *Salome and the Dance of Writing,* 16–17. The authors she cites are less confused than following different traditions of naming.

12. Josephus names Herod's half-brother Herod also; the gospel takes the name Philip not from Herodias's first husband but from her son-in-law, the husband of Salome. *Jewish Antiquities,* XVIII, cix, cxxxviii, 77, 93.

13. Bruce D. Chilton suggests that Jesus as a child or adolescent may have seen John; see "John the Baptist: His Immersion and His Death," in *Dimensions of Baptism,* ed. Stanley E. Porter and Anthony R. Cross (New York: Sheffield Academic Press, 2002), 25–44. Others argue Jesus was a follower or convert of John; see Steve Mason, "Fire, Water and Spirit: John the Baptist and the Tyranny of Canon," *Studies in Religion/Sciences Religieuses* 21:2 (1992): 163–80; William Badke, "Was Jesus a Disciple of John?" *Evangelical Quarterly* 62 (July 1990): 195–204; J. Murphy-O'Connor, "Why Jesus Went Back to Galilee," *Bible Review* 12 (1996): 20–29, 42–43; Leif E. Vaage, "Bird-watching at the Baptism of Jesus: Early Christian Mythmaking in Mark 1:9–11," in *Reimagining Christian Origins,* ed. Elizabeth A. Castelli and Hal Taussig (Valley Forge, Pa.: Trinity Press International, 1996), 280–94. Although Jesus had doubtless heard of John, the entire relationship may also be the tradition's or Mark's invention, taking John's head for Christianity.

14. Richard Broxton Onians, *The Origins of European Thought about the Body, the Mind, the Soul, the World, Time and Fate* (1951) (Cambridge: Cambridge University Press, 1988), 530–43; Ewa Kuryluk, *Salome and Judas in the Cave of Sex* (Evanston, Ill.: Northwestern University Press, 1987), 201–7, 337–40; l'Abbé Pardiac, "Les Feux de Saint-Jean," *Revue de l'art chrétien* 16 (1873): 115–40; Maurice Vloberg, *Les Fêtes de France* (Grenoble: B. Arthaud, 1936), 154–69.

15. John McManners, *Death and the Enlightenment* (Oxford: Oxford University Press, 1981), 29. Isabel Combs Stuebe, "The *Johannisschüssel:* From Narrative to Reliquary to *Andactsbild,*" *Marsyas* 14 (1968–69): 3.

16. Saint John Chrysostom (ca. 354–407), *Homilies on the Gospel of Saint Matthew* in *A Select Library of the Nicene and Post-Nicene Fathers of the Christian Church,* 14 vols., ed. Philip Schaff (New York: Christian Literature Company, 1886–90), vol. 10, 298–99, 301. Edgerton, *Pictures and Punishment,* 142, 174, 183. The Order of St. John of Jerusalem, founded in the eleventh century in the Holy Land, took John's head as emblem; see Stuebe, "The *Johannisschüssel,*" 13–15.

17. In Luke, the angel appears to John the Baptist's father in the temple on the Day of Atonement, so John is conceived mid-September and born nine months later in mid-June. When Elizabeth is six months pregnant, in March, the angel appears to Mary to announce her pregnancy. So Jesus is born in December.

18. The Chartres manuscript, Bibliothèque Nationale de France, Paris, is reproduced in Dottin-Orsini, *Salome*, 11, discussed in Kuryluk, *Salome and Judas*, 196. For Toulouse, see Linda Seidel, "Salome and the Canons," *Women's Studies* 11 (1984): 29–66. Salome dances on her hands in the cathedrals at Lyon and Rouen.

19. The fish and John's head are in identical bowls. Ewa Kuryluk, *Salome and Judas*, fig. 112, 206–7.

20. Martin D'Arcy Gallery of Art, Loyola University, Chicago.

21. The York Breviary, cited by Jessie L. Weston, "Notes on Grail Romances Caput Johannes = Corpus Christi," *Romania* 49 (1923): 273–78; Stuebe, "The *Johannisschüssel*," 7, 16.

22. Stuebe, "The *Johannisschüssel*," 1–16; Hella Arndt and Renate Kroos, "Zur Ikonographie der Johannesschüssel," *Aachener Kunstblätter* 38 (1969): 243–328.

23. Sixten Ringbom, *Icon to Narrative: The Rise of the Dramatic Close-Up in Fifteenth-Century Devotional Painting*, 2d ed. (Doornspijk, Netherlands: Davaco, 1984), 59, 40–41, 68–70, 48–49.

24. *Salome dans les collections françaises*, 18.

25. Erwin Panofsky, *Studies in Iconology* (New York: Oxford University Press, 1939), 12–14; Stuebe, "The *Johannisschüssel*," 1, 5–7, 11. Stuebe locates eleven tondi, based on a lost original by Dirc Bouts (ca. 1415–75), painted on circular panels serving as the charger to produce a sculptural and realistic effect, 9.

26. The image attributed to Zoppo by Adolfo Venturi has been assigned to Giovanni Bellini, but without universal acceptance. Stuebe, "The *Johannisschüssel*," 9n. 57. Venturi, *Storia dell'arte italiana, VII, La Pittura del quattrocento, Parte III* (1914) (Nendeln, Liechtenstein: Kraus Reprint, 1967), figs. 17, 40. On the attribution question, see Giovanni Paccagnini, *Andrea Mantegna*, exhibition catalog (Mantua: Palazzo Ducale, 1961), 92–93, plate 81. The Musei Civici, Pesaro, where the image is held, continues to assign it to Zoppo, the artist of the altarpiece of the Church of St. John Baptist, Pesaro.

27. Sylvie Béguin attributes the inception of the motif in Italy to Gentile Bellini and a lost work of Leonardo da Vinci, *Andrea Solario en France* (Paris: Ministère de la Culture, 1985), 28. David Alan Brown doubts the lost Leonardo original. *Andrea Solario* (Milan: Electa, 1987), 161.

28. Ringbom, *Icon to Narrative*, 11–13, 15.

29. Ringbom, *Icon to Narrative*, 12.

30. Esther Cohen, "Towards a History of European Sensibility: Pain in the

Later Middle Ages," *Science in Context* 8:1 (1995): 47–74; Robert W. Scribner, "Popular Piety and Modes of Visual Perception in Late Medieval and Reformation Germany," *Journal of Religious History,* 15:4 (1989): 452–53, 455; Mitchell B. Merback, *The Thief, the Cross and the Wheel: Pain and the Spectacle of Punishment in Medieval and Renaissance Europe* (Chicago: University of Chicago Press, 1999), 20–21.

31. Brown, *Andrea Solario,* 162. Brown argues that the reflected image represents the patron, Béguin the artist. Béguin, *Andrea Solario en France,* 28, 37.

32. Brown, *Andrea Solario,* 206.

33. Brown, *Andrea Solario,* 207–9, 217–19.

34. Béguin, *Andrea Solario en France,* 94–95.

35. Paul Joannides, "Titian's *Judith* and its Context: The Iconography of Decapitation," *Apollo* 135 (1992): 163–70.

36. Domenichino, Guercino, Pacheco (*Arte de la Pitura,* Seville, 1638); Valdés Leal, 1658; Ribera, at Naples, 1647. Stuebe, "The *Johannisschüssel,*" 11–13.

37. Antonio-Ignacio Meléndez Alonso, *Time to Hope/Tiempo de esperanza: Treasures of Castilla y León,* Cathedral of St. John the Divine, New York, 27 September–24 November 2002.

38. Bartholomeus Ströbel, *Feast of Herodias and the Beheading of St. John the Baptist,* Madrid, Prado, reproduced in Natalie Zemon Davis and Arlette Farge, *A History of Women in the West,* vol. 3, *Renaissance and Enlightenment Paradoxes* (Cambridge, Mass.: Harvard University Press, 1993), 205.

39. Wintermute, *1789: French Painting during the Revolution,* 148. Mary Tavener Holmes correctly sees a Baptist in the Denon, but then misidentifies the Villeneuve as a Baptist. Perrin Stein and Mary Tavener Holmes, *Eighteenth-Century French Drawings in New York Collections* (New York: Metropolitan Museum of Art, 1999), 229n. 6.

40. Wintermute, *1789: French Painting,* 148. In the group version printed in *Eighteenth-Century French Drawings in New York Collections,* the head shows the left side, but the image was accidentally reversed in printing, according to Perrin Stein and Eileen Sullivan.

41. The wax head of Robespierre at Madame Tussaud's Museum is reproduced in D. Bindman, *The Shadow of the Guillotine* (London: British Museum, 1989), 75.

42. Marie-Anne Dupuy-Vachey, "Quelques têtes de révolutionnaires par Denon (1747–1825)," *Revue du Louvre* 4 (October 2003): 52, 57, 117; Udolpho van de Sandt, in *Dominique-Vivant Denon: L'oeil de Napoléon,* ed. Pierre Rosenberg and Marie-Anne Dupuy (Paris: Réunion des musées nationaux, 1999), [96].

43. van de Sandt, *Dominique-Vivant Denon,* [96].

44. Merback, *The Thief, the Cross and the Wheel,* 80, 198.

45. Nina Athanassoglou-Kallmyer, "Géricault's Severed Heads and Limbs: The Politics and Aesthetics of the Scaffold," *Art Bulletin* 74 (1992): 614.

46. The Ribera and Valdés Leal images reproduced by Stuebe lie on one ear, facing the viewer (figs. 13, 14); see Stuebe, "The *Johannisschüssel*," 6.

47. Athanassoglou-Kallmyer, "Géricault's Severed Heads and Limbs," 602. The obtrusion of the wound is common to Maineri and Zoppo.

48. Solario's St. John had traveled from Rouen, Géricault's natal town, to Paris by 1841. Tantalizingly, the tomb in Rouen cathedral opposite the tomb of Solario's patron, the Cardinal Georges d'Amboise, presents a death agony remarkably similar to the expression on Géricault's drawings of guillotined heads, at Besançon. The tomb of Louis de Brezé (1536–44) represents the governor of Normandy with his dead body writhing, head thrown back, mouth gaping. In Willem Key's or a follower's *La décollation de Saint Jean-Baptiste* (between 1520 and 1568), Musée des Beaux Arts, Rouen, the eyes of the Baptist handed to Salome are slightly open; the arm of the Baptist in the front of the picture plane curls rather like an arm in Géricault's paintings of mutilated limbs.

49. Athanassoglou-Kallmyer, "Géricault's Severed Heads and Limbs," 603. Athanassoglou-Kallmyer also observes that the blood on the sheets is invented, since the female's head produced no blood, and the head of the thief from Bicêtre must have been long drained of blood by the time Géricault obtained it.

50. Géricault's women consist of an attractive black; two old, ugly madwomen; the severed head; a child; a paralytic scowled at by another woman passing; the mother dropped from the *Raft of the Medusa*; some classic nudes embracing or being raped; and finally an "Amazon" on a spotted horse—an elegant lady in black riding dress, side-saddle, on a magnificent horse. See *L'opera completa di Géricault,* ed. Jacques Thuiller and Philippe Grunchec (Milano: Rizzoli, 1978). Had the Amazon got down and walked forward into the frame, upstaging her horse, she would have made an early nineteenth-century Salome.

51. "Géricault's Severed Heads and Limbs," 609, 606–8.

52. Quoted in Athanassoglou-Kallmyer, "Géricault's Severed Heads and Limbs," 611.

53. Lorenz E. A. Eitner, *Géricault: His Life and Work* (London: Orbis, 1983), 194–96.

54. "Géricault's Severed Heads and Limbs," 610, 617.

55. André Joubin, ed., *Journal de Eugène Delacroix* (Paris: Plon, 1950), III, 71. Athanassoglou-Kallmyer, "Géricault's Severed Heads and Limbs," 617–18. "Ce fragment de Géricault est vraiment sublime: il prouve plus que jamais qu'*il n'est pas de serpent ni de monstre odieux,* etc. C'est le meilleur argument en faveur du Beau, comme il faut l'entendre."

56. Eitner, *Géricault*, 214, 192–93.

57. Linda Nochlin, "Géricault, or the Absence of Women," *October* 68 (1994): 45–49.

58. At the salon of 1831 with Delacroix's *Liberty Leading the People*, Delaroche showed *Cromwell before the Coffin of Charles I*, Musée des Beaux Arts, Nîmes. Commemorating the bourgeois revolution of 1830, Delaroche sets Charles I against Cromwell, figuring Louis XVI and Napoleon, as well as the overthrow of France's Charles X, Louis XVI's last brother. Suggesting nostalgia for inevitably departed aristocratic glory, the powerful but troubled strength of the future meditates upon the aristocratic elegance and spiritual beauty of the world it has been constrained to destroy. Brown-habited, heavily booted, his hand gloved in yellowed leather, split at the seam, Cromwell holds open the black coffin. He frowns, his bull-dog plebeian face furrowed. Below him gleams Charles's delicate face, unearthly in hue. A fragile hand emerges from white lace against the coffin's blue silk lining, the colors of the Virgin ascending. The only trace of violence is a bloody, vaginal wound where the neck meets the torso.

59. The Église Saint-Vincent was destroyed in 1944; the glass has been in the new church of Ste. Jeanne D'Arc since 1979. Rouen Cathedral's tympanum is regularly cited as the inspiration for Flaubert's dance of Salome in "Herodias."

60. Veronique Chaussé, *Rouen Eglise Sainte-Jeanne D'Arc Les Verrières*, No. 67 Itinéraires du Patrimoine (Rouen: Connaissance du Patrimoine de Haute-Normandie, 1994), 6; Françoise Gatouillat, *Pont-Audemer Eglise Paroissiale Saint-Ouen Les Verrières*, No. 103 Itinéraires du Patrimoine (Rouen: Connaissance du Patrimoine de Haute-Normandie, 1996), 10–12, 16. Gatouillat calls the reconstruction described below "fantaisiste"; Chaussé calls it an "erreur."

61. Glass screen, Musée Carnavalet, Paris.

62. Michael Mason, *The Making of Victorian Sexuality*, 57–58, 119–21, 132; Bram Dijkstra, *Evil Sisters*, 3–7.

63. Alexandre Masseron, *Saint Jean Baptiste dans l'art* (Paris: Arthaud, 1957), 136.

64. In *Les Dieux antiques* (1880), Patricia R. Kellogg, "The Myth of Salome in Symbolist Literature and Art," Ph.D. diss., New York University, 1975, 5.

65. *Odilon Redon: Catalogue Raisonné*, 4 vols. (Paris: Wildenstein Institute, 1994), II, #1152, 209.

66. Aimée Brown Price, *Pierre Puvis de Chavannes* (New York: Rizzoli, [1994]), pl. 11, 14, pl. 57, 129. The painting is dated 14 December 1769. On 11 July 1869, he had made a caricature of himself as baby, swaddled, carried by her.

67. Dijkstra, *Idols of Perversity*, 390.

68. *A Rebours*, Paris, 1907, ARTFL, 76–77; *Against the Grain* [no trans. credited] (New York: Dover, 1969), 54–55; Pierre-Louis Mathieu, *Gustave Moreau* (Paris: ACR Edition, 1998), 175.

69. Mathieu, *Gustave Moreau*, 175.

70. Mathieu, *Gustave Moreau*, 168–69.

71. Even in parody, the valorization of the Baptist's head continues. Jules Laforgue, tweaking Flaubert's "Herodias" and *Salammbô* in his "Salome"

(1886), assimilated the dead head not to Christ, but to Moreau's Orpheus. A frustrated revolutionary to a transcendental, metaphysical, Salome savante, Laforgue's Baptist is a "visionary, scribbler . . . bastard son of Jean-Jacques Rousseau," conspirator and publicist; see Jules Laforgue, *Moral Tales,* trans. William Jay Smith (New York: New Directions, 1985), 98. Vain, pathetic, sweetly childlike in life, he is last seen sopping up the ink from a spilled inkwell, his hopes of having come to power in his own country equally spilt, equally absurd. Death, however, transforms him: "On a cushion . . . shone the head of John . . . coated with phosphor, washed, rouged, curled, grinning at these twenty-four million stars." Salome places an opal in his mouth, kisses his mouth, and then throws "that inspired noddle" into the sea. Once thrown, "like the head of Orpheus of old," the head of John floats on the sea, a "phosphorescent star," 108–9. Securing a meaning it did not possess in life, the absurd head of the living St. John is in death serene, sacramental, beyond strife. Alive, ridiculous, and dead, a saint.

72. Mathieu, *Gustave Moreau,* Salome and John with dove, pl. 368–69; *Salome (Deuxième Empire),* 171, 174.

73. Kellogg, *Myth of Salome,* 44.

74. *Salome and the Dance of Writing,* 18.

75. For an alternative view, see Victor Provenzano, "'Hérodias,' or the Self-Annihilation of the Absolute Work," *MLN* 115:4 (2000): 761–82.

76. Gustave Flaubert, *Trois Contes* (Paris: Nelson Editeurs, 1935), 276–77.

77. Béguin, *Andrea Solario en France,* 96. In Dubois's 1841 catalog of the collection of the Comte de Portalès Gorgier at Paris, rue Tronchet, it was sold at auction in 1865, purchased by Lecomte, donated to the Louvre three years later, and put on display.

78. *Correspondance—1868* (Paris: L. Conard, 1926–54), 138.

79. Sylvie Béguin describes it as a copy or study of a *Mise au Tombeau* sketched on the same sheet; however, Redon's placement of the sketch seems purposeful. R. Bacou dates the sketch shortly after Redon's other Louvre sketches, 1866–69; Béguin, *Andrea Solario en France,* 99.

80. Michael Wilson, *Nature and Imagination: The Work of Odilon Redon* (New York: E. P. Dutton, 1978), 30.

81. Douglas W. Druick et al., *Odilon Redon: Prince of Dreams, 1840–1916* (Chicago: Art Institute of Chicago, 1994), 18; Carolyn Keay, ed. *Odilon Redon.* Intro. Thomas Walters (New York: Rizzoli, 1977); *Odilon Redon, Gustave Moreau, Rodolphe Bresdin.* Museum of Modern Art (Garden City, N.J.: Doubleday, 1961); Gilberte Martin-Méry, René Huyghe, and Robert Coustet, ed., *Odilon Redon, 1840–1916* (Bordeaux: Galerie des Beaux Arts, 1985).

82. *Civilization and Its Discontents,* trans. James Strachey (New York: Norton, 1961), 19.

83. Emile Hennequin, *La vie moderne* (1881), in Keay, ed., *Odilon Redon,* 6.

84. *A rebours*, ARTFL, 84–85.

85. Druick, *Odilon Redon: Prince of Dreams*, 226–8, 371, fig. 32.

86. Druick, *Odilon Redon: Prince of Dreams*, 347, fig. 111.

87. Michael Kennedy, *Richard Strauss: Man, Musician, Enigma* (Cambridge: Cambridge University Press, 1999), 159.

88. Kennedy, *Richard Strauss*, 145.

89. "Tonal and Dramatic Structure in *Salome*," in *Richard Strauss: "Salome*," ed. Derrick Puffett (Cambridge: Cambridge University Press, 1989), 95.

90. Derrick Puffett, "Salome as Music Drama," in *Richard Strauss: "Salome*," 62.

91. Stewart Robertson, Conductor, "Lecture on *Salome*," Glimmerglass Opera, 24 July 2000; Roland Tenschert, "Strauss as Librettist," and Puffett, "Salome as Music Drama," in *Richard Strauss: "Salome*," 44–48, 66–68, 78–82; Edward W. Murphy, "Tonality and Form in *Salome*," *Music Review* 50:3–4 (1989): 215–30; Norman Del Mar, *Richard Strauss: A Critical Commentary on His Life and Works*, 3 vols. (London: Barrie and Rockliff, 1962), I: 239–80, esp. 259–60, 268; Cynthia Annmarie McGregor, "The Musical Language of Dramatic Monologues: A Study of Wotan, Tristan, Salome, Boris, and Guimas," Ph.D. diss., Northwestern University, 2001.

92. John Williamson summarizes the negative "Critical Reception" of John's music in *Richard Strauss: "Salome*," 137–38. In the same volume, Tethys Carpenter calls John's music "pseudo-symphonic . . . over-blown . . . stilted" (100). Robin Holloway finds one theme "superb"; otherwise, the Baptist's is an "unctuous strain" in "full flatulent flower" (145–47), with its "oleaginous appeal to 'higher things'" (148). Charles Osborne, *The Complete Operas of Richard Strauss* (North Pomfret, Vt.: Trafalgar Square, 1988), 46–49, disapproves more mildly, but still finds that "religious fervour" did not engage Strauss as did love or sexual obsession.

93. Puffett, "Salome as Music Drama," in *Richard Strauss: "Salome*," 62.

94. *The Complete Operas of Richard Strauss*, 49.

95. "The Musical Language of Dramatic Monologues: A Study of Wotan, Tristan, Salome, Boris, and Guimas," 105.

96. Puffett, "Salome as Music Drama," in *Richard Strauss: "Salome*," 62.

97. To Stefan Zweig, 5 May 1935, in Kennedy, *Richard Strauss*, 145.

98. Sigmund Freud, "Notes on Medusa's Head," *Standard Edition of the Complete Psychological Works of Sigmund Freud* (1940 [1922]), trans. James Strachey (London: Hogarth Press, 1955), XVIII, 273–74. Sandor Ferenczi, "On the Symbolism of the Head of Medusa" [1923], *Further Contributions to the Theory and Technique of Psycho-analysis*, ed. John Rickman, trans. Jane Isabel Suttie et al. (New York: Basic Books, 1952), 360. Freud credits Ferenczi with the discovery in "The Infantile Genital Organization" (1923), in *Standard Edition*, XIX, 144n. 3.

99. *Civilization and Its Discontents*, 80.

100. An anecdote from 1901, in Sigmund Freud, *The Psychopathology of Everyday Life*, trans. Alan Tyson, ed. James Strachey (New York: Norton, 1960), 197–99.

101. Laurence Sterne, *The Life and Opinions of Tristram Shandy, Gent.* 1760–67, III, chap. xvii.

102. *Aspects of Death in Early Greek Art and Poetry*, 99.

103. *Mortals and Immortals*, 64–65.

104. Ssu-ma Ch'ien, "Letter to Jen An," in *Anthology of Chinese Literature from Early Times to the Fourteenth Century*, ed. Cyril Birch and Donald Keene (New York: Grove Press, 1965), 95–102.

105. Sigmund Freud, *A General Introduction to Psychoanalysis* (1935), trans. Joan Riviere (New York: Simon and Schuster, 1963), 185, 278, 322–23, 169–70, 238, 136–48.

106. Charles Bernheimer, "Fetishism and Decadence: Salome's Severed Heads," in *Fetishism as Cultural Discourse*, ed. Emily Apter and William Pietz (Ithaca, N.Y.: Cornell University Press, 1993), 62.

107. Julia Kristeva, "Women's Time," trans. Alice Jardine and Harry Blake, in Nannerl O. Keohane, Michelle Z. Rosaldo, and Barbara C. Gelpi, eds., *Feminist Theory: A Critique of Ideology* (Chicago: University of Chicago Press, 1982), 41; Toril Moi, *What Is a Woman? And Other Essays* (Oxford: Oxford University Press, 1999), 344–46; Bronfen, *Over Her Dead Body*, 119, 406.

108. "(Re)Writing the Body: The Politics and Poetics of Female Eroticism," *Poetics Today* 6:1/2 (1985): 49.

109. Jacques Lacan, *Ecrits: A Selection*, trans. Alan Sheridan (New York: Norton, 1977), 287–88.

110. Sigmund Freud, *Complete Letters of Sigmund Freud to Wilhelm Fleiss 1887–1904*, trans. Jeffrey Moussaieff Masson (Cambridge, Mass.: Harvard University Press, 1985), 295–96. Square brackets in Masson's translation.

111. *Judith: Sexual Warrior*, 191–93.

NOTES TO CHAPTER 5

1. *Conrad's Western World* (Cambridge: Cambridge University Press, 1971), 59.

2. Joseph Conrad, *Heart of Darkness*, ed. Robert Kimbrough (New York: Norton, 1963), 58.

3. Peter Edgerly Firchow, *Envisioning Africa: Racism and Imperialism in Conrad's "Heart of Darkness"* (Lexington: University Press of Kentucky, 2000), 111–13, 121–22, 128–32, 139, 224n. 7, 229–30n. 1, 234n. 6.

4. A Bengali babu, having passed the appropriate civil service exams and served the requisite apprenticeships, is promoted to head a frontier district, but

he is able neither to control his district nor to keep his head. The story ends as the babu's head rolls across the floor of his office, still wearing his gold-rimmed spectacles (so like Kipling's), an irrefutable sign of Bengali inadequacy to the manly tasks of empire. The rolling head stops at the feet of the imperial English master, who picks it up, looks it over, and identifies it as the babu's brother: these savages never get anything right. Whether the Bengali babu looks east or west, to savagery or civility, there is no help: someone is after his head.

5. *Dreams of Adventure, Dreams of Empire* (New York: Basic Books, 1979), 86. The exception to the no-white decapitations rule, Kipling's "Man Who Would Be King" (1890) is a loafer, not a gentleman, who loses his head not to a darker-skinned race, but to a tribe blue-eyed and white. Like Kurtz, he goes native, his ambition foundering on a marriage.

6. *Dreams of Adventure,* 287, 289–93, 230–31.

7. Nicolas Tredell, ed., *Joseph Conrad: Heart of Darkness* (New York: Columbia University Press, 1998), 20, 37–38, 106.

8. Roxann Wheeler, *The Complexion of Race: Categories of Difference in Eighteenth-Century Culture* (Philadelphia: University of Pennsylvania Press, 2000), 289–99; Ivan Hannaford, *Race: The History of an Idea in the West,* 187–324.

9. In *Resident Evil: The Movie,* the first victim is an attractive, elegant black woman. Trying to slither out of an elevator to release her companions, she is decapitated as the elevator system suddenly starts to move again. An important moment and the only frightening or effective scene in the film, she is the first victim and the only decapitee. In *A.I.* the anti-robot fête incinerates and tortures various mechanical persons of many ages, sexes, and shapes. Yet the one blown from a cannon to lose his head is the genial black robot-man. His head is displayed for us, stuck between the wires of the cage. When the white robot-boy knocks the head off his twin, we see the headless body, but not the separated head. The viewer does not contemplate the blond severed head of Haley Joel Osmont.

10. *The Grand Scribe's Records,* vol. 7: *Memoirs of Pre-Han China by Ssu-ma Ch'ien,* ed. William H. Nienhauser, Jr. (Bloomington: Indiana University Press, 1994), 316.

11. Sima Qian [Ssu-ma Ch'ien], *Selections from Records of the Historian,* ed. Zong Shi (Beijing: Chinese Literature Press, 1999), 222.

12. Paul Varley, "Warriors as Courtiers: The Taira in *Heike monogatari,*" in Amy Vladeck Heinrich, ed., *Currents in Japanese Culture* (New York: Columbia University Press, 1997), 62, 67–68; Kenneth Dean Butler, "The *Heike Monogatari* and the Japanese Warrior Ethic," *Harvard Journal of Asiatic Studies* 29 (1969): 93–108. For a contrary view that draws the lines as we now do, see Herbert S. Joseph, "The *Heike Monogatari*: Buddhist Ethics and the Code of the Samurai," *Folklore* 87 (1976): 96–97, 99, 103.

13. *The Tale of the Heike,* trans. Hiroshi Kitagawa and Bruce T. Tsuchida (Tokyo: University of Tokyo Press, 1975), book 9, chap. 13, 556.

14. *The Tale of the Heike,* book 11, chap. 2, 652.

15. John B. Gabel, Charles B. Wheeler, Anthony D. York, *The Bible as Literature,* 4th ed. (New York: Oxford University Press, 2000), 43.

16. *Oxford Study Bible,* ed. M. Jack Suggs, Katharine Doob Sakenfeld, and James R. Mueller (New York: Oxford University Press, 1992), 384; 2 Kings 10:1–14n.

17. Cristelle L. Baskins, "Typology, Sexuality, and the Renaissance Esther," in James Grantham Turner, ed., *Sexuality and Gender in Early Modern Europe* (Cambridge: Cambridge University Press, 1993), 44.

18. Herodotus, *The History,* Issedones, IV.26: 289; Scythians, IV.64, 65: 303–4; Tauri, IV.103: 319; Massagetae, I.212–14, 216: 129–30; Man-Eaters, IV.105: 319.

19. Edith Hall, *Inventing the Barbarian* (Oxford: Clarendon Press, 1989), 27, 126; Pierre Vidal-Naquet, *The Black Hunter,* trans. Andrew Szegedy-Maszak (Baltimore: Johns Hopkins University Press, 1986), 2–4, 6, 16. Hannaford, *Race: The History of an Idea in the West,* 55, 75.

20. Hall, *Inventing the Barbarian,* 26–27.

21. Vidal-Naquet, *Black Hunter,* 16.

22. *Discovery of the Mind,* cited in Charles Taylor, *Sources of the Self: The Making of the Modern Identity* (Cambridge, Mass.: Harvard University Press, 1989), 118.

23. Maggie Kilgour, *From Communion to Cannibalism: An Anatomy of Metaphors of Incorporation* (Princeton, N.J.: Princeton University Press, 1990), 11, 13–14, 23–24; Neil L. Whitehead, "Hans Studen and the Cultural Politics of Cannibalism," *Hispanic American Historical Review* 80:4 (2000): 721–51.

24. Donald Earl, *The Moral and Political Tradition of Rome* (Ithaca, N.J.: Cornell University Press, 1967), 68.

25. In particular, the Oppidum of Entremont, north of Aix-en-Provence; the Sanctuary of Roquepertuse, near Marseille; and two lintels from Nîmes. Remains from these sites are at the Musée Granet, Aix-en-Provence; the Musée d'Archéologie Mediterranée, Marseille; and the Musée d'Archéologie, Nîmes.

26. Ovid, *Fasti,* I, 543–86, V, 647; Livy, *Ab Urbe Condita,* 13 vols., trans. B. O. Foster (London: Heinemann, 1919), I, 26–27.

27. Ralph Merrifield, *The Archaeology of Ritual and Magic* (New York: New Amsterdam, 1987), 27–29, 37–38, 45–46, 60, 74, 82, 101; Anne Ross, *Pagan Celtic Britain* (1967) (Chicago: Academy Chicago Publishers, 1996), 106–7, 141–43.

28. Lucan mentions Caesar's visiting Troy after Pharsalia, *Civil War,* trans. J. D. Duff (Cambridge, Mass.: Harvard University Press, 1928), IX, 964. Appian

describes him as pursuing Pompey through Asia Minor but does not refer specifically to Troy. *Civil Wars*, book 3, chap. 13, secs. 88–89, pp. 388–91.

29. David Garland, *Punishment and Modern Society* (Chicago: University of Chicago Press, 1990), 233–35.

30. Carol Houlihan Flynn treats cannibalism and slavery, but misses the head as marker, in *The Body in Swift and Defoe* (Cambridge: Cambridge University Press, 1990), 149–59.

31. *Robinson Crusoe*, ed. J. Donald Crowley (New York: Penguin, 1972), 204. The footprint appears at 153–54.

32. Michael Banton, *Racial Theories* (Cambridge: Cambridge University Press, 1987); Patrick Brantlinger, *The Rule of Darkness: British Literature and Imperialism 1840–1914* (Ithaca, N.Y.: Cornell University Press, 1988); Eric Cheyfitz, *The Poetics of Imperialism: Translation and Colonization from "The Tempest" to "Tarzan"* (Oxford: Oxford University Press, 1991); P. C. Emmer and H. L. Wesseling, eds., *Reappraisals in Overseas History* (The Hague: Leiden University Press, 1979); V. G. Kiernan, *The Lords of Human Kind: European Attitudes towards the Outside World in the Imperial Age* (London: Weidenfeld and Nicholson, 1969); Adam Kuper, *The Invention of Primitive Society: Transformations of an Illusion* (London: Routledge, 1988); Edward Said, *Culture and Imperialism* (New York: Alfred Knopf, 1993); Bernard Semmel, *The Liberal Ideal and the Demons of Empire: Theories of Imperialism from Adam Smith to Lenin* (Baltimore: Johns Hopkins University Press, 1993); Pat Shipman, *The Evolution of Racism* (New York: Simon and Schuster, 1994); Eileen P. Sullivan, "Liberalism and Imperialism: J. S. Mill's Defense of the British Empire," *Journal of the History of Ideas* 44.4 (1983): 599–617; H. L. Wesseling, ed., *Expansion and Reaction: Essays on European Expansion and Reaction in Asia and Africa* (The Hague: Leiden University Press, 1978).

33. "An Image of Africa: Racism in Conrad's *Heart of Darkness,*" *Massachusetts Review* 18 (1977): 782–94; rptd. in Joseph Conrad, *Heart of Darkness*, 3rd ed., ed. Robert Kimbrough (New York: Norton, 1988).

34. Don C. Ohadike, *Anioma: A Social History of the Western Igbo People* (Athens: Ohio University Press, 1994); Simon Ottenberg, *Leadership and Authority in an African Society: The Afikpo Village Group* (Seattle: University of Washington Press, [1971]).

35. Mda is South African. His decollator is, like Kurtz, a European entrepreneur, and the heads of the ancestors, procured in Xhosaland, now collect dust in the backrooms of the British Museum. *The Heart of Redness* (New York: Farrar, Straus and Giroux, 2002). In Mda's neighborhood, the British cut off, pickled, and circulated in a barrel the head of Bambata, leader of the Zulu rebellion of 1906. Bryan, *Off with His Head*, 162.

36. Interview, 1991, *Contemporary Authors*, vol. 138 (Detroit: Gale, 1993),

338; Abioseh Michael Porter, "Ben Okri's *The Landscape Within:* A Metaphor for Personal and National Development," *World Literature Written in English* 28:2 (1998): 203–5.

37. In *My Life in the Bush of Ghosts,* four thousand heads with hands grow on "faithful Mother's" body. When some are cut off in battle, they cry until they are put back on her body. So fecund an image staggers, and overwhelms, the psychoanalytic treatment it seems to demand; *My Life in the Bush of Ghosts,* 1954 (New York: Grove Press, 1994), 109–10.

38. *Simbi and the Satyr of the Dark Jungle,* 1955 (San Francisco: City Lights, 1988), 12. Further page citations in text.

39. Observing that as many as twenty slaves might be killed in a day, E. J. Glave, Conrad's contemporary, described such a singing, dancing, executing scene at the death of a chief in his *In Savage Africa, Or Six Years of Adventure in Congo-Land,* 1892, cited in Firchow, *Envisioning Africa,* 121–22.

40. This episode is curiously instrumental: the gnome, a helper figure (rescued by Simbi as a snake), arranges the death of the king's daughter so that Simbi can restore her to life with the help of the hunter's head. That is, Simbi needs the hunter dead and the king grateful, and the head is the life that saves and restores life. So the gnome arranges a death in order to get the hunter's life. Symbolic signification links up with practical (political) tactics.

41. At the end of Victor Nwankwo's story in *The Insider,* everyone splits up and goes back to "his mother's kitchen"; *The Insider: Stories of War and Peace from Nigeria* (Enugwu, Nigeria: Nwankwo-Ifejika, 1971).

42. Bernth Lindfors, citing the last sentence, agrees that "Simbi, too, has a lesson to teach," but does not comment on the nature of the lesson; "Amos Tutuola: Literary Syncretism and the Yoruba Folk Tradition," in *European-Language Writing in Sub-Saharan Africa,* ed. Albert S. Gérard, 2 vols. (Budapest: Akadémiai Kiadó, 1986), II, 641.

43. For novelistic accounts of African women's autonomy, see Onuora Nzekwu, *Highlife for Lizards* (1965), Cyprian Ekwensi, *Jagua Nana* (1961); Alain Severac, "The Igbo Novelists," in *European-Language Writing in Sub-Saharan Africa,* II, 712, 706. Modern chapbook fiction seems intent on creating the sentimental heroine of western bourgeois fiction, for whom love is her whole existence; Juliet Okonkwo, "Popular Urban Fiction and Cyprian Ekwensi," in ibid., 652–54.

44. Nancy Tanner, "Matrifocality," in *Woman, Culture, and Society,* ed. Michelle Zimbalist Rosaldo and Louise Lamphere (Stanford, Calif.: Stanford University Press, 1974), 146–50; Nancy B. Leis, "Women in Groups: Ijaw Women's Associations," ibid., 223.

45. Raoul Granqvist, "Orality in Nigerian Literature," *Moderna Spreak* 77:4 (1983): 339–40.

46. Tutuola shares with Latin American writers of the 1930s and '40s the in-

terest in folklore; the practice of inventing folklore links him more specifically to the Guatemalan writer Miguel Angel Asturias, who was redirected to Mayan folklore by French surrealists. Eileen Julien, "Of Traditional Tales and Short Stories," in *Toward Defining the African Aesthetic,* ed. Lemuel A. Johnson, Bernadette Cailler, Russell Hamilton, and Mildred Hill-Lubin (Washington, D.C.: Three Continents Press, 1980), 83–94. Bernth Lindfors, "Indigenizing British Language and Culture in Yorubaland," in *Language and Literature in Multicultural Contexts,* ed. Satendra Nandan (Suva, Fiji: University of the South Pacific, 1983), 226. For comparisons between Fagunwa and Tutuola on specific passages, see Bernth Lindfors, "Amos Tutuola: Literary Syncretism and the Yoruba Folk Tradition," in *European-Language Writing in Sub-Saharan Africa,* II, 635–36, 644–47; see also Abiola Irele, "Tradition and the Yoruba Writer: D. O. Fagunwa, Amos Tutuola, and Wole Soyinka," in Biodun Jeyifo, ed., *Perspectives on Wole Soyinka: Freedom and Complexity* (Jackson: University Press of Mississippi, 2001).

47. For the controversy over Tutuola's English, see Abiola Irele, *The African Experience in Literature and Ideology* (London: Heinemann, 1981), 182–83, 163, 51; Harold Collins, *Amos Tutuola* (New York: Twayne, 1969), 110–16; Bernth Lindfors, ed., *Critical Perspectives on Amos Tutuola* (London: Heinemann, 1980); Lindfors, "Amos Tutuola," 647–49; Bernth Lindfors, "Characteristics of Yoruba and Ibo Prose Styles in English," in *Common Wealth,* ed. Anna Rutherford (Aarhus, Denmark: Akademisk Boghandel Universitetsparken, 1971). Tutuola's English is not uniform from work to work; the contrast is particularly striking in *The Village Witch Doctor and Other Stories* (London: Faber and Faber, 1990). Tutuola offered his first publisher the right to correct his "WRONG ENGLISH," but the publisher declined. Bernth Lindfors, "Amos Tutuola's Search for a Publisher," in *Toward Defining the African Aesthetic,* ed. Lemuel A. Johnson et al., 100–101.

48. *Myth, Literature, and the African World* (Cambridge: Cambridge University Press, 1976), 144.

49. Christopher Wise, "Excavating the New Republic: Post-colonial Subjectivity in Achebe's *Things Fall Apart,*" *Callaloo* 22:4 (1999): 1054–70.

50. R. Victoria Arana, "The Epic Imagination: A Conversation with Chinua Achebe at Annandale-on-Hudson, October 31, 1998," *Callaloo* 25:2 (2000): 524.

51. *Things Fall Apart* (Greenwich, Conn.: Fawcett Books, 1959), 75. Further citations in text.

52. For a summary of critics on this issue, see Emeka Nwabueze, "Theoretical Construction and Constructive Theorizing on the Execution of Ikemefuna in Achebe's *Things Fall Apart,*" *Research in African Literatures* 31:2 (2000): 164, 170.

53. *No Longer at Ease* (1960) (New York: Anchor Books, 1984), 157–58.

54. *Myth, Literature, and the African World,* 88–89. Relations between the Yoruba Soyinka and the Igbo Achebe have often been vexed; see Adebayo Williams, "The Autumn of the Literary Patriarch: Chinua Achebe and the Politics of Remembering," *Research in African Literatures* 32:3 (2001): 8–21.

55. For a different view, see R. N. Egudu, "Colonialism and Postcolonialism in Nigerian Literature," in *Language and Literature in Multicultural Contexts,* ed. Nandan, 120–22.

56. Firchow, *Envisioning Africa,* 113.

57. There was a period when we did, when Norse antiquities were more in fashion. On 12 April 1778, James Boswell urged Thomas Percy, translator of *Northern Antiquities,* to make short work of a traveler who had complained that helmets were no longer hung out to invite to "the hall of hospitality": "(Humouring the joke,) Hang out his skull instead of a helmet, and you may drink ale out of it in your hall of Odin, as he is your enemy; that will be truly ancient. *There* will be *Northern Antiquities";* see *Life of Johnson,* 933.

58. Nwabueze, "Theoretical Construction and Constructive Theorizing on the Execution of Ikemefuna in Achebe's *Things Fall Apart," Research in African Literatures* 31:2 (2000): 170.

59. *No Longer at Ease,* 121–22, 45; *Arrow of God* (1964, 1974) (New York: Anchor Books, 1974), 30, 31, 33.

60. Firchow, *Envisioning Africa,* 116, 120, 42–43.

61. *Arrow of God,* 39.

62. *A Man of the People* (New York: John Day, 1966), 121, 129, 123.

63. Chinua Achebe and C. L. Innes, eds., *African Short Stories* (London: Heinemann, 1985), 29.

64. "Civil Peace," in *African Short Stories,* 30.

65. "G.B.'s Dance," in *The Insider: Stories of War and Peace from Nigeria.*

66. John C. Hawley, "Ben Okri's Spirit-Child: *Abiku* Migration and Postmodernity," *Research in African Literatures* 26:1 (1995): 31; Ato Quayson, "Protocols of Representation and the Problems of Constituting an African 'Gnosis': Achebe and Okri," *Yearbook of English Studies* 27 (1997): 142–49; Ato Quayson, *Strategic Transformations in Nigerian Writing* (Bloomington: Indiana University Press, 1997).

67. "In the City of Red Dust," in *Stars of the New Curfew* (London: Secker and Warburg, 1988), 51–53.

68. Joshua W. Sempebwa, "Religiosity and Health Behaviour in Africa," in *Health and Development in Africa,* ed. Peter Oberender, Hans Jochen Diesfeld, and Wolfgang Gitter (New York: Verlag Peter Lang, 1983), 34–44.

69. In South Africa, murders for the sake of body parts are called *muti,* from the Zulu word for medicine. Heads bring higher prices than other parts ($1,300 for a head vs. $230 for brain, eye, and kneecaps), and the heads of children are

especially prized. Sharon LaFraniere, "Toddler's Killing Exposes Ghoulish South Africa [*sic*] Practice," *New York Times,* 28 September 2003, A3.

70. Chantal Mouffe, "Foreword," in Saint-Amand, *The Laws of Hostility* (Minneapolis: University of Minnesota Press, 1996), xi.

NOTES TO THE EPILOGUE

1. Georges Bataille, *Visions of Excess: Selected Writings, 1927–39,* ed. Allan Stoekl (Minneapolis: University of Minnesota Press, 1985), xix-xx; Denis Hollier, ed., *The College of Sociology (1937–1939),* trans. Betsy Wing (Minneapolis: University of Minnesota Press, 1988).

2. Vladimir Velickovic, *Descente Fig. XXI,* 1989, *Le Monde de L'Education: Science,* 245, February 1997.

3. Ralph Waldo Emerson, *Representative Men* (Philadelphia: Henry Altemus, 1895), 279.

4. Henry S. F. Cooper, Jr., "Origins: The Backbone of Evolution," *Natural History,* 105:6 (June 1996): 31–44.

5. "Braincase" does not appear in the OED until 1989, with a single citation from Monro's *Anatomy,* 3rd ed. (1741), referring to the human head.

6. Yudhijit Bhattacharjee, "With an Evolutionary Milestone, the Race for Survival Began," *New York Times,* 18 February 2003, D3.

7. "Have Animals Souls?" *Atlantic Monthly,* 1874, cited in James Turner, *Reckoning with the Beast* (Baltimore: Johns Hopkins University Press, 1980), 62.

8. *On Human Nature,* in Charles Taylor, *Sources of the Self* (Cambridge, Mass.: Harvard University Press, 1989), 406–7.

9. Stephen Jay Gould, "On a Toothed Bird's Place in Nature," *Natural History* 105:2 (February 1996): 88.

10. Among the achievements of the Age of Reason is its recognition of the limited role of reason in human endeavor and motivation, a position conspicuous in Swift, Pope, Hume, Johnson, Burke; see Albert O. Hirschman, *The Passions and the Interests* (Princeton, N.J.: Princeton University Press, 1977), 14–31. As Pope puts it, "And Passions are the elements of Life," *Essay on Man,* I, 170; "On life's vast ocean diversely we sail, / Reason the card, but Passion is the gale," II, 107–8; *Poems of Alexander Pope,* ed. John Butts (New Haven: Yale University Press, 1963), 510, 519.

11. Emmanuel Lévinas, *Entre nous/On Thinking-of-the-Other,* trans. Michael B. Smith and Barbara Harshav (New York: Columbia University Press, 1998), 4; Donald B. Calne, *Within Reason: Rationality and Human Behavior* (New York: Pantheon Books, 1999).

12. Alexander Pope, *Moral Essay I: On the Characters of Men,* ll. 29–30, 35–36; *Poems of Alexander Pope,* 551.

13. Michel de Certeau, *Heterologies*, trans. Brian Massumi (Minneapolis: University of Minnesota Press, 1986), 15, 24.

14. Taylor, *Sources of the Self,* 509.

15. "Where Will Psychoanalysis Survive?" *Harvard Magazine,* January–February 1997, 38.

16. Vittorio Fagone, ed.. *Carlo Carrà: La matita e il pennello* (Milan: Skira, 1996). Renato González Mello and Diane Miliotes, eds., *José Clemente Orozco in the United States, 1927–1934* (New York: Norton, 2002), 257, figs. 274, 273.

17. Raquel Tibol, *Siqueiros* (Mexico, D.F.: Universidad Nacional Autónoma de México, 1961), fig. 77, *Paisaje humano;* fig. 78, *Adoración;* fig. 96, *Nuestra Imagen;* fig. 71, *Nueva democracia.*

18. "Head eats, Head looks, Head hears, Head speaks. Always above or in front of the trunk, the head is first exposed to the unknown. It is responsible for the rest of the body as a leader for its herd." http://www.walkerart.org/resources/res_msg_mapframe.html. An Abakanowicz field of bodies also appeared in *To the Rescue: Eight Artists and an Archive,* 1999, curated by Carole Kismaric.

19. Edward O. Wilson, *Consilience* (New York: Alfred A. Knopf, 1998), 127.

20. George Johnson, "Mindless Creatures, Acting 'Mindfully, *New York Times,* 23 March 1999, F1, 4; Mark Kingwell, "Viral Culture: A Fashionable Theory Takes the Self Out of Consciousness," *Harper's,* April 1999, 83–90.

21. New Haven: Yale University Press, 1998.

22. Dana Mackenzie, "The Science of Surprise," *Discover* 23:2 (February 2002): 61. For a demonstration of the artificial birds in motion, visit www.red3d.com/cwr/boids. Lane A. Hemaspaandra and Mitsunori Ogihira, *The Complexity Theory Companion* (New York: Springer, 2002).

23. Mas'ud Zavaradeh and Donald Morton, "Theory Pedagogy Politics: The Crisis of 'The Subject' in the Humanities," *boundary* 2, 15:1–2 (Fall 1986/Winter 1987): 1–22; rpt. in *Theory/Pedagogy/Politics* (Urbana: University of Illinois Press, 1991), 1–32; *Decolonizing Tradition,* ed. Karen R. Lawrence (Urbana: University of Illinois Press, 1992).

24. Foreword, in Alain Renaut, *The Era of the Individual* (Princeton, N.J.: Princeton University Press, 1997), xii.

25. *Discipline and Punish,* trans. Alan Sheridan (New York: Vintage Books, 1979), 217, 308; *The Order of Things* (New York: Random House, 1970), 387 (no trans. named).

26. Carolyn Dean, "Law and Sacrifice: Bataille, Lacan, and the Critique of the Subject," *Representations* 13 (1986), 42. There is, of course, considerable question as to how "rational" and "stable" the Enlightenment concept of self was. Stability and rationality were contested terms from the beginning.

27. So Jane Gallop: "This orthodoxy will here be called 'antihumanism' so as

to avoid the current problem of distinguishing between structuralism proper and poststructuralism"; see *Intersections: A Reading of Sade with Bataille, Blanchot, and Klossowski* (Lincoln: University of Nebraska Press, 1981), 2.

28. Scott Manning Stevens, "Sacred Heart and Secular Brain," in *The Body in Parts: Fantasies of Corporeality in Early Modern Europe,* ed. David Hillman and Carla Mazzio (New York: Routledge, 1997), 263–82. In *The Body in Pain* (New York: Oxford University Press, 1985), 363n. 71, Elaine Scarry rejects "cerebral primacy," her only reference to the head.

29. *The Pleasure of the Text,* trans. Richard Miller (New York: Hill and Wang, 1975), 67.

30. Jacques Derrida, *Dissemination,* trans. Barbara Johnson (Chicago: University of Chicago Press, 1981), 20.

31. D. E. Harding, *On Having No Head: Zen and the Rediscovery of the Obvious* (London: Arkana, 1986). My thanks to Joel Smith for this text.

32. Kingwell, "Viral Culture," 83–90; Lawrence M. Friedman, *The Horizontal Society* (New Haven: Yale University Press, 1999). Todd Gitlin's review of Friedman concludes, "The vertical cannot hold. . . . Roll over, authorities—the culture of the next millennium is not going your way." *New York Times Book Review,* 23 May 1999, 32.

33. Jonathan Glover, *Humanity: A Moral History of the Twentieth Century* (New Haven: Yale University Press, 2000), 406. Glover does not refer to Lévinas, but would appreciate him. Martin Jay cites Lyotard's tribute to Lévinas, "his books have been my companions for twenty years." *Downcast Eyes: The Denigration of Vision in Twentieth-Century French Thought* (Berkeley: University of California Press, 1993), 546. Luce Irigaray and other feminists are more critical of a position that ignores female difference. Lévinas is reluctant to recognize that the first face-to-face is not God to man, but mother to infant. See Luce Irigaray, "The Question of the Other," trans. Noah Guynn, *Yale French Studies* 87 (1995): 7–19; Hélène Cixous, "A la source Lévinas," *magazine littéraire* 419 (April 2003): 51–52 ; Lisa Walsh, "Between Maternity and Paternity: Figuring Ethical Subjectivity," *differences: A Journal of Cultural Feminist Studies* 12:1 (2001): 79–111. Lévinas was the subject of a "Dossier," *magazine littéraire* 419 (April 2003): 22–61.

34. *Entre nous/On Thinking-of-the-Other,* 148.

35. Jacques Derrida, "Violence and Metaphysics: An Essay on the Thought of Emmanuel Levinas," in *Writing and Difference,* trans. Alan Bass (Chicago: University of Chicago Press, 1978), 125. Martha Nussbaum's eloquent tribute to Rawls moves from Rawls's self to the other, the general good, "Making Philosophy Matter to Politics," *New York Times,* 2 December 2002, A21.

36. Jay, *Downcast Eyes,* 556–57.

37. *Entre nous/On Thinking-of-the-Other,* 10, 185, 195–96.

38. *The Gay Science,* sec. 335, in Glover, *Humanity,* 13.

39. *Entre nous/On Thinking-of-the-Other*, 188–96, 216–17.

40. "Levinas' Ethical Interruption of Reciprocity," *Salmagundi* 130–31 (2001): 124. Although he does not cite Lévinas, Pierre Saint-Amand concludes his account of the Enlightenment's failure to theorize violence with a call not "for a return to religion, but for a new relation: one of obligation," in *The Laws of Hostility: Politics, Violence, and the Enlightenment*, trans. Jennifer Curtiss Gage (Minneapolis: University of Minnesota Press, 1996), 156.

41. *Entre nous/On Thinking-of-the-Other*, 9.

42. *Entre nous/On Thinking-of-the-Other*, 114. The evil of the order of being includes its laws of survival and justice—retribution and revenge.

43. *Entre nous/On Thinking-of-the-Other*, 9–10, 7.

44. *Entre nous/On Thinking-of-the-Other*, 114.

45. Will Self, *My Idea of Fun* (New York: Vintage International, 1993), 4–5.

46. Witkin arranged with a Mexico City morgue for corpses picked up daily from the streets, and his artistic needs gentled the handling of the bodies. Those picking up the bodies learned to be careful not to damage the faces when they slung them in the truck. In the autopsies performed to determine cause of death, the skull is opened to remove the brain, facilitating Witkin's later placement of vegetation in the head. If as John Fraser argues, good violent art shocks the artist as well as the bourgeoisie, Witkin has shocked himself on occasion; see *Violence in the Arts* (Cambridge: Cambridge University Press, 1974), 116. He found the dead baby and severed arms and legs for "Feast of the Insane" floating in a drawer with eyes, penises, and other children: "Because the bureaucracy is so incredibly corrupt, no one had said 'get this stuff out of here.' No one had the balls to do it. That time I did say, 'Why am I doing this?' . . . I did have the belief that there was a purpose to my being there, that I could make something beautiful" (interview with Michael Sand, before opening of Guggenheim retrospective). From *World Art* 1/96, the interview is quoted at www.zonezero.com/exposiciones/fotografos/witkin/jpwdefault.html and www.dir.salon.com/people/bc/2000/05/09/witkin/index.html.

47. Guggenheim 1995; "Dossier," *Photo* 367 (March 2000): 74–85; Cintra Wilson, "Joel-Peter Witkin," www.dir.salon.com/people/bc/2000/05/09/witkin/index.html.

48. "Still Life, Marseilles," "Harvest," and "Le Baiser (The Kiss)" appear in Germano Celant, *Joel-Peter Witkin* (New York: Scalo, 1995) and at www.smog.net/photographers/witkinO/ypwx17.php?alD=25; "Story from a Book" (1999) and "Queer Saint" at www.zonezero.com/exposiciones/fotografos/witkin2/index.html. Others at www.art-forum.org/2_witkin.

49. José van Dijck, "Bodyworlds: The Art of Plastinated Cadavers," *Configurations* 9:1 (2001): 104.

50. An exception to these strictures is Witkin's "Glass Man," an autopsied man, sewn back up. His eyes are open, he looks at the viewer, serene, as if alive.

Working on the body, the pathologist and Witkin agreed that something had transfigured the corpse, and Witkin's photograph catches that effect. Nothing distracts the viewer from the body; the artist does not intervene, drawing attention to other objects, himself, and his intentions.

51. *Joel-Peter Witkin*, 10, 25. Celant also invokes the therapeutic to defend the "Artist-Creator," performing "diabolical surgery" (9). "[N]ot . . . sadistic or barbaric," Witkin arrives "at a healing, a defense against the intolerable reality of life's end" (22).

52. www.zonezero.com/exposiciones/fotografos/witkin2/index.html.

53. Maria Christina Villaseñor, "The Witkin Carnival," *Performing Arts Journal* 53, 18:2 (1996): 82.

54. "A Career's Worth of Corpses and Severed Limbs," *New York Times*, 20 October 1995, C32.

55. Arthur Yorinks (New York: Farrar, Straus and Giroux, 1983).

Index